WIND'S TRAIL

WIND'S TRAIL

THE EARLY LIFE

☙ OF ☙

MARY AUSTIN

BY

PEGGY POND CHURCH

EDITED BY

SHELLEY ARMITAGE

MUSEUM OF NEW MEXICO PRESS

Manufactured in the United States of America.

Library of Congress Cataloging-in-Publication Data

Church, Peggy Pond, 1903–
    Wind's trail : a biography of Mary Austin / by Peggy Pond Church ; edited by Shelley Armitage.
        p.   cm.
    Includes bibliographical references.
    ISBN 0-89013-200-3. — ISBN 0-89013-201-1 (pbk.)
    1. Austin, Mary Hunter, 1868–1934—Biography. 2. Authors, American—20th century—Biography.   I. Armitage, Shelley, 1947–
II. Title.
PS3501.U8Z57   1990
818'.5209—dc20
[B]   89-14562
                                                                             CIP

Designed by Helen McCarty

MUSEUM OF NEW MEXICO PRESS
P.O. Box 2087
Santa Fe, New Mexico 87504-2087

TABLE OF CONTENTS

I
INTRODUCTION

Shelley Armitage

Mary Austin at home in Santa Fe, August 7, 1927.
Photograph by Carol Stryker, courtesy of Museum of New Mexico Archives.

In 1967, at the encouragement of Crowell publishers, Peggy Pond Church began a biography of Mary Austin. Both women had been longtime residents of Santa Fe, Austin from 1921 until her death in 1934. During this time, she reached the height of prodigious national success as a novelist, nature writer, folklorist, poet, and feminist and took a leading role in community causes. Her last eight books were published during this time.

Peggy Pond Church (1904–1986), the youngest writer to be associated with the Santa Fe writers' colony in the 1930s, was a native New Mexican whose parents settled in Santa Fe during her college days. She was known primarily as a poet, but the Austin biography was her second long nonfiction project with a woman as subject. The first was a book about Edith Warner, a Pennsylvanian who came west for her health before the Manhattan Project and the development of the atomic bomb, settling at Otowi, New Mexico, on the Rio Grande, between San Ildefonso Pueblo and what was to become the town of Los Alamos. Church's treatment of

Warner's life in *The House at Otowi Bridge* employs Warner's journals and letters and Church's journals and recollections of this
woman whose life touched many people who passed over that bridge
between the two worlds: the Pueblo Indians and other local people and such nuclear scientists from elsewhere as Niels Bohr and
Robert Oppenheimer. Church was inspired by an admiration for
the strength, centeredness, and quiet growth upon which Warner's grateful friends drew during World War II. She found in
"the woman who dwells in singing by the river" (Warner's Indian
name) an antidote to her own turbulent, sometimes bitter, and
rebellious self. They knew each other during the years when the
development of nuclear warfare not only threatened human life
worldwide but forced Church and her husband to leave the Los
Alamos Ranch School where he taught—disinherited from their
land on the Pajarito Plateau where the beauty of New Mexico and
the visible history of the Anasazi had been Church's heritage since
girlhood. In her moving depiction of Warner, Church reveals also
her own coming into self-understanding, "the worth of my own
woman's life." In her book, published in 1959, eight years after
Warner's death from cancer, the biographer examines her own life in
the light of her subject's life and writings and of their friendship.

Church's approach to Austin's life was somewhat different, yet
the biographer's fascination was similar: to work out in another's
life the corresponding issues in one's own. Church's attraction to
Austin was a complex one, linked to Austin's subject matter, her
personal life, and her life as a woman writer. "I myself was smitten
with the landscape and some of her philosophical essays and felt
that she expressed some of the things I was groping for,"[1] * Church
wrote John Espey, professor of English at UCLA, in 1977.

Though the two did not meet until 1929, Church knew of Austin's activities and interests in Santa Fe through summer visits,
the Santa Fe newspaper, and conversations with her parents. When
Austin visited Santa Fe in 1918, Church was at a boarding school
in the East. In the fall of 1919, she attended the Marlborough

*Notes begin on page 199.

School in Los Angeles where she later discovered Mary Austin's niece was a day scholar. Church attended Smith College in the fall of 1922 and left in 1924 to marry Fermor Church, a teacher at the Los Alamos Ranch School, which her father had managed for some years. She summarized that "on the whole Mary Austin was a legendary character"[2] to her at that time, adding that in the 1930s, when along with Austin she was connected with the Writer's Editions and the Poets' Roundups (publishing and public reading convocations encouraging regional writers), "I was so terrified that I remember all the occasions as one."[3] In the brief span during which Church knew Mary Austin—1929 to 1934—they remained passing acquaintances, with the younger, shy, beginning writer taking note of the older, acclaimed professional.

Yet there were two contacts between them that Church noted as important to her. In October 1929, Church exchanged two letters with Austin, asking for the older author's advice about her poems. At that point, Church had published a few poems in *The Atlantic Poetry* magazine, *Parents Magazine*, *Scribner's*, *Scope*, *The Southwest Scene*, *Literary Digest*, and Alice Corbin Henderson's *The Turquoise Trail: An Anthology of New Mexico Poetry*. She had been consciously working as a poet since childhood, encouraged by teachers and later, in Santa Fe, by Haniel Long, whose reputation as a poet far outstripped Mary Austin's. Austin answered Church's first query by complimenting her technique while criticizing the slightness of the poems, as Church's reply to that Austin letter reveals:

> *Your criticism of the verses coincided exactly with my own opinion of them except that I am sure I would not have credited the techniques with as much. I realize they are "distinctly minor" in content though I had hoped the level would appear to have been rising slightly. But I am not disappointed as I might be had I ever had my heart set on a "literary career." To write poetry, with me, is no life's work but a form of intellectual or spiritual (it is hard for me to know which of these overworked words I really mean) exercise which affords the exhiliration on its own plane that brisk swimming or swift riding or climbing a tall mountain might on the other.*[4]

There is a tone of stung pride in the letter—Church's claim on the one hand that the poems were even more minor than Austin had said and on the other that she hoped they showed improvement. Austin was known at that time in Santa Fe for her bossiness, a dominant personality that often appeared overbearing, egotistical, overweening: overcompensation for what she admitted late in life was her loneliness. She needed to feel important publicly, through acknowledged success and her claims to be both mystic and singularly gifted. Church, though shy, countered in the same spirit. To say she did not want a literary career and therefore could not be disappointed by criticism was a way of maintaining an upper hand in the exchange. Yet her claim that writing poetry gave her spiritual and intellectual exhilaration coincided with the spirit of Austin's writing, which was closely connected to self-discovery and intellectual and spiritual growth.

Church continues to reveal, in this letter to Austin, other similarities between the two women. Citing her practice of meditation, interest in psychic powers, and study of a wide range of fiction and nonfiction writings, including *The Golden Bough, The Mansions of Philosophy,* Katherine Mansfield's *Letters,* Spinoza's *Improvement of the Understanding,* and Eddington's *Nature of the Physical World,* Church attempts to show the older writer that they indeed had much in common, for Austin's career attested to her lifelong interest in the subjects these books addressed. Furthermore, Austin had experienced much of what she wrote about, most notably the physical aspect of her love affair with nature and the cultures of the Southwest as reflected in her California and New Mexico works. She remarked near the time of her death that she most regretted losing the power of the senses to directly experience life. Church mentions the relationship between writing and inner experience that both women shared:

> My dearest ambitions are fulfilled in any experience which comes through the avenue of the mind or the senses. For while we may develop other faculties for experiencing after death, that they will be just these is doubtful, so I am eager to make the fullest possible

*use of them while they are mine. A paralyzing shyness and reti-
cence has always made it difficult for me to go forth to seek such
experience (except in books) and so I sit and wait for it to arrive.
So far the best of it has always come from inside and has seemed
too personal to be written down except in the private journal I
always keep at my elbow.*[5]

The young poet may have added as well that, like Austin, whose
childhood and young womanhood involved an intimate, mystical, and solitary relationship with nature, Church found a similar
experience, not only in books, as she says in this letter, but in
the New Mexico landscape that was an intimate part of her life,
particularly during childhood and young womanhood. The phrase,
"beauty-in-the-wild, yearning to be made human," which Austin
used to describe the complex relationship between mankind and
nature in her autobiography, *Earth Horizon,* becomes a refrain in
Church's perceptions of her own life and, as her biographer, of
Austin's. The theme of writing about this experience as a way to
overcome shyness, separateness, and to express their unique perception occurs in both women's writings. "Writing nature" was
the way in which both became a tongue for the wilderness.

The other situation that identified for Church inner correspondences with Austin was a meeting over a pot of pepper-pot
soup at Austin's home on Camino del Monte Sol, a stone's throw
from where the Churches later would live for a number of years.
In this domestic setting, Church noted the difference in the two
women's lives—one a professional woman, the other a wife and
mother. Yet there remained a basic similarity that made them
kin. "I had chosen the safe framework of marriage and maternity,
a conventional woman's life, at least outwardly—she had chosen
commitment to her career for the sake of which she put away
'childish things.' I admired her and felt guilty before her—and yet
felt most of all what we really had in common, the fact of being
women, with the mysterious, instinctive wisdom of the importance
of the secret ingredients of the pepper-pot soup."[6] Though her
conclusion is humorously expressed, Church later clarified that

this domestic reference had a deeper import. She identified with the essential woman in Austin—the "woman-soul," she called it—instinctive, feeling, connected with the unconscious and creativity. Later, when her direction and energy flagged while she worked on the biography, she wrote in her journal: "We cleave to the woman to find the woman within ourselves. . . . I must go on with the biography for the sake of the creative spirit."[7] This search for the nature of Austin's creativity, what fed and thwarted it, and its consequences for Austin the woman is the drama that Church recognized and with which she sympathized. After her comment on the creative spirit, she added that she must also go on with the project for "the sake of redemption." Clearly in pursuing the sources of women's creativity and how it impacted on femininity and traditional womanhood in Austin's life, she saw a way of explaining similar conflicts in her own.

The quest for the essential Austin, if not for the "essential woman," has been that of several biographers to date, and like them Church went to the obligatory sources—collections of primary source material at the Huntington Library in California, the T. M. Pearce Collection at the University of New Mexico, and Austin's published works, including more than one hundred articles and her autobiography, *Earth Horizon*. Church had special qualifications as a biographer of Austin. Not only was she intensely interested in the issue of women's creativity, the dilemmas of the woman writer, and the connection of landscape and nature to woman's genius, she also was aware in her own life of the conflicts between the subjective and objective selves—the faith in inner-knowing and the conflicts over expressing these perceptions as they conflict with the expectations of society. As a writer and intense individual, yet a wife and mother, she could identify her own guilt in the face of Austin's single-minded dedication to her career and the guilt she hypothesizes Austin felt in the face of her failed marriage, the birth and later relinquishing of a mentally disabled child, and her stated regret that she never had been "taken care of" by a man.

Church, moreover, was a fine poet, with the ability to identify the motifs, key imagery, and psychology inherent in Austin's style and themes. These perceptions contribute to a new and convincing interpretation of what motivated the young Austin. In addition, because Church knew Austin in her last years and interviewed people who were friends or acquaintances of Austin, she was better able to address the challenge of reconciling the personality of what appeared to be a lonely, bitter, irrascible, unhealthy, and egotistic woman with Austin's contrasting creative theories and writings. Church not only sought to unravel the mystery of the many Marys but to explain how her almost Delphic creativity might have a dark side: how the writer indeed might be possessed by her talent to the exclusion of her tenderness.

Though she originally planned a full-scale biography, Church's fascination with her subject's first twenty years, this formative period, seems to have exhausted the biographer's resources. Central to Church's bold and sometimes seemingly harsh interpretation is her Jungian orientation. She studied Jung's theories with Jungians in California and in Santa Fe and read intensively in psychological and Oriental studies throughout her life. She severely applied Jung's theory of the animus to explain Austin's denial of her femininity and her projection of an ideal mate in her fiction that, as Church believed, she was unable to locate in her life. She related these conclusions to Austin's fantasy life, mythic themes, and her relationship to her family in a way that agrees with Austin's own philosophy of a patterned life. (Dudley Wynn in *A Critical Study of the Writings of Mary Austin*, New York University, 1941, has remarked that these related theories of Austin's predated Jung's theory of racial memory, archetypes, and primordial behavior.) Thus, Church's analysis of Austin's growing consciousness is based on theories Austin herself endorsed.

In the course of her work on the biography between 1967 and 1977, Church's focus and methodology underwent some changes. Her publisher, Crowell, initially wanted a contribution to a series on notable American lives for young readers, and that emphasis at first set the tone and direction. Church began chronologically, attempting to establish Austin's activities year by year and, in some cases, month by month. In attempting to confirm factual data, Church was at first confounded as she discovered that Austin omitted or inadvertently changed dates in her autobiography, *Earth Horizon*. Church soon discovered the value of the metaphorical quality of Austin's rendering of her own life: "Innocently expecting to find the most accurate chronology in her own writing, I might have taken a look at my own difficulty in recalling when various events in my own life happened. Or even how they happened—the tendency to exaggerate or make metaphors of one's own experience."[8]

As one example of this tendency, Church noted that the date of a drought recorded by Austin as having happened during her early years in California could not be verified. Finally she consulted a vineyardist, who reconstructed the record of drought cycles from the record of grape growing, paralleling Austin's description and dates. Church soon realized the importance of this discovery was not the accuracy of the dates but what this discrepancy signified in Austin's life—how she felt in that strange environment, under hard, even primitive, circumstances. "What she felt was a drought in her soul," Church concluded.[9] For the biographer, this discovery signaled the important realization that "reality" was more a matter of attitude than absolute facts. "I might have remembered how awfully puzzled I was sometimes during my teens when I looked at myself in the mirror," Church wrote.[10] "That was the way I looked to myself, for sure, but how could I tell if it was the way I really looked—if things looked the same way to my eyes as they did to other people's? I might have gotten some kind of lesson from my own experience of the way history gets written."[11] With this discovery, Church's focus subtly began to change to emphasize and interpret the growth of Austin's attitudes. As she struggled with the conflicts in Austin's life and realized they were so much like her own, she began to keep dream logs in an attempt to analyze a series of dreams she was having about those conflicts.

By August 1968, she had completed most of her preliminary research, and two sample chapters had been approved by Crowell. By May 1972, however, when Church sent the remaining sections, the publishers agreed with the author's enclosed comment: the tone and emphasis had changed. The work had evolved from being a juvenile piece to a more sophisticated study. After a visit from Augusta Fink in May 1973, Church all but relinquished the project. Fink's biography was further along than hers and "Ms. Fink has a secretary,"[12] she noted. Yet by November, Church was back in California touring Austin country and working at the Huntington Library with a firmer resolve than ever. Church was encouraged during this time by readings of her manuscript by Harriet Stoddard, an English professor at Blackburn College who knew the Austin material. As she continued to try to resolve her shift in tone and intent, she was advised by John Espey to write a memoir.

Finally, Church concluded she must trust her original instinctive feelings for Austin, what had interested her in writing the biography in the first place: "I'm an instinctive trail-follower. There's nothing I've loved better to do since I was 'going on eleven' and went to live on the Pajarito Plateau. It was full of Indian trails and game trails and horseback trails and the kind of trails your imagination gets you into when you pick up pottery shards and arrowheads, to find your way around by blazes on trees, or if there aren't any, just by the lay of the land. If you got lost, you depended more on a feeling in your bones, a sort of inner compass, than on anything in your mind to get you out again."[13] Though she had criticized Austin for "getting her inner experiences mixed up with her outer," Church now saw Austin's method—the confluence of subjective and objective experiences—as the way in which her own story of Austin would best be told.

Primarily, then, Church shaped the biography to demonstrate the struggle within Mary Austin for her creative life. Church identified in Austin's youth the seeds of the many Marys that Church alternately quarreled with and embraced. She notes the struggle of the woman artist for acceptability and notability ("I hate this

Siamese-twin self and I wish I could kill one of them,"[14] Austin once wrote of her publicist and creative sides), the contrary pull of conventionality and instinctive womanliness, the challenge to Austin's mystic voice. In Jungian terms, Church thought her shadow-side or animus destroyed the "noticing eye" that gave Austin's nature writing "a strain of pure gold." She described Mary as "a human being who struggled with her own nature, and wrote a great deal about her inner world, both explicitly and implicitly, with enormous flashes of insight and with enormous naîveté," noting her test in the desert was recorded "in loving, selfless attention which she gave, on the one hand, to her desert world, while fighting tooth and nail to get herself out of it on the other—yet could never get free of it, and realized at last that her heart truly was among the sequoias and the flocks."[15] Church interprets the experience in the Carlinville woods as contrasting with the later experience Austin had in the desert where the wildness of nature was felt as "a wilderness of spirit." While Church saw Austin's writing as having been born of this land's lack of cooperation, she recognized Austin's ability to advocate this experience as ultimate meaning and through her storytelling to give meaning to it.

The contrast between the conventional pressures of Austin's Midwest, Methodist girlhood to be "good" and the young girl's love of the wilderness are emphasized by Church. She further demonstrates how the absence of emotional support and love from her family (particularly her mother) and the social and professional discriminations against intelligent, independent, and artistic women led Austin to be even more disappointed in her womanhood. Because of the recurring theme of rejection in Austin's life and works, Church believed that men did not awaken or support Austin. She addresses the need, in the experiences of the young woman, for a man who could understand and cherish the feeling self, the feminine nature. When Austin met young McClure, editor of the *Blackburnian* at college, who declared Austin to be a genius, Church believes this aroused "visions of glorious destiny" in Austin. "This clash between the rich and unconscious fantasy life and the austere and intellectual conscious aspiration was particularly fateful when its representation appeared as McClure, the young man who represented the ideal inner figure—the 'dream man.' "[16] Church then questions the relationship between the "fire of eros" and soul-making: "I believe this inner figure to be important in the life of any woman artist. He is a manifestation of that fiery imagination out of which all creation rises. He was not known as such by Mary. . . . Much had been repressed by the mores of her time; much more of that had never been allowed to come to life except as sparked by her imaginative reading."[17] Moreover, in her marriage and motherhood, Church thought Austin struggled with, almost resisted, the tenderness that she had learned to repress in childhood. No wonder that Austin sought to uphold other qualities in women besides vanity and motherliness or the "charm" she associated with Frances Willard.

The longing for love, its absence, and the substitution of reputation appears, according to Church, in autobiographical characters and situations in Austin's fiction. The predominance of a negative self-image may be read in the thoughts of the hero of *The Lovely Lady*, Peter Weatheral, who was infatuated with his archetypal dream woman: "He had lost the capacity for loving through having been made to feel unable to love," Austin writes.[18] And in her *No. 26 Jayne Street*, Neith falls in love with a man of vast theories and windy words, who reminds her of her father; but when he wants to marry her, she rejects him because of an abstract theory about how a man should behave in his relation to women. As Neith sits alone, living with only her principles, she feels "the worm of the future gnawing at her heart."

Church suggests that because of being unloved in early life—her longing for her father's approval, her feeling of her mother's rejection, the unacceptability of her spontaneous, imaginative self—Austin came to view deviation from the social norm as expressive of the creative individual. To be herself, Church argues, Austin had to deny the "normal" human woman within. Ultimately, Church sees this as a threat to woman's creativity: "I understand this so well from the lifelong tension and conflict between my own creative side and my own domestic life and relation to my husband, worked out with much pain and rebellion over many years before understanding that a woman must do violence to neither side, but try to do justice to both by keeping them in balance."[19] She also sees Austin's conflict as one between the world of knowledge and the archetypal world of myth and story. Though Church identifies the egoist in Austin, she sees her also as one who sought to bring ancestral wisdom to a culture that had lost its spirituality, awe, and connection to nature.

In bringing together Church's biography of Austin in her youth with Austin's essay "The Friend in the Wood," written six years before her death in 1928, a significant balance is struck in the consideration of the woman artist and her life. The two pieces address the formative period of Austin's life as key to her creative patterns and her struggle to realize them. Yet, it is their varying perspectives that establish a fulcrum from which the "truth" of a life emerges: the portrayal of the whole sense of a person—the relationship between the public ideal of herself, which she holds as a personal "mythology," and the inner fears, longings, and spirited aspirations that call it forth. This dynamic of personality—the evolving sense of self as it is and as it would like to be—emerges in each of these works separately. Austin, writing "The Friend in the Wood" as a kind of synthetic microcosm of her youthful experience and mature thought, reviews the origin, development, and impact of the "presence" in the woods that shaped many of her philosophical, spiritual, and creative theories. Church, writing essentially about a woman who late in life would assume an often repugnant egoism that some friends felt belied her own mystical beliefs, searched her subject's early life for clues to her struggle to resolve the culturally imposed contradictions between femininity and creativity in the emerging self. Church astutely identified Austin's proclivity for "inventing herself," a practice long associated with the American character, but not often with women. As Carolyn Heilbrun has pointed out in her book on women's biography, *Writing a Woman's Life*, the female life must pass through the veil of predetermined ideas about the patterns of men's lives, and often, even if addressed autobiographically, the subject must struggle behind the masks she adopts in response to conventional expectation or for the purpose of telling some truth safely.[20]

Both Church and Austin utilized myth and metaphor to map the inner development of the personality. Much of Church's application of folklore and fairy-tale elements was to define the myth that ordered her subject's experience and that offered the key to her nature. Given this intimate act of life-telling—particularly when it addressed her own forbidden, Bluebeard-like keys to the conscious and subconscious levels—Church finally trusted her intuitive ability to decipher the mythic power of Austin's life. Perhaps fittingly, even logically, she relied most heavily upon what she called Austin's own invented facts about herself, the material in her autobiography *Earth Horizon*.

The publication of *Wind's Trail: The Early Life of Mary Austin* offers some insight into the nature of the collaboration between biographer and subject as the writer struggles to understand meaning in another's life. Though Church often is critical, her tone reveals the pain in this joint affair, for the issue of her own redemption as a creative woman was at stake. While the metaphors for Austin's struggle for her creative self seem not to have been exactly Church's—the irony of the desert landscape, at once compelling and repelling; the disappointment in womanhood associated with family rejection and the unfulfilled search for a "male muse"; the consequent cultivation of reputation as creative deviation to compensate for the loss of tenderness—each writer sought an integration of the personal and public worlds, and each has written memorably about the mythic power of a woman's personality and art.

❧

II
MARY AUSTIN:
WRITING NATURE

🖎

Shelley Armitage

Mary Austin in 1888 on graduation day from Blackburn College.
Courtesy of The Huntington Library, San Marino, California.

i

Whehn Mary Hunter Austin died in August of 1934, 135 jars of jams and jellies were found in storage in her Camino del Monte Sol residence in Santa Fe, New Mexico. This domestic expression of the essential country woman in Austin was often overlooked by those who knew her. Most people, even friends, chiefly noticed her domineering nature—the "I-Mary" some believed signified the egoist or at least the outspoken author of more than thirty books and some one hundred articles. Mabel Dodge Luhan most astutely located the storyteller in the domestic sphere:

> She was one of the best companions in the world in a house or on a trip. She loved to put on a big apron and go into our big old kitchen and toss a couple of pumpkin pies together. She loved to hob-nob, to sit and spin out reasons for strange happenings, to hear and tell about all the daily occurrences in both our lives. She

was a romantic and loved the romance of the mystical and occult and often induced in herself peculiar symptoms. She could see and hear and truly experience more than the rest of us, so when she least knew it she really became fascinatingly delphic and sibylline. [1]

In an article entitled "Greatness in Women," Austin linked the domestic or homemaking quality—"givingness to others," she called it—with the intellectual, prophetic, and intuitive qualities in women that make their acts or arts contributory. Thus, the great woman who is a storyteller realizes her intellectual and intuitive gifts, as they are centered, unlike those of men, says Austin, "on the recipient rather than on the act." [2] Moreover, as Austin observed in her autobiography *Earth Horizon*, the writer herself is a recipient—a vessel through which the story is told:

From the time I was thirteen there has been nothing new in my life. What I should do later was pretty clear to me then. I realized that I should be interested in people, for I was then. I liked the place where I lived and the people with whom I lived, though there was nothing dramatic about my life, and no contacts which could be called literary.

What I did in the way of study of people, of cities, of the Indians in their villages, of literary folk in art communities has been directed by some design in my life for which I am not responsible. I knew when I was very young that I should have a good deal of mystical experience, but I have always felt that I was not doing it, that something outside me was responsible, that I was not the shaper but the shaped. [3]

Confronting the issues of women's sphere, the equation of art with masculinity, and her era's culturally imposed contradictions between femininity and creativity, Austin discovered a self and a voice that argued for certain artistic qualities particular to women. She noted too that creativity could be inspired by daily life, which itself is revelatory. Her life and work signify what Eudora Welty notes as the connection between autobiography and art: "The events of

4

our lives happen in a sequence in time, but in their significance to ourselves they find their own order, a timetable not necessarily—perhaps not possibly—chronological. The time as we know it subjectively is often the chronology that stories and novels follow: it is the continuous thread of revelation."[4] The story of this revelation, implicit in all of Austin's works, is that of the woman writer's struggle for self, a voice, and a contributory relationship to society.

Just why Austin found this essential relationship with society so conflicting may be first seen in her youthful struggles to recognize, faithfully pursue, and share her creative life. She noted that the most serious deterrent to the success of women greatly and originally endowed was society's incapacity to recognize original genius when it occurred in a characteristic womanly fashion. In her interior life as a child, she often found herself at odds with the very "womanly" attributes she later championed as key to the creative life.

Austin was born in 1868 to a Midwest family in which the father was an invalid and the mother an ardent Methodist, activist in the Women's Christian Temperance Union (WCTU), and later taxed supporter of four children. She recalled her childhood as deprived, her early creative and mystical experiences ignored. This sense of loneliness and isolation she related to being the middle child, unwanted, as she believed, because of physical and financial stress in the family. Further, she was unusual in that she early preferred intellectual interests, announcing her plans to become a writer. Also, she lacked conventional attractiveness, which the family feared would preclude her marrying. In her inner-directed alienation from typical American extroversion, she was enraptured from childhood with the solitary cosmological experience—and one not bound to religious creed or formal practice. By the age of ten, the major losses of a father who had shared her love of books and nature and her sister Jenny ("the only one who loved me") had intensified Austin's isolation and reliance on her inner resources.

Austin's account of her discovery of "I-Mary"—the independent and imaginative self, which as an identity crucially countered "Mary-by-herself," the socially dictated Mary, meeting the expectations of the external world—centers on two experiences through which this inner self made itself known. While she was learning her letters at her older brother's elbow in the kitchen one day, when she was around two and a half years of age, they came to the "i" in the vowels and Austin pointed to her eye. Her mother explained, "No, I, myself, *I* want a drink, I-Mary," and pointed to the girl. For the first time, Austin perceived herself as existing significantly separately in the adult-ordered world. She had a self; moreover, a self connected to letters, words, and reading. Later when she relied on the inner knowledge of this self to describe events as she imagined they had happened, her mother accused her of lying—"storying," as she called it. Also, when Austin truthfully claimed to be able to read when she first attended public school, the teacher, too, accused her of lying. Her important and precocious gift for "stories" apparently signified to the outer world willful, independent behavior inappropriate in a girl.

Austin further confirmed the authenticity of this developing inner voice when she found that her storytelling thrilled her playmates in the woods near her Carlinville, Illinois, home. Away from the stifling conventions of home, community, and school, Austin became a kind of pagan priestess. Here the "totem" friends in the woods were paid homage through the properly told story and acts of daring and occasional pranks of rebellion against the adult world. Moreover, nature was a sanctuary for this newly discovered self. The "little bird on the tongue," which at home leaped out with sometimes ill-mannered truths to her mother's displeasure, in the woods enjoyed a clear, uncaged cry. And—someone answered. In her account of the mystical experience under the walnut tree, Austin experienced a confirming response not found in any of her other "outside" experiences in Carlinville. Of the "presence" under the walnut tree she asked "God? God?" and felt a reply to her inward spirit. Austin's mystical experiences in the woods clearly confirmed her writer's vocation and the story's authenticity. Further, the story became a bridge between this precocious, prophetic, and isolated child and the outside world.

Later, at Blackburn College in Carlinville, Austin again felt her identity and purpose sanctioned, this time in an intellectual community that, unlike the milieu of her family and Carlinville society, offered opportunities to both young men and women to develop their gifts. Yet here, perhaps because she was anxious to prove herself intellectually equal to men and also to gain her family's approval, she chose to major in science rather than English. She may also have turned to the objective study of nature as a way of factualizing her awe. Through this intellectual approach to her feelings, she sought to reconcile her inner life with the outer—to validate her genius while assuaging a lack of fundamental affection. In the study of botany, she could re-create the kind of emotionally charted life she had found in her girlhood reading of Hugh Miller's *The Old Red Sandstone*, a scientific yet philosophical and poetic work centered on natural history study.

In the essay "Woman Alone," Austin writes:

Long before I came to the intellectual understanding of the situation I had accepted as fact that I was not liked and could not expect the normal concessions of affection. . . . I had learned that it was only by pushing aside all considerations of liking and insisting on whatever fundamental rightness inhered in a particular situation, that I could secure a kind of factual substitute for family feeling and fair play. . . . Out of this I developed very early an uncanny penetration into the fundamental ethics of personal situations which my mother was too just to refuse and not always clever enough to evade. By the time I was old enough to discuss our relationships with my mother the disposition to seek for logical rather than emotional elements had become so fixed that I had even made myself believe that being liked was not important. I had, at least, learned to do without it.[5]

At Blackburn College, there was justice or "rightness" in Austin's success as assistant editor and contributor to the literary magazine, *The Blackburnian*, where her intellectual gifts were praised.

When removed against her will to a homestead claim in the Southern California desert immediately upon her graduation from college, Austin at once felt exiled both from the garden of her childhood, the Carlinville woods, and from her sanctioned success and intellectual stimulation at Blackburn. Initially, she felt the rigors and bleakness of the desert denied her a vocabulary and her mysticism: This was a "wordless wilderness" for which her reading of Hugh Miller, Emerson, Tennyson, and the Romantic poets hardly prepared her. At first she was spiritless and voiceless as the desert erased her familiar ways of seeing, but slowly, forced into a psychic pioneering not unlike the resourceful "mother-wit" she admiringly championed in her female forebears, she interpreted for this setting a longing that matched her own deep self, a "beauty-in-the-wild, yearning to be made human."[6] Much as she had discovered the magic of words as a child, here as a young woman she discovered the magic of the desert and its people, which would frighten, temper, and inspire her.

Austin recognized in the ancient rhythms of the land and indigenous lives a primordial truth akin to her initial inner awareness of the "presence" in the Carlinville woods. The discovery of "self behind the self," as she later called it, allowed her to finally "begin to write in my own character." Seeing a kinship between the feminine principles she recognized and the ancient patterns of life in the desert, Austin experienced this landscape as both test and confirmation. "The friend in the wood" returned to companion her in her maturing life, not as faun or fairy but as the "ultimate Pan,"[7] "the voiceless passion of spirit toward form."[8] In her new world of Paiute and Shoshone, sheepherders and homesteaders, she further learned the difference between knowing something and knowing *about* it. Direct experience of what she had previously sensed imaginatively activated her creativity as a voice for ancient wisdom.

As her creative life took new energy from the environment, her marriage to Stafford Wallace Austin and the birth of their mentally disabled child made writing a practical necessity as well. From 1884 to 1912, the years Austin lived in California, she was displaced a number of times due to her husband's failures or restlessness. On a trip to San Francisco, she was befriended by Ina Coolbrith, a former editor of the *Overland Monthly*, whose habit it was to encourage young writers. Austin's first work to be published, a story entitled "The Mother of Felipe," subsequently appeared in the *Overland Monthly* in November 1892.

During 1898–99, the family homesteaded at Tejon Pass on the Beale Ranch, where Austin learned much lore from Wallace and the Mexican sheepherders. Then she and Wallace took up a claim on a series of rocky ridges near Owens Lake called the Alabama Hills. Here Austin explored the mysteries of the arroyos and befriended the local miners, enjoying their folksongs, card tricks, and country dances.

In 1899, she was invited to teach at the Los Angeles Normal School by Dr. Edward T. Pierce, head of the school and a friend of Charles Fletcher Lummis. Lummis at that time had published nearly a dozen books and was editor of *Out West* magazine. Through him, Austin met local writers Sharlott Hall, Edwin Markham, anthropologist Frederick Webb Hodge, Charlotte Perkins Stetson (later Gilman), and Grace Ellery Channing, among others. Lummis advanced the opinion that Austin had talent but no genius. Nevertheless, in July of 1900 she published a story, "Shepherd of the Sierras," in the *Atlantic Monthly*. A number of her early writings appeared in various publications in the period between 1897 and 1904 before her success with her nonfiction work *The Land of Little Rain* in 1904. Austin sold poems and stories to *Munsey's Magazine, Cosmopolitan, St. Nicholas,* and the *Atlantic* while Lummis continued to publish her stories in *Out West*, along with the writings of Eugene Manlove Rhodes, Emerson Hough, and Ernest Thompson Seton. Lummis no doubt influenced her interest in Native American and Hispanic culture, while with David Starr

9

Jordan, a scientist and later first president of Stanford and a member of the Lummis circle, she shared the belief that nature shaped human societies.

Though her creative efforts provided needed funds for them, her family still rejected the idea that she could be a writer. True, her mother had once ferreted one of her discarded poems out of the trash and given it to Frances Willard for publication in the WCTU newsletter. Still, this gesture seemed to the girl solely in her mother's own interest. Austin claimed that though she always sensed she would be a writer, was indeed "endowed" for it, the family's attitude was "What makes you think *you* can write?" She confesses:

> In truth, I did not know. Looking back on the idea of a literary career which prevailed in the Middle West of that period, it was probably well for me that nobody knew. I won a college degree by dint of insisting on it, and by crowding its four years into two and a half. My brother had a full four years. That I got so much was partly a concession to the necessity of my earning a living. With a college education I could teach, and teaching was regarded then as a liberal profession, eminently suited for women. Being "plain," and a little "queer," it was hoped rather than expected that I would marry. My queerness consisted, at that time, in . . . stoutly maintaining against all contrary opinion that I would some day write, and in the—to my family—wholly inexplicable habit of resting my case on its inherent rightness rather than upon emotional reactions it gave rise to. [9]

The conflict between writing, marriage, and mothering came to seem overwhelming at such times as after the birth of her mentally disabled child Ruth, when Susanna Hunter remarked: "I don't know what you've done, daughter, to have such a judgment upon you." Ironically, Susanna Hunter thought marriage and childbirth would settle Austin down—cure, in fact, the ill health from which she suffered throughout her life. Austin herself believed marriage and writing totally compatible—under normal circumstances: "I thought two intelligent young people could do about as they liked with life."[10] Later she claimed to have realized this freedom only through tragedy. In 1905, she committed her child to an institution, where Ruth remained until her death at twenty-two. Austin wrote in 1927, "In a way this tragic end to my most feminine adventure brought the fulfillment of my creative desire, which had begun to be an added torment by repression. Caring for a hopelessly invalid child is an expensive business. I had to write to make money."[11]

The failure in this personal arena, while thrusting Austin into a writing career, encouraging her radicalism, and creating a practical necessity for the expression of her imaginative abilities, also encouraged her to translate the feminine principle into "man's sphere," the professional world outside the home. Here, certainly through her intellectual and intuitive faculties and often with tenderness, she addressed nature, religion, feminism, and folklore.

The last cause Austin and her husband shared was that of the Owens River water issue in which water promised to develop the Owens Valley was diverted, through political maneuvering, to Los Angeles. The Austins were heartbroken over the turn of events, and Mary saw the outcome as a blow to her faith in cultural evolution—the growth of people in harmony with natural resources. The couple separated during part of this time and later divorced. Austin sought once again, as she had with Lummis, a larger family unit, this time in the artist colony of Carmel.

The power of the desert life of Southern California and its people emerged in her successful first books, *The Land of Little Rain, The Flock, Isidro, Santa Lucia,* and *Lost Borders.* With the proceeds from these books, she built a house at Carmel in 1905 where she could share her creative life with Jack London, Harry Leon Wilson, Charles Warren Stoddard, and later George Sterling. For an outdoor study, she built a wickiup in the fashion of the Paiutes and there began to experience the "larger life":

Released thus to the larger life which opened to me with literary success, I found plenty of reasons for being a feminist in the injus-

11

tices and impositions endured by women under the general idea of
their intellectual inferiority to men. . . . I thought much that was
said at that time about Home and Mother sentimental tosh; I thought
it penalized married love too much to constitute the man she loved
the woman's whole horizon, intellectual, moral, and economic.
I thought women should be free to make their contribution to soci-
ety by any talent with which they found themselves endowed, and
be paid for it at rates equal to the pay of men. I thought everything
worth experiencing was worth talking about; I inquired freely into
all sorts of subjects. . . . I talked freely of art as though it had a
vital connection with living. [12]

Austin was to participate in this larger life as one of the leading
American women writers of her time, living in writers' colonies
in Carmel, New York, and later Santa Fe, traveling abroad as a
speaker and gaining an enviable reputation as a lecturer in the
United States, and, toward the end of her life, recognized for her
many creative contributions.

In 1908, she became the first prominent woman writer from
the American West to tour England. She traveled to Italy as a
guest of the Herbert Hoovers, meeting the Joseph Conrads and
H. G. Wells, and attended the meetings of the Fabian Summer
School, where she conversed with George Bernard Shaw. When
she returned from Europe, Austin established residence in New
York City to produce her play *The Arrow-Maker* and publish the
works *Fire* and *Outland,* based on life in the Carmel colony.

Her New York period, which lasted from 1912 to 1924, is distinguished as her most productive. There she was occupied with
the feminist movement, largely reflected in her books during this
time, the war effort, and a furthering of her interests in Indian
myths and poetry. *Love and the Soul Maker,* a lengthy philosophical dialogue between the author and Valda McNath, expresses the
idea that true love is a creative force governed by influences outside of man. Austin notes in this work that the structure of married love can be a creative force governing the great artist, shaping

something beautiful, honest, and permanent. This force she calls the Soul Maker and at other times Wakonda, the Friend of the Soul of Man, Everyman's Genius, and the Sacred Middle. Speaking of these same ideas earlier at the New York Legislative League in 1912, Austin advocated the instruction of women in the psychology of the sex relationship, organization of marriage on an equitable financial basis, and investigation into the ancestors of each member in the relationship. Her pragmaticism as well as the personal experience of her failed marriage emerge in this plea.

Never solely a theorist, Austin involved herself in the war effort by working on the Mayor's Committee for National Defense, disbursing food to the needy. She also sponsored a war garden that provided fresh vegetables. Her novels during this period, *A Woman of Genius, The Lovely Lady, The Ford,* and *No. 26 Jayne Street,* reflect her contribution to the feminist movement of the time. *The Man Jesus* (which she preferred to be titled *A Small Town Man*), a psychological biography of Christ based on her experiences in Italy, indicates her continued interest in religion and mysticism. *The Trail Book,* a collection of animal stories, and *The American Rhythm,* translations of Indian songs, illustrate her work with Amerindian materials and her role as popularizer and interpreter of this folklore.

A trip to New Mexico at the invitation of Mabel Dodge Luhan, whom she had met in Greenwich Village earlier, and a lecture tour to the Plains states in 1921 reconfirmed Austin's belief in the vitality of regional America. She noted the importance of musical instruments, festivals, local art exhibits, and community theaters in the cultural life of each region. In New York City she had found that "I was bothered by the rage for success; the idea that an immediate success was the sign of capacity; that the little whorls of success that kept appearing on the surface of affairs were final and invincible."[13] New Mexico now succeeded New York as her essential creative environment. Serving as a surveyor of Taos County Hispanic cultural institutions for the Carnegie Institution's Americanization program in 1917–18, she toured northern New Mexico and, the next summer, traveled with the Gerald Cassidys down the Rio Grande and into southern Arizona, sketching and writing, collecting materials for what would become *The Land of Journeys' Ending*.

Austin decided New Mexico would be her permanent residence and built "the Beloved House" in Santa Fe in 1924. In the decade that she lived there, though she was accused of being uncommunicative, preoccupied, and unfriendly, she pursued relationships with those who shared her interest in indigenous cultures, the preservation of arts and the land, and the regeneration of American literature through regional roots. At Mabel Dodge Luhan's house, she met the D. H. Lawrences. Lawrence satirized both her and Mabel's attitudes in his unpublished play, *Altitude*, but Austin shared with Lawrence a deep faith in the power of the collective unconscious, the meaning of primitivism to modern man, and a love of the New Mexico landscape's beauty and creative force.

Largely through her efforts, there was a revival of interest in their music and drama among the Hispanics of Santa Fe. She had collected Penitente hymns during her visit in 1919 and argued that they were "authentically as American as the Negro Spirituals." In her leadership to preserve both Hispanic and Indian art and culture, Austin was instrumental in the restoration of the Santuário at Chimayó, joining Frank Applegate and architect John Gaw Meem, then-president of the Society for the Preservation and Restoration of New Mexico Mission Churches. She and Applegate established and nurtured the Spanish Colonial Arts Fund to preserve and promote the creation of these native works.

Along with other Santa Fe and Taos colony members, Austin helped rally national support for the defeat of the Bursum Bill that would have deprived the Pueblos of vast tracts of agricultural and grazing lands. Reacting to Commissioner of Indian Affairs Charles H. Burke's order to ban dances among the Pueblos, Austin fired a strong letter to Burke accusing him of depicting the Pueblos as "half animals" and interfering with their religious freedom. She and other members of the community brought enough pressure on Burke so that he relaxed his order. Austin further argued that

Congress should adopt laws guarding Native American rights. She worked for federal legislation to emphasize Indian arts and crafts in the federal Indian-school curriculum. So well-known was her reputation as an advocate of Indian culture and welfare that the Mexican government in 1930 appointed her a consultant to assist in that country's effort to restore its own Indian arts and culture.

Working with Witter Bynner on language experiments affecting Hispanics in an Anglo-dominated school curriculum, Austin strongly advocated bilingual education in New Mexico's public schools. She also promoted the local library and community theater and for several years urged federal officials to establish a national department of arts and letters (the forerunner to the present National Endowment for the Arts and Humanities) so that creative people could turn from "struggling for place and honor among themselves" to "developing art of the people."[14] As an environmentalist, Austin was appointed in 1927 to the Seven State Conference on Colorado River Basin Development, during which she lobbied for recognition of the river as both a national asset and of international importance to Mexico.

As a professional public speaker during this period, she was booked by L. J. Alber World Celebrities Lecture Bureau and other agencies. Austin lectured on college and university campuses, was a particular favorite at Yale University, and for years lectured annually to the Women's University Club in Los Angeles. In 1926, she spoke at Clark University as a guest of the Department of Psychology's "Symposium on Psychical Research." Some of her topics were "Southwestern Literature and the Common Life," "Primitive Drama," "Genius and the Subconscious Mind," and "American Fiction and the Pattern of American Life." In 1930, she addressed the Seminar on Latin American Cultural Relations in Mexico and, while there, lectured at the National University on "American Indian Art."

The tremendous productivity of this period centered on Austin's protective attitude toward Santa Fe and issues affecting the Southwest and its native elements. Her poetry of a regional emphasis appeared in *Poetry, Saturday Review of Literature, Literary Digest,* and several anthologies; articles, both interpretative and popular, were featured in *Ladies Home Journal, Art and Archaeology, New Republic,* the *Nation, Collier's,* and the *Saturday Evening Post.* In her ten years in Santa Fe, Austin published eight books, including her acclaimed autobiography *Earth Horizon* ("A profoundly original interpretation of the American spirit," one reviewer applauded) and the highly acclaimed *Starry Adventure* and *One Smoke Stories.*

Austin's tremendous accomplishments were acclaimed by critics in her lifetime and upon her death in 1934. T. M. Pearce noted her ability to write of one locale yet create universal stories of lasting import. Henry Seidel Canby, the founder and first editor of *Saturday Review of Literature,* memorialized Austin as "one of the greatest American women of letters of our time," deserving a "prominent place in American literature."[15] Despite her primarily southwestern identification, she was compared with Tolstoy in her ability to utilize regional materials to express the universal. Some critics recognized her insightful and mystic influences while others still saw these tendencies as dubious. In answering one such critic who challenged her to produce her research in developing her theory of the American rhythm, Austin had retorted:

> I recognize no such objection as you lay upon me to demonstrate an American Rhythm "by means of vast documentation, special reference, and detailed analysis." This is a matter I had out with myself many years ago, after I discovered myself in possession of a field of scholarly research that had not been entered by many of my contemporaries. I see myself, primarily, as a creative thinker—a creative writer, whichever term suits you best—which I feel to entail a higher obligation than that of stodgy and meticulous demonstration for the uninitiated of what has come to me through regular channels of scholarly experience. I felt that I couldn't be faithful to my primary obligation if I must go dragging after me all the fructifying sources, as a queen bee trails the entrails of her mate.[16]

Thus, Austin asserted that her intuitive certainty had a fundamental rightness—that feeling could be argued in the outer world as fact. As critic Carl Van Doren expressed after her death: "She was the master of the American environment . . . whose books were wells that drive into America to bring up water for her countrymen, though they might not have realized their thirst."[17]

Austin claimed an ability to "read patterns," through which, as storyteller, she could anticipate life patterns and meanings, the significance of "man turning his insides out"—the manifestation of universal archetypes, coming from the subjective unconscious in behavior and beliefs. Though her claim to these intuitive powers often seemed egotistical, Austin argued as a storyteller of place and universal elemental experiences the value of these primary resources for the psyche of mankind. For her fellow Americans, she said that she wrote not of survival but of a life, lived harmoniously upon the land, which conveyed "elemental truths which are antidotes to those provided in industrial slums where minds are torn and bodies worn."[18] Moreover, the wells she drove deep, which her countrymen often ignored, held antidotes to the characteristic criticism of Americans as Babbitts. Shouldering her mantle of intuitive power as surely as a medicine woman her manta, Austin ultimately created a new image of the American woman writer as seer, sayer, and healer—a role expressing the feminine principles she advocated. This "calling," her sacrifice for it, and the heroic stature she thereby won, she explained during the celebration of the publication of her *Earth Horizon* in 1932. Noting that she had been lonely most of her life, she said she nevertheless joyously paid the price for the intuitive and intellectual gifts with which she served society: "I knew that I had lived symbolically, that I had done what any woman perhaps could have done, but which for some reason or other most of them do not. I was the medium, the tool of forces I could not control."[19]

17

ii

The American Southwest landscape and its people contributed to Mary Austin's sibylline voice and her identity of woman writer as a kind of prophetess. Nature also offered external proof of what she claimed intuitively: that people were significantly tied to environment and those people who had lost this basic contact could revivify themselves through close observation of lives still harmoniously part of the land. Art—in Austin's case, "writing" nature—could reunite nature and human nature. The subconscious common ground for what Austin called the "Sacred Middle," the "middle ground between art and knowledge"—distinctively Mary's own—was the source of a "feeling-knowledge" Austin believed could heal by restoring a psychic wholeness. Art, as it emerged from the rhythms of landscape, contained the imprint nature made on individuals and societies and the imprint the subconscious made, in customs, ritual, and ceremony, on the land. In that microcosm of her thoughts on this subject, *The Friend in the Wood,* Austin says this interpenetration calls "the grass to be man." She also shows in her nature-centered fiction and nonfiction writing that this interpenetration of "Life on lives" also calls the writer to respond to "the ever living and as yet uncreated Life, pressing to be shaped as tree and shrub"[20]; or to, as she says elsewhere, "the voiceless passion of spirit toward form."[21] Giving form in her writing to this spirit was Austin's ultimate declaration of the meaning of nature, chronicled in her work from an essentially romantic, transcendental view to a political, social, and finally aesthetic and feminine one. As a tongue for the wilderness, Austin relates most of her mystical, critical, literary, and cultural theories through nature's meaning.

Her initial identification of the nature essay with religious and philosophical matters came through her reading of Emerson, Thoreau, John Muir, and Hugh Miller, whose *Old Red Sandstone,* a philosophical natural history, was the first book Austin purchased with her own money as a young girl. Charles Robertson, her biology teacher at Blackburn College, inspired her study of natural adaptation; with her husband, Stafford Wallace Austin, something of a botanist as Registrar of the United States Land Office in Inyo County, she shared field trips in which they studied the flora and fauna of the desert and the Sierras. Years of observing the Shoshone and Paiute Indians in Owens Valley acquainted Austin with a primitive faith analogous to that of Emerson's faith in Spirit. The animal stories of Ernest Thompson Seton, with which she was familiar, incorporated philosophical and botanical observations and exemplified the fruitful combination of the factual and the mystical and their relationship to the primitive mind. But as Dudley Wynn has observed, perhaps the most crucial matter of Austin's early "membership" among American nature writers is that she took transcendentalism to the desert: a land bereft of the conventionally sublime or picturesque. Unlike Emerson or Muir, Austin claimed that no part of nature—even the desert—lacks beauty or the power to inform the spiritually perceptive. No doubt her own hard experiences pioneering in Southern California desert areas, which altered forever her girlhood conception of the "friend" in the woods, awakened her sensitivity to a unique and primarily ignored aspect of American landscape.

In her first book, *The Land of Little Rain,* Austin, though working in the romantic, transcendental tradition, noted the beautiful and the redemptive qualities of the Southwest desert, creating from it a new way of seeing. She attends to the adaptive facts of flora and fauna, people, places that speak of the ancient definition of beauty based on harmony. As she sets the geological and botanical background—the wind and water trails, the habits of buzzards, the rare gorges, mountains, and forests with their particularized plants—she also emphasizes that life is naturally religious when lived in proper adjustment to nature. Linking natural rhythms and human rhythms, she speaks of the relation of people and place— the significant connection between the individual (such as the carefully drawn Basket Woman or the old prospector) and the communal. The specific details emphasize uniqueness yet suggest that these elements of man and land represent larger primordial "history" or truth. Describing the grand in the commonplace, the beautiful in the average, she suggests a democratic way of seeing that nevertheless reaches epic proportions.

Within the minute observation, which Austin articulated loyally through local place names, Spanish and Indian words not known to the larger American public, is the transcendental rapture that suggests this new American epic is both ancient and ongoing, both a storied landscape and real. Even in this Muir-like passage, Austin communicates the awe she feels in a distinctly direct, personal, yet magnificent way:

> The shape of a new mountain is roughly pyramidal, running out into long shark-finned ridges that interfere and merge into other thunder-splitted sierras. You get the saw-tooth effect from a distance, but the near-by granite bulk glitters with the terrible keen polish of old glacial ages. It is terrible; so it seems. When those glossy domes swim into the alpenglow, wet after rain, you conceive how long and imperturbable are the purposes of God. [22]

Austin's tone is often that of a friendly travelogue, yet her resonances are those of poetry as she utilizes the conversational in the service of the spiritual. Her method in experiencing the landscape, aside from her rich direct situations, involves a use of poetry to clarify the images and thoughts of prose. She once told Charles Minton, a young acquaintance in Santa Fe, that direct perception, rendered in poetry then realized in prose, came closest to the revelatory event. "There's a figure of speech, for example," she remarked to Minton one day as they passed some goats on a road outside of Santa Fe: "Brown goats like the sunny sides of winter hills." [23] In her book, The Flock, she practiced this approach, ably demonstrating that the history of sheep raising in California contained certain mimetic elements. This book is at once an account of her history of sheep raising and the effect of the rhythm of the returning flocks, the ways of the shearings, festivities, and hireling shepherds. To effect the rhythmical significance of this historical and political event on the greater meaning of the rightness of harmonious adjustment to the natural environment, Austin sometimes employs an archaic language, suggesting the ancient, even everlasting, quality of the present activity:

> *Here I heard at intervals the flute, sweet single notes as if the lucid air had dripped in sound. Awhile I heard it, and between, the slumberous roll of bells and the whistling whisper of the pines, the long note of the pines like falling water and water falling like the windy tones of pines; then the warble of the flute out of the flock-murmur as I came over the back of the slip where it hollowed to let in a little meadow fresh and flowered. . . .*[24]

Ambrose Bierce, favorably reviewing the book, noted the important connection between Austin's power of observation and her style. "The best of her reading is her style," he said. "What a knack of observation she has! Nothing escapes her eye."[25] Thus, Austin created a style that both recorded and elevated; she suggested in it the landscape as activator, the writer and reader as discoverers, the artistic American plain as connected to the primordial.

In her next book, *California, the Land of the Sun,* the rhapsodic voice is placed in service of the prophetic as she argues for the recognition and preservation of the beauty she discovered in California. The sweep is broad as it is deep, indicating through the encompassing horizons of California geography the ancient truths (vertical, subconscious, primordial) lost on what she called "the most impotent—culturally and spiritually impotent"[26] American society of her time. Seeking to awaken this society to truths visible in its own landscape, yet ignored, commercialized, or managed without stewardship for profits, she often characterizes the land as feminine, applying the Native American concept of Mother Earth. Such chapters as "Mothering Mountains" exemplify Austin's belief of the feminine principle of the land also expressed in some of her fiction, for example "Lone Tree" and "The Last Antelope." The land is nurturing, spiritual, and resilient. Austin believed that despite the (largely) Anglo destroyers, "the land would have its way."[27] She connects the feminine aspects of the land with the aesthetic—the feminine with the beautiful and the perseverance of the landscape with art and culture. "With their low and flat pitched roofs they [modern houses] present a certain likeness to the aboriginal dwellings which the Franciscans found scattered like wasps' nests among the chaparral along the river, which is only another way of saying that the spirit of the land shapes the art that is produced here."[28] Not only do these shapes survive in future revivals, but the very patterns of art and civilization are manifestations of the shapes, rhythms, essence of this life force. Austin sees this outer world bringing influence to bear on the "patterns of the mind of man which existed before they were ever extroverted in carved bones or reduced to painted figures on bits of pasteboard."[29] In this book, Austin prophesies an ongoing battle within man to retain this inner awareness, what she calls his "genius," and hence his art and culture. In *The Trail Book*, a later book designed for juveniles but with similar themes, Austin traces ancient trails, and ancient stories told there of the rapport of prehistoric men and animals, with the hope that such stories might lead modern man to subtle spiritual perceptions lost in contemporary sophisticated society.

Thus, in the face of the lost or altered landscape, the storied landscape becomes crucial: story, style, and teller are the guides for the lost genius of humankind. In two of her plays, *The Arrow-Maker* (1911) and *Fire* (1913), Austin anticipated her psychological and philosophical ideas on the subject that were substantially developed in *Everyman's Genius* and *Experiences Facing Death*. She remained concerned with the searching for the "soul" of man through the concepts of racial memory and Jung's notion of collective unconscious. Like *The Arrow-Maker*, *Fire* is an allegory of the artist's relationship to society. In relating the story of Coyote, the fire-bringer, and his connection to the tribe, Austin addresses the idea that the artist's power and ability to benefit society depend on his or her intuitive feeling of kinship with the whole world.

22

Evind, the fire-bringer who is told by brother Coyote how to seize
fire from the mountains for the tribe, comments to his wife, Laela,
about the significance of the tribe's demand that he reject Coyote, his fellow creature:

> Sometimes, Laela, I have thought—
> If I could find my brother beast again
> And with him follow
> The viewless track which leads
> The moth of moonless nights to honeyed hollows;
> To windy pastures where the wild sheep are;
> Where the keen eagles wheeling high
> Seek for their meat afar—
> If I could feel that rock and tree again,
> And every creeping thing were sib to me
> I should be more unto my fellow man.[30]

The play suggests that in order for modern man to get inside
the Amerindian's psychic processes he must cultivate his relatedness to animals. The necessity of this intuitive effort to engender
kinship and creativity is vital. Austin insists that Evind's (Pro-
metheus's) gift is a deep, implicit sense of connectedness, and her
experience and literal acceptance of Indian lore shape her notion
of the storyteller as guide, capable of *relating* man to nature through
the telling of the story.

In a speech delivered before the Unitarian Church in New York
City, Austin said that the primary value of mystical experience—
the instinctive ability to perceive subconscious truths—was the
relatedness it enabled one to feel. "The average man wants not so
much an explanation of ultimate reality as some sort of relation
to it which will 'work,' " she explained—not a new doctrine, a
new definition, but a "freedom of experience." She went on to
say that the mystical faculty had been rendered impotent by modern education, psychoanalysis, and intellectuality. This "studied
release," as she termed it, of the creative faculty, she argued, denied
the significance of the inner act and often shifted what happened

to one in search for God to simply how one thought about it. As a practical equivalent of these ideas, Austin argued for the settling of the Colorado Basin according to the village pattern of small-scale communalism, local integrity, self-sufficiency, and "aesthetics as a mode of life behavior."[31] These aesthetics, in her sense, included the search for relatedness of one individual to another, of culture to culture, of human nature to nature.

In Austin's literary theories—her methods for translating Native American poetry, the idea of the American rhythm, the landscape line, and the value of regionalism to American literature—background, environment, the land were basic. Her theory of the landscape line established a direct relationship between what people look at daily and their art. Austin claimed that she could listen to any poem, chant, or song and trace its origin by connecting its rhythms to the landscape source. This theory also influenced her method of translating Native American materials, as in the poems in *The American Rhythm* and *The Children Sing in the Far West*. She maintained that to accurately translate from the original linguistic sources, interpreters must be used, but also one must achieve a prayerlike mood so that she may absorb the correct rhythm into which the poems are translated. Her book, *The American Rhythm* (1923), antedates William Carlos Williams's *In the American Grain* and anticipates Williams's and other American writers' reclaiming of vital local, regional, and indigenous elements. In her poem "Western Magic," she says there "are no fairy folk in our Southwest," then proceeds to make a case for the powerful native sources of folklore, myth, and legend. Out of a distinct environment, therefore, comes particular lore and literature. In a 1922 forum on the novel, Austin expressed the idea that the pattern of a story and the arrangement of its elements must occur in true relationship to the social structure by which they are displayed—"a revelation of place, relationships, solidarity."[32] American writing would be authentic, she said, only when it revivified these elements; in fact, American writing could be a "democratic" art to the degree to which it tapped into the patterns available through the collective unconscious. The loss of the meaning of landscape was for Austin the loss of culture as well.

In her final nonfiction nature book, *The Land of Journeys' Ending*, Austin convincingly connects the significance of nature, the individual's intuitive self, and culture, as represented by the larger social group and its art—ceremony, stories, writing. In the section entitled "The Left Hand of God," she writes of the model of the Indian's wholeness, his "unselfconscious translation of first-hand contacts with the environment into rhythm of color and design," his keeping of cultural interests in one pattern, his group-mindedness running "higher than the individual can reach":

> *Behind this cultural wholeness, making it possible, is a psychic unity, so foreign to our sort of society that we have not yet a name for it. Sometimes in intervals of the Corn Dance, when the wind comes up and blurs the long, rhythmic line in the dust of its own dancing, or waiting outside the governor's house in Taos, where the sky over Pueblo Mountain holds on blue until long after midnight, while the council deliberates within and the young men are singing to the moon between the North House and the South, the word swims up and circles, flips its bright tail, and vanishes. It is a word woven out of the belief that there is god-stuff in man, and the sense of the flow of life continuously from the Right Hand to the Left Hand. But why seek for a word defining the state of the Whole, who have not achieved wholeness? Somewhere at the edge of the experience the word lingers, intuitively felt, and still to be brought to con-sciousness by some happy observer if the Pueblos live long enough.*[33]

How well Mary Austin must have understood this eternal search of the woman aware—the writer! Her line, "beauty-in-the-wild, yearning to be made human," is another expression of this search for the word that would encapsulate the cultural wholeness of the Pueblos; or, as anthropologist and curator Peter Sutton said recently at the exhibition of aboriginal Australian art in New York City, "The land is already a narrative—an artifact of intellect—before people represent it. There is no wilderness."[34]

iii

Within the pattern of Mary Austin's life and works is the development of the familiar "American Self"—the myth of the self as connected to the American romantic story of self-discovery and self-transformation. Yet what is unique about Austin is that she applied this story to the woman writer, thus including her in what Carolyn Heilbrun calls "the masculine wilderness of the American novel"[35]—that almost solely masculine arena of questing, self-reliance, and individuality that typifies the predominantly male experience with nature in our literature. Austin, who lived and wrote about the necessity for individuality and lone heroism, knew that individuality and individuation, in the Jungian sense, are not the same. The fully integrated individual searches for the shared myth, the universal language represented by the collective unconscious, thus accomplishing in her inner awareness a tribal connection. Despite the sometimes lonely, isolated, renegade, or outcast conditions of her characters, Austin advocates the eternal wholeness of the family of man and the conscious actions that bespeak this integration.

Her image of the woman writer as vessel for the creative spirit is a significant twist both to the American ideal of the created self and the nineteenth-century idea of the woman as vessel—and vassal—for the dominant male culture. As Austin listened to the narrative of the landscape and came to represent it, she activated the myth of the continual pilgrimage in search for the word, the alchemy that could call back to life the spirit of the closed, tribal world.

Austin's belief in the power of the image or the word was similar to that of the Imagists, some of whom lived or lectured in Santa Fe during Austin's tenure there. Like the Imagists, she sought to restore a direct relation between the concrete and the emotional, discarding abstract verbosity. As her friend, Alice Corbin Henderson, said of Imagism:

> *In looking at the concrete object or environment, it [this poetry]*
> *seeks to give more precisely the emotion rising from them. . . .*
> *Great poetry has always been written in the language of contem-*
> *porary speech, and its theme, though legendary, has always breadth*
> *and direct relation to contemporary thought, contemporary imagi-*
> *native and spiritual life.* [36]

Since Austin believed the past to be ever-active, ever-present in
the person of genius whose intuition could recall or activate it,
she believed also that the revitalized word encapsulated and delivered this past to the present. With Pound, who believed that the
reverberating image mirrors the moment, making the language and
the thing one, Austin thought that the intellectual and emotional
energies generated by capturing the moment implied a complex
of desires and memories. In her essay, "The Walking Woman,"
she explains:

> *All building is out of the deep self; in whatever name the Friend*
> *is called upon it answers. To me it answers most completely out of*
> *the back of beyond sleep, from which also our Lost Others drew*
> *their wisdom. Times when I wake seeing all our ancient life falling*
> *into perspective behind me in the swiftly vanishing illumination of*
> *sleep, I know where I have been and what doing. I have been walk-*
> *ing in the Wild Hills with the beast figures of ancient wisdom,*
> *which will little by little clarify in my intelligence, according to its*
> *capacity. Then I know that the recovery of lost wisdom does arrive*
> *not at finality in the figure of the suffering Man-God any more*
> *than it did the Animal Helper; but in the continuing recovery and*
> *reapplication of that wisdom to the way of life. That is why I call*
> *the friendly presence masked as beast or god, Never-Was and Never-*
> *to-Be. It is my own lost self I run with as the Coyote Brother, my*
> *own unrecovered self that beckons in the Wild Hills.* [37]

This Walking Woman is the eternal quester, who, in searching for
the word as wisdom, is continually "pressing toward life adventure." Austin conceived of this articulation—physical movement

and word—in terms of the life, death, rebirth cycle, as is implicit in this passage from her poem, "Going West":

> Lay me where some contented oak can prove
> How much of me is nurture for a tree;
> Sage thoughts of mine
> Be acorn clusters for the deer to browse.
> My loving whimsies—will you chide again
> When they come up as lantern flowers?[38]

In her poem, "When I Am Dead," she repeats this theme of vegetal consciousness when her "happy ghost/Walk(s) with the flocks again . . . and is one with his thought at last/And the Wish prevails."[39] Thus, the cycle of the story is in its process the ongoing pilgrimage itself.

Developing this central mythic idea, Austin demonstrates that myth can enter the work as a dominant theme existing below the surface, or as an allusion to or incorporation of specific myths of a culture, either shared or borrowed, or by the invention of new fictions that attain mythic stature in the work, perhaps because they offer new versions of old patterns. Certainly, Austin accomplished the first two of these, often implying the theme of the inward journey either comparatively, say to the Paiute, Shoshone, Pueblo, or Mexican cultures, or stylistically through a narrative voice that expresses a journeying experienced by the writer. Austin also created new fictions out of old myths, reviving archetypal stories.

In her early novel, *Isidro*, she utilizes the prosaic setting of a dime novel, with a conventional hero, to suggest a new twist: the male character is a woman in disguise who accomplishes heroic feats and, in the tradition of the pard ("chum") character in the later dime novels, "saves" the hero and establishes herself as noble, resourceful, and independent. In *The Lovely Lady*, she attempted a juvenile treatment of *A Woman of Genius*, trying to popularize a serious feminist theme of the intellectual, talented, and successful new woman. Most notably in the creation of male-female relationships, she rewrites the conventional and, to her mind, failed interplay of men's and women's expected roles and behavior. Many of her male characters are child-men, innocent, naive, molded into soul mates by the strong mother or woman figure. In these stories, if men reject women as equals and refuse to adopt broad liberal attitudes as standards for personal relationships, they fail to successfully adjust to life. Women fall short of fulfillment when they do not develop intellectually and do not assert independence from masculine domination. Sex is a satisfying experience in these novels only if it reflects a democratic and spiritual alliance.

Many of Austin's women characters reflect her ideas on the satisfactory realization of their own genius or talents. In *The Basket Woman,* Olivia in *A Woman of Genius,* and the Chisera in *The Arrow-Maker,* we see the culture hero realized as a strong, intuitively wise, and healing woman. Yet in some of these fictions, the price for exceptional ability and action is ultimately the sacrifice of the individual to the larger society. The medicine woman in *The Arrow-Maker,* after losing her mystic abilities and asking to live as a normal woman, is shot and killed with her own poison arrow by the man she professes to love.

Though the price of the woman protagonist often is sacrifice of the self, Austin makes clear this sacrifice is not to society's inequities but for the ultimate change of societal patterns. It is almost impossible not to read her reworking of these conventional and archetypal aspects in her stories biographically, since she knew the price of "genius" and the sacrifice to be an artist. Also, these new fictions, ultimately creating new roles for men and women who, valuing both their respective "male" and "female" sides could be whole, functioning, creative individuals, reflect Austin's own continuing inner conflict. Calling this inner division her Siamese twin selves (the conflict between the publicist and the poet), she struggled between the dictates of the rational, external world of knowledge and the inner world of myth and story. Restoration, she argued in "Woman Alone," could come through a strengthening of character from sources other than the superficial role definitions of modern American society:

As for not being under the necessity of being liked which began as a defense, it has become part of my life philosophy. I see now that too many of the impositions of society upon women have come of their fear of not being liked. . . . It is in this weakness of women displayed toward their sons which has fostered the demanding attitude of men toward them. It puts women as a class forever at the mercy of an infantile expectation grown into adult convention. . . . But it is women I am aiming at, women and their need for detachment from the personal issue. At present the price for refusing to "manage" men is high, but not too high for a self-respecting woman to pay.[40]

Just how prophetic Mary Austin was may be noted in the timeliness of her considerations of ethnicity, class, and gender, the role of the woman artist, and the consequence of landscape. Her timelessness—the universality of her themes, the primary myths forming her work—lies in more than her historical worth as naturist, folklorist, mystic, or feminist. In fact, the reader, observing that neither Southern California, the lives of Native Americans, nor the role of women are exactly the same as during her lifetime, may justifiably ask what the "value" of Austin is today. Perhaps it is the world within the word that speaks to us so resonantly, for in many cases, it is the word, the style of the work, that still exists to make magic for us in the way in which experienced nature did for Austin. In the unfolding pattern of her life realized in her various works is a special meaning of the pilgrimage, the search. In her own continual expulsion from gardens that harbored her imagination, she had to travel the journey to yet another phase or state, and in so doing discover that one is always in the midst of the pilgrimage—writing—because one does not know the whole story.

"The true emergence of self," Austin wrote, "is dependent upon discipline, upon the *doing* of effective acts rather than the acceptance of dogmas or the practice of selected emotions."[41] As she said of the "friend" in the woods, it is neither form nor symbol but the substance of experience that in its illumination sets in motion the search for words, the pressing toward life adventure. For readers largely estranged from the mysterious and awesome world Austin knew—from the association, say, of the seasons with festival—such universals touch them only when a writer can provoke a deep recognition, a sense of personal relevance in them. Because these events happened to Austin and live in her works, the reader may experience a sense of the sacred though he or she has had no direct contact with the event. As Denise Levertov observes: "Man is the animal that perceives analogies. Even when cut off from tradition, the correspondences that, if he holds open the doors of his understanding, he cannot but perceive, will form images that are myth. The intellect, if not distorted by divorce from the other capacities, is not obstructive to the experience of the mysterious."[42] Renewal and inspiration may be found, if not directly through a set of conscious beliefs or in dream, vision, or archetypal revelation then in the events and intuitions of daily life as re-created in the story. Therefore, style—the process of the story with its recognizable analogies—is itself the journey toward understanding.

Mallarmé observed that convictions that do not find their proper language are not poetry, for poetry is made not of ideas but of words. If Mary Austin's words speak to us today, it is not solely through her polemics on women, creativity, art, or the environment. It is because, at her best, the myths still speak as the words do: Having discovered "Pegasus among the cockleburs," she reveals to us what we forgot we knew.

ᏏᏘ

31

III

WIND'S TRAIL

THE EARLY LIFE OF MARY AUSTIN

🐦

Peggy Pond Church

Peggy Pond Church in 1985.
Photograph by Cynthia Farah.

WEDNESDAY'S CHILD

Monday's child is fair of face;
Tuesday's child is full of grace;
Wednesday's child is full of woe;
Thursday's child has far to go. . . .

If the child who was to become Mary Austin could have chosen her own birthday, it would most certainly have been Monday. No one ever longed more than she to be fair of face nor felt more deprived all her life because she obviously wasn't.

But she came into the world "on the stroke of midnight, between a Wednesday and a Thursday" (*Earth Horizon* 38),[*] and her life saw

---

[*]Editor's Note: Parenthetical documentation has been retained throughout in Church's references to Austin's fiction and nonfiction. For a fuller accounting, the reader is referred to the Selected Bibliography.

a mingling of both days' fates. The uncle who had been waiting around to carry word of the mother's safe delivery to the child's grandfather could think of nothing more flattering to say about her than that she was the " 'noticingest' baby he had ever seen" (*E.H.* 38). Though "noticing" turned out to be the most important habit the child had, she was to suffer all her life because she felt she was not beautiful. She learned to pretend that she didn't care, that she would much rather be thought knowing, but her disappointment shows in almost all her stories.

From the position of the planets at the moment of the child's birth it appeared that she would suffer conflict between the feminine and masculine sides of her nature. She was Virgo with a Gemini moon; she also had Cancer rising, but these feminine influences tended to be outweighed by the dominant positions of the planets Mercury, Uranus, and Mars. According to the astrologers, Mars stands for qualities related to the will, and Mary Austin still is remembered as one of the most self-willed of women. The planet Uranus is associated by some astrologers with revolutionary social change; others think of it as "a planet of genius, the secret magical power in man," which unless accompanied by a good sense of humor—and this was not a noticeable ingredient of Mary Austin's character—can turn to poison. Who can forget that Mercury was once upon a time the god of thieves? He was believed to be a trickster whose cleverness could turn equally to good or evil, a demonic spirit that impels to an insatiable search for knowledge; he also appears as a messenger of the gods. Coyote in American folklore is very much like him, and Mary Austin would often refer to the coyote as her animal brother—which he seems to have been in more ways than she ever realized. Whether or not the planets had anything to do with it, there is little doubt that this newborn child's life was determined by the historical moment she was born into and by the ancestral qualities that strove to come into expression through her.

"It has always been a profound realization of my life that there was a pattern under it," Mary Austin would write in her autobiography, published in 1932 (*E.H.* vii). Like the old Paiute Basket Maker in *The Land of Little Rain*, a book of descriptive essays published in 1903, she wove the pattern out of the materials that were given her and the sense of design that was hers from the beginning.

The particular midnight on which this Wednesday–Thursday child began her life's long journey fell on the ninth of September in 1868, when "the War Between the States"—the Civil War—had been for some three and a half years over. The place was a small town called Carlinville in central Illinois. In 1868 the county commissioners were engaged in building an extravagant courthouse that would be, at the time of its completion, the largest county courthouse in the nation, with the single exception of that in New York City. It was built at such a crushing expense to the taxpayers that the burden of debt would hang over them and their children for more than forty years.

Only a few decades earlier, Illinois had been a wilderness of trees and grass and sluggish streams that meandered toward the larger rivers that feed the rolling Mississippi. Along these rivers Indians once glided in their long canoes, noiseless among the grazing animals, the rustling birds. They sowed their fields of corn in the summer seasons and respected the land for its bounty. The graves of their ancestors made them feel that the land had always belonged to them and would belong to them forever.

Down the rivers in the eighteenth century came Frenchmen exploring out of the Great Lakes, their eyes big with the beauty of the still-unspoiled continent, their minds eager with never-to-be-realized dreams of empire. Upriver from the south, pushing the Spaniard from his precarious toehold along the Gulf of Mexico, and at almost the same time from the east, past the Appalachian Mountain barrier and over the blowing seas of grass, came the land-hungry settlers of the newborn American nation. The bewildered Indians were driven back from their traditional hunting grounds. The earth they had thought of as their ancient mother became, in the white man's hands, mere property to be bought and sold as opportunity for possession or profit came along. Men used the land they snatched from the Indians and from the French not only to dwell on but each for his own financial gain. Forests gave way to fields, to mines, to rutted roads. Animals and birds were hunted without respect or gratitude to the indwelling spirit of all life.

To begin with, each man cleared his own few acres and built a rough cabin for his wife and children, around which wolves still came to sniff at night. Slowly the cabins gave way to neighborly clusters of houses. Towns sprang up, each with a square and a church and streets in even rows. The houses along the streets had picket fences and yards where shrubs and flowers bloomed that had grown from slips brought by the pioneer women from far-off remembered gardens.

It was in one of these houses that Susanna Savilla Hunter, age twenty-five, brought her fourth child to birth, her second daughter. Susanna's first two children had died, the one an infant girl in an officer's tent in a swampy Civil War encampment; the other a boy who had lived not even long enough to have a name. The third child, a little boy called Jim, now hardly more than two years old, had been born in the little house on First South Street in Carlinville. He was just beginning to toddle and from the first was Susanna Hunter's treasure. Only lately she thought he showed signs of a slight limp, which troubled her. Her own father, Milo Graham, had been lame since boyhood. Her husband, Captain George Hunter, had returned from the Civil War unwounded but with his health permanently impaired by malarial fevers. He suffered from asthma and from persistent pain in one leg that was never satisfactorily explained. Susanna couldn't help wondering whether her husband's or her father's infirmity could have been passed on to her little boy. In those days not much was known about heredity, and facts were often mixed with old wives' tales.

Susie had been only a little more than eighteen when she and George Hunter were married. He was a handsome young Englishman who had opened an office for the practice of law upstairs in the drugstore building that Milo Graham owned. The wedding took place in the first summer of the Civil War, a few months after George had enlisted. Susie spent her first married years in army camps, returning to her father's home only to bear her first two babies. In the seven years since her captain-husband took her away from her father's house upon his military arm, Susanna Hunter had grown from a girl to an experienced woman. She had given up the vague dreams she once had of a literary career when her high school compositions were often praised in the local paper. Her pretty mouth was already set into firm lines. She disciplined her thick brown hair to lie flat against her head without a sign of a wave. Her young husband had turned into an often moody invalid who was none too happy with his lawyer's occupation. The glories of war that had been sung so valiantly at its beginning had blackened with the memories of those years of army life, the swamps, the rains, the sickness, the wounded and the dying, and for Susie the birth giving, the tiny bodies so soon buried. It had been evident almost from the beginning of her marriage that it was up to her to be the strong one of the family.

Without her religion Susie would surely have become discouraged. Her father was a devoted Calvinist. Her mother came of strong Methodist stock. Susie's grandfather organized the first Sunday school in Carlinville, and Susanna at the time of her marriage was teaching the infant class. She believed in salvation through repentance for sin and in something called the Joy of the Lord, which was an inward experience she could usually count on to sustain her in her troubles.

What were her thoughts in that first faint hour after midnight as she inspected the infant newly laid beside her? Should she be glad that she had a little girl again? This baby couldn't have been much to look at. The wide down-turned mouth and the chin disappearing into the creases of its neck must have reminded Susanna of her own grandmother, Polly Dugger. Grandmother Polly had become so heavy that she overflowed her chair when she sat down. The baby, however, seemed a scrawny mite. The pointed nose gave her a gnomelike look. Like a bird just out of the egg, she must have seemed all beak and ravenous. Her eyes were too big, and, as brother Otis said, they were noticing, almost too noticing. They kept glancing everywhere as though they were already trying to uncover the world's secrets, or as though something very ancient and wise and knowing was looking out.

Well, one could never tell what an infant's face might grow into. It was just as well for a girl not to be too pretty; the less trouble to keep her from becoming vain, and vanity was one of the sins that Susie Hunter's church most frowned on. Perhaps she sighed a little as she remembered the rosy look of the little girl she had lost almost before her arms had grown used to holding her. It was best for a mother not to let her heart grow too tender. The Lord gave and the Lord too often took away. If such thoughts as these passed through Susie Hunter's mind, she would have had to dismiss them at once. A good Christian like herself must never seem to question the Lord's ways. We can see her settling back upon the pillow, leaving the facing of this new uncertain burden until another day.

THE NAME OF MARY

The midnight child was given the name of Mary. It could have been for her great-great-grandmother of Revolutionary days. It could have been for Great-grandmother Polly McAdams, who married Jarrot Dugger and came to Illinois riding in the tail of a lumbering ox cart. It could have been for her father's sister, Mary, an independent lass who took the money her brother had loaned her to set herself up in the millinery trade and then ran off to marry the Confederate colonel she was in love with. The colonel became a mining engineer; he may have been one of the models for the mining engineers who would play important parts in several of Mary Austin's stories. She could have been named for several other Mary kin on her mother's side, each of whom gave her a silver spoon, a string of beads, or a ring for the namesake. With a twinkle, her father said, "Let them fight it out among them" (E.H. 39).

Our Mary preferred to believe that she was secretly named for an old flame of her father's, Mary Patchen. Though the romance—if romance there ever really was—had happened several years before her father married and at least ten years before Mary was born; though she met Mary Patchen only once, and that rather late in her own life; and in spite of the fact that the beautiful Miss Patchen had thrown George Hunter over for a scoundrel who turned out already to have another wife, Mary Austin liked to imagine, even when she had become an aging woman, that she was really meant to be Mary Patchen's child rather than the child of her own mother and that her father secretly had his own true love in mind when he approved the family name of Mary for his daughter. It seems that Mary was a spinner of legends from the very start; even her autobiography is partly the story of her legendary self. Since her father died when she was only ten years old, she was able to make him over in her mind into the kind of hero that he never was. She was sure that she got her love of books from him, as well as the coppery tints in her heavy hair, which was her only real beauty.

George Hunter, as Mary tells his story, blue-eyed and wearing his hair long "after a fashion of the time" (E.H. 10), had come out of Yorkshire, England, with his brother William in 1851. The young brothers had worked their way from New Orleans to St. Louis on a Mississippi River packet boat. George would later tell his children about this voyage as though it were the most unforgettable adventure of his life, remembering for them "the vast clouding flood . . . the huge rafts . . . the whining clouds of flies and mosquitoes . . . how the Negroes sang, and how the tall loose-jointed 'hands' on the rafts whiled their drifting by betting their wages on the range of their spitting capacity" (E.H. 3–4). His daughter Mary especially loved to hear him repeat that hoary joke about the Irishwoman who had been told of a strange American insect that put down its snout and sucked your blood. When the woman landed at the port of New Orleans, she saw an elephant that was part of the menagerie of a traveling circus being unloaded.

When the elephant waved its trunk, the Irishwoman cried out, "Holy Jaysus, and is *that* a muskaytoe!" (*E.H.* 5).

Mary was sure that it was only in *her* presence that her father dared to use the expression "Holy Jaysus" when he told the story. If her mother were anywhere in sight, he would substitute "Holy Moses." This convinced the small Mary that she and her father were joined in a special conspiracy about "things that weren't to be said in front of Mothers!" (*E.H.* 5).

George Hunter had settled first at Alton, a bustling town "set eagle-wise on the cliffs" (*E.H.* 6) above the Mississippi in the State of Illinois. The whole American West lay wide before him. A few miles south of Alton, the Missouri River entered the Mississippi with its roiling foam of mud and sand washed down from the mountains so far away that they were almost impossible to imagine. The rivers, George learned, had been the chief trails of commerce since the days of the fur traders. Then the railroads began spinning their iron webs throughout the region east of the Mississippi, linking the growing industrial cities and the scattered towns along the route. Who would believe that in another decade construction would be started on a railroad that, reaching out to the goldfields of California, would span the continent?

George Hunter's dreams did not reach as far as California. He had brought with him from England more of a love of farming and growing things than of fortune hunting. The year after his arrival in Illinois, news began to go around that there was still good land to be taken up around Carlinville. The span of railroad from Alton to Carlinville had just been finished, and George was one of those to arrive on the first train, "sharp with the English hunger of land" (*E.H.* 7), as his daughter would always insist.

What persuaded him to take up the study of law instead of farming we can only imagine. There was no doubt the need of making money. The best opportunities for young men at this time in Illinois history seemed to be in politics, and the first step toward politics lay in the law. No doubt George heard considerable talk about men, such as Abraham Lincoln of Springfield, who had gone up

42

from nowhere to be first lawyer, then congressman, and who knows what next. Carlinville, being the county seat, had several notable lawyers already practicing. George, after some years completing his education at Shurtleff College back in Alton, returned to read law in the office of one of Carlinville's prominent citizens, and in 1858, some eight years after his arrival in the United States, he was admitted to the bar. He was then around twenty-five years old.

It was about this time that he and the young schoolteacher, Mary Patchen, began "keeping company." George Hunter had first met her at her brother's home. He discovered that she shared his love for books and intellectual discussion. They read books and attended lectures together. According to legend, Miss Patchen was not only intellectual, she was beautiful. Her hair was golden and her eyes were blue. Her skin was white and rosy like any princess in a fairy tale. This may have made it an even more severe blow to his pride when, after being led to believe that he had spoken lightly of her, she returned his books and letters and forbade him to see her again.

A short time later, Miss Patchen married the out-of-town lecturer who had spread the story. Before the couple returned from the wedding journey, a sheriff arrived with a warrant for the bridegroom's arrest on a charge of bigamy. A lynching was barely prevented. The lecturer was returned to his lawful wife in the custody of the sheriff. Miss Patchen went into seclusion; some months afterward, she married a second time and moved away from Carlinville. Mary Austin claims that her father made no effort to be reconciled with his faithless love, but one of Miss Patchen's brothers claimed years later that Hunter tried to make up and she wouldn't; she expressed her satisfaction that she had got rid of him.

No matter how little or how deeply he had really been involved with Mary Patchen, George Hunter's pride must have taken an awful beating. A blow to the ego is often harder for a man to bear than a blow to the heart, and one wonders whether Mary's father ever really recovered. He managed to hide his feelings, went on with the study of law, and in a year or two opened his own office on the second floor of Milo Graham's drugstore building. A little before this, he began going out with Milo Graham's younger daughter Susanna Savilla, who was soon to become his wife.

According to Miss Patchen's brother, his sister Mary and Susie Graham were pals at school and co-editors of a manuscript paper called the *Morning Star*. They must have been pretty nearly of an age, and we know that George Hunter was eight or ten years older than Susie. Whatever went on in Susie Graham's heart when she became engaged to her friend's cast-off suitor, Mary Austin, her daughter, does not think it important to mention in the autobiography, not even the fact that Mary Patchen and Susie had been friends. In two of her novels, however, the young hero, after being rejected by the glamorous lady of his dreams, marries the hometown girl, or the straightforward playmate, and one wonders whether Mary had been affected by her father's disappointment more than she let herself realize. What Mary wanted to believe—or what she wanted the readers of her autobiography to believe—was that George, in marrying Susie, had been untrue to the one great love of his life. She had always felt that Susie Hunter didn't understand her, in fact, didn't even like her. Like so many children who think they are misunderstood, she had a dream image of a different kind of mother, one who would see her as she wanted to see herself and who would always be loving and praising, never chiding, as a busy mother often has to be. She must have carried this dream deep within her all her life. Mary Austin was more than forty years old, lecturing in a far-off California, she tells us, when a Mrs. Snyder called at her hotel.

"You don't know me," she said; "would it help if I told you I am Mary Patchen?" (*E.H.* 316).

As reported in her autobiography, Mary said yes, she had seen the name in some of her father's books. The two women talked of George Hunter all afternoon. Mrs. Snyder told Mary how she and her husband had called on the Hunters in Carlinville the summer before Mary, Susanna Hunter's fourth child, was born. "It came over her," Mrs. Snyder said (*E.H.* 316), that Susie Hunter didn't really want this baby. How she wished it could have been hers and George's. Though nothing was said, Mrs. Snyder felt as though that was just what George must be thinking. She had followed Mary's career, she said, and showed herself "familiar with the most intimate of my [Mary's] writing" (*E.H.* 317). As they talked, it seemed to Mary Austin that her long-lost father "moved beside us there in the room" (*E.H.* 317).

"I never saw her again, but I never forgot her," Mary Austin tells us (*E.H.* 317).

From the report of Mary Patchen's kin, it seems unbelievable that this story could have happened anywhere but in Mary Austin's imagination. Perhaps in a moment of weariness and discouragement in a lonely hotel room, her need to feel herself the child not of her mother but of her father and his "one great love of his life" (*E.H.* 318) emerged again in dream to reassure her that from the first hers had been a special destiny. All her life, the child named Mary would find it difficult to distinguish between dream and reality, between "story-telling" and the truth of every day, between her father and mother as actual people and the characters she gave them in her own life's drama.

THE CUCKOO'S EGG

"Whatever in Mary makes her worth so much writing about has its roots in the saga of Polly and Hannah and Susanna Savilla, in the nurture of which she grew up" (*E.H.* 14). Polly was Great-grandmother Polly Dugger, who had been born Mary McAdams in 1792, had married Jarrot Dugger in 1811, and, after several migrations, had come with him to settle in Carlinville in 1833.

There was a family tradition that Mary Austin very much wanted to believe that Dugger was originally spelled Daguerre and that the American Duggers were collateral relatives of "the distinguished French chemist, Louis Jacques Mandé Daguerre, inventor of the daguerreotype" (*E.H.* 13). Unfortunately, Mary was unable to trace the original Daguerre, due to the expense and effort required, so she had to be satisfied with just the hint of an aristocratic connection and with a cousin's assurance that his grandmother, Polly Dugger, had once been referred to by the wife of President James A. Polk as "my earliest young friend" (*E.H.* 13). Aside from these rather wispy claims to fame, "the Duggers . . . were plain people, neither rich nor poor, devoid of airs, loving the soil, good bargainers, the women rather outmatching the men in that quality indispensable to pioneer society, known as mother-wit" (*E.H.* 14).

To tell the truth, if the Duggers had much love of the soil, as Mary liked to claim, they seem to have loved it in the typical American way, for the profit they could gain from it. Indeed, Jarrot Dugger had hardly settled in Carlinville before he became a storekeeper. He organized the first Sunday school and served acceptably for several terms as county commissioner. His son Samuel established the first newspaper in the town—though it passed into other hands after the first two years. Of all that the Duggers accomplished, Mary Austin insists, "so much was of the soil, of the solidly middle class, Middlewest, that considering the odd, the unconformable gesture she has made, except for Polly, you might suppose that Mary was hatched from a cuckoo's egg" (*E.H.* 14).

One can't be sure just why Mary Austin likes to make an exception of Polly. She knew her ancestress as a real person only slightly, for her great-grandmother died at the age of seventy-nine when Mary was only three. The child's impressions were of "a sibylline and rather fearsome old lady, who overflowed her chair completely when she sat . . . so that, at her funeral . . . the body had to be brought out of doors to the casket, which could not be conveniently carried in" (*E.H.* 19).

It was from Polly's side of the family, Mary confesses, that the Duggers "took the disposition toward portliness that characterized them all in middle age" (*E.H.* 19). A picture of Polly and her twin sister, that must have been taken in their middle years, shows two shapeless, sagging figures with the heavy features and the drooping mouth that seem to have been a family trait, skipping Susanna Savilla, who was thin as a folded umbrella, to show up in Mary, at least in her worst moments. People who remember Mary Austin in her later years still tell the story of how she was once overheard through the thin walls of a hospital bath reciting over and over the phrase, "Oh, my beautiful body! Oh, my beautiful body!" according to the formula recommended by Dr. Emile Coué, a psychologist of that day famous for his insistence on the powers of autosuggestion (Ruth Morrison, correspondence, PPC papers).

In Mary's imagination, Polly loomed as the type of pioneer woman who stood shoulder to shoulder with her man confronting the wilderness, fulfilled in the awareness and use of her own feminine powers, her "intuitional" approach as contrasted with the "male ritual of rationalization" (E.H. 15). Austin writes, "It is to the things that the Polly McAdamses discovered in their westward trek that Mary's generation owed the success of their revolt against the traditional estimate of women at the rating of an effect produced, and reëstablished for them the criterion of a result achieved" (E.H. 15).

Chief of the discoveries of the Polly McAdamses, as it was told to Mary, or as Mary persuaded herself it had been told,

> was the predominance of happenings of the hearth, as against what happens on the battlefield and in the market-place, as the determinant of events. What they found out was that the hope of American democracy and the justification of the Declaration of Independence depended precisely on the capacity of the Polly McAdamses to coördinate society, to establish a civilization, to cause a culture to eventuate out of their own wit and the work of their hands, out of what they could carry with them into the wilderness . . . with no more labored equipment than a wooden pestle and a mortar of Indian make, a tin grater for corn meal, a deep pot and a frying-pan, and their own intention (E.H. 15).

In the figure of Polly, Mary was probably praising her own intention, for it seems doubtful that Polly, in that day and age, was really so self-conscious. The actual stories Mary remembered from her childhood are concerned with the down-to-earth aspect of Polly, the real Polly, who in spite of all intellectual interpretation must have existed deep within Mary's blood and bone, the woman she herself might have been had not "her own intention" driven her to a far different destiny.

"One heard, when one was young and had a listening ear" (E.H. 17) how Polly, the wife of Jarrot, came into the country of the "Eellanoy," as the old songs had it, "sitting on a bundle of pieced quilts and blankets of her own spinning, on the tail of an ox cart, and with an unrelinquished claim on all the sanctions of civilization and the preciousness of womanhood in her heart" (E.H. 15). One can't help suspecting that the "preciousness of womanhood" was another of Mary Austin's ideas which she liked to think came to her from Polly. In 1833, when Polly and Jarrot Dugger settled in Carlinville, Polly was forty-one years old and had already borne all but one of her ten children. It is unlikely that she had time or inclination to consider the "preciousness of womanhood," if indeed the phrase had even been invented then.

What Polly obviously did possess was "mother-wit" (E.H. 14), the practical wisdom of women that is always concerned with the realities of every day. It was Polly who, somewhere along the way, had persuaded Jarrot to build a waterwheel to which the spinning wheels of the neighbor women could be attached so that their hands the while could go on with the piecing and quilting. When Jarrot's apple orchard, the first in Carlinville, came into bearing, Polly invented a way to put up the fruit in wide-mouthed crocks, long before screw-topped jars were invented. Polly's recipe for "spiced apples" was handed down in the family at least as far as her great-granddaughter Mary, who would always seem her most real and human self when she was stirring a savory kettle or ladling out glasses full of jelly from her own currant bushes.

The Dugger women not only enjoyed good cooking, they obviously enjoyed good eating. "Polly's 'spiced apples' went notably with the venison pot-pie, which was the local company dish, or with tom-turkey stuffed with pecan meats and roasted before the fire" (E.H. 17). The spirit of Polly shone at its best in Mary Austin

48

when, visiting friends with whom she felt most at home in later life, she would put on a big apron and go into her hostess's kitchen to toss a couple of pumpkin pies together. In her autobiography, she recalls vividly "houses where pumpkin pie was two inches thick and served with a great gob of new comb honey" (*E.H.* 69).

Despite Mary's normal accomplishments in the literary world and her lifelong spiritual aspirations, her flesh remained very much that of Polly Dugger. When asked if he knew the exact cause of her death, which was officially noted as heart trouble, the attending physician told a young acquaintance bluntly, "she died of overeating," for in spite of all his warnings about the importance of restricting her diet, Mary would get up as soon as the doctor's or the nurse's back was turned and devour the refrigerator's contents.

It was Polly's fourth daughter, Hannah, who in 1841 married Milo Graham and became the mother of romantically named Susanna Savilla, Mary's mother. Hannah inherited both Aunt Polly's ingenuity and her "aptitude for cookery." "Aunt Hannah's smokehouse" and "Aunt Hannah's gingerbread" (*E.H.* 20) were family bywords long after Hannah herself had passed away. The time Milo's drugstore caught fire in the night and burned totally to the ground, Hannah was up at daybreak selling hot gingerbread to the bystanders. "All that day, as the countryside came in to the rare spectacle of smoking ruins, she sold them bread and gingercakes, and kept on selling until the store could be rebuilt and business restored" (*E.H.* 20).

Hannah Graham died when her daughter Susie was only ten, so Mary knew her grandmother only through her mother's recollection. The story she liked best was the one "about the tailor-made dress. . . . On their wedding journey to St. Louis, . . . Milo . . . bought for his handsome bride a fine length of broadcloth, which . . . he [who had once been apprenticed to a tailor] made up for her at home" (*E.H.* 19).

No one in Carlinville had ever heard of such a thing as a tailor-made dress, let alone a man who would make a dress for his wife with his own hands. A little later, when a visiting daguerreotypist came through town in his traveling van, "Milo had his young wife pictured in the very dress, . . . for which she was promptly 'Disciplined' " by the Methodist church (E.H. 19). This meant that, due notice having been given all around, she was called to the front seat on the following Sunday to have the Church Discipline regarding vanity real aloud and then a sermon preached on the subject. "One must suppose that the church was well filled on that occasion, and that it was at the properly dramatic moment . . . the young matron walked down the aisle with her limping and totally unperturbed Scotchman beside her, *wearing that particular dress!" (E.H. 19–20).*

"It was so exactly the thing Mary would have done!" Mary Austin declares (E.H. 20), but one suspects that Mary would have done it out of bravado rather than out of the assurance of love that obviously surrounded Hannah.

In Hannah's twelve years of married life, she bore seven children to the man she loved, of which only three survived her. She died trying to deliver her last child. "That was the hazard of early American women, and husbands were supposed to accept it as the inscrutable will of God," Mary Austin comments (E.H. 20–21). Sixteen months later, Milo Graham married again, a widow named Eliza Boring, with a young son of her own. Eliza bore two children to Milo and raised her stepchildren kindly, taking care to instruct Susie and Mary Ann in the elements of young ladyhood, "the use of Cucumber and Elder-Flower Cream, steeped in buttermilk," for their complexions, carefully lacing "them into their hourglass corsets for the preservation of their figures" (E.H. 21).

After thirteen years of marriage, Eliza, too, died. Her stepdaughters were by then grown and married with homes of their own. Her own children were still in their teens. Barely a year later, Milo Graham, a dignified patriarch of fifty-one, again brought home a wife. Her name was Sophia Applegate, and although the third wife survived him, along with his five children, Mary Austin never mentions her except in a footnote in her autobiography (see E.H. 369, Note 6).

MILO GRAHAM

One can't help wondering about the things Mary Austin chooses *not* to tell us about Milo Graham, her mother's father, whose blood flowed in her veins as surely as Polly Dugger's ever did. She presents him, both in her autobiography and, thinly disguised, in her last novel, *Starry Adventure,* as a venerable and kindly man whom she loved and of whom she was also a little afraid. "She worked him endless perforated cardboard book-markers, and learned whole chapters of the Bible" (*E.H.* 67) to please him, proud when she won the $5 he had offered to the first of his grandchildren to convince him he or she had read the Bible all the way through. Once she dug up a Scotch harebell and gave it to her grandfather in a pot because she thought it romantic that "he was Scotch" (*E.H.* 67). He kept the plant in the window until it bloomed, though Mary never felt sure he understood the feeling that went with it or whether he just kept it "because he was the gentlest-hearted old darling that ever lived, who wouldn't for anything have hurt the child's feelings" (*E.H.* 67).

Milo Graham, the father of Susanna Savilla, she tells us, "had come into Illinois from Ohio in 1839. Milo's father had apprenticed him, lame from his early youth, to a tailor, much against the choice of his soul which had been for the study of medicine. Making the best compromise possible between inclination and necessity, the young man had worked at his trade until he could teach himself pharmacy, traveled alone on horseback to Carlinville, and in the course of a few years established himself in a drugstore which he built and owned" (*E.H.* 12).

This is all Mary Austin reveals about her grandfather's background. She never seems to consider the possibility that she and he might have more in common than their Scottish blood or that "whatever in Mary makes her worth so much writing about" may have had its roots in her Graham lineage as well as in the "saga of Polly and Hannah and Susanna Savilla" (*E.H.* 14) in which she takes so much pride.

"I am trying to trace out in the family connection the source of my literary gift," she tells her cousin, Anna Burns, in a letter written February 9, 1933, not long after her autobiography was published. "I can find nothing at all in the family history in the past except a little talent for music and of course the literary gifts my father had." Her father's literary gifts seem to have existed chiefly in Mary's imagination. As far as one knows, George Hunter's writing consisted mostly of papers read at local farmers' or horticultural society meetings, on such subjects as the culture of vines and the breeding of fancy hogs. He also is known to have written legal papers and letters concerning soldiers' pensions. Among those who knew him as a young lawyer, "his well-stored memory, his ready gift of words, his flexible and argumentative turn of mind are favorably remembered. For the whole of his life thereafter his name appears in the local papers as connected with every forward community interest" (*E.H.* 9). We have only Mary's word for it that he harbored special literary ambitions.

Curiously enough, it was Susie Graham, the girl George Hunter married, whose schoolgirl compositions were indeed "faithfully reported in the local papers" (*E.H.* 23); Susie, rather than George, had "even aspired to a writing career, of which," says Mary Austin patronizingly, "except as she observed it through the women contributors of 'Godey's Lady's Book,' she had not the faintest idea" (*E.H.* 23). Not for anything could Mary bring herself to admit that her mother was at least the intellectual equal of her father or that Susie's literary ambitions were ever worth considering. Only when she wished to rebuke her mother for appearing not to understand her daughter's work does she declare inconsistently that Susie "had been all her life a devoted reader of 'Scribner's,' 'Harper's,' and the 'Atlantic Monthly.' " (*E.H.* 255).

It looks as though, in her effort to build up her chosen image of herself, Mary felt forced to run her mother down. Perhaps she really wanted to believe she had been "hatched from a cuckoo's egg" (*E.H.* 14) or that her own intellect had sprung like the motherless goddess Minerva from the head of Jove.

However, with all her accomplishments, it is obvious that Susanna Hunter was not a poet, and this may have been the crucial difference between her and her daughter. Moreover, Susie was musical and Mary was not. Susie had a sweet contralto voice and sang in the church choir. Mary was the only one in the family who could never carry a tune. Susie's father, Milo Graham, loved to play the flute for hymn singing, white beard and all, at his house on Sunday afternoons. Mary does not mention that he could also play the violin.

When Mary Austin began to write her autobiography in 1929, her cousin, Mrs. Anna Burns, the daughter of Susanna Savilla's sister Mary Ann, sent her some details about the Graham family history that Mary apparently had never seen and that for some reason she fails to mention in her own account:

> *Janot [sic] Graham: Born in Scotland n. d. Came to America and settled near New Canaan, Conn. Later moved to Nelsonville, Ohio. A school teacher. A violinist of more than ordinary ability and something of a poet. A lover of the beautiful in Art and Nature. Tall, fair, blue eyes, light hair, a typical Scotchman. His wife, Theda Case, was born in north Ireland of Protestant parentage. Described as being one of the most placid and lovable women of her time. Gentle, kind, beloved by all.*
>
> *One of Janot and Theda's sons was Milo Graham, born June 18, 1817. A druggist. He played the violin and the flute. He was an artist of some ability and a great lover of nature. He loved to experiment with unusual varieties in flowers and plants. In his young manhood he had a swelling of the knee which left him lame for the remainder of his life. He was a man of lovable disposition and mild temper. . . . Milo Graham was a Calvinist. Besides his love of music, he could draw with considerable skill and also wrote interesting rhymes* (Mary Austin Collection, Huntington Library).

The love of beauty and nature, the vein of poetry, even the eye for "unusual varieties in flowers and plants" that were to distinguish the best of Mary Austin's writing were plainly evident in her Graham forebears. One would have expected this to have excited Mary greatly in her search for her antecedents. Yet in thanking her cousin for the information, all she says is, "I was especially interested in the note of Jaret Graham; in my family Bible, however, it is spelled Jarrot. I had nothing about this."

Could there have been something about her grandfather that Mary didn't wish to see, something she had been taught, perhaps, to be afraid of, something she concealed, even from her own eyes, behind the facade of the kindly Bible-reading patriarch?

An early photograph of Milo Graham reveals a young man with sensitive features and the burning eyes of a poet, the delicate, almost feminine look of a Keats, a Shelley. One likes to imagine him on that long, solitary horseback ride across almost the whole width of three states, from Ohio through Indiana to Illinois, through forests and prairie openings that blazed with wildflowers. How much there would have been to invite his beauty-loving eye, the forests still largely virgin, oak trees and hickory, black walnut and tulip trees, dogwood and wild crab apple. Here and there the oldest half-decaying trees would be festooned with vines, woodbine, clematis, wild grape, and bittersweet. Interested as he was in growing things, he would already have known most of the flowers by name, the phlox, the lilies, the mints, the goldenrod.

The young man would have found himself surrounded by nature's music as well as by her beauty. If he had his flute or his violin with him—the naturalist Audubon is known to have traveled with his—he would have made music of his own, at dusk before sleeping or at noontime under the trees. He was twenty-two years old. One wonders whether the struggle with his own passionate feelings was already strong within him, for Milo Graham had been reared a Calvinist, which faith seems more afraid of the spell of beauty upon the human heart and of the quality of human tenderness than any other.

Milo Graham not only loved music and nature, he also loved beauty in women, as the labor of love in fashioning the tailor-made dress for his young bride showed. Unlike most Calvinists, he seems to have been unusually indulgent toward his daughters. Mary Ann, Susanna Savilla's sister, somehow always managed to be well dressed. Her father used to take the girls, each in her turn, on his semiannual buying trips to St. Louis to replenish his drugstore stock. From one of these Mary Ann returned "with the roomiest possible hoopskirt, inside which she swam elegantly down the church aisle the next Sunday, only to discover that no amount of tilting it this way and that would get it between the benches, so that she had finally to sail out again amid the discreet smiles of the congregation" (E.H. 24–25). According to one of Mary Austin's nieces, there was a family legend that Milo Graham had altogether had five wives. "He seems to have been quite a ladies' man, and when a wife died there was always another waiting to take over" (Mary Hunter Wolf, personal communication). There seems to be some hint of this in Mary Austin's novel, *Starry Adventure*, which she wrote at almost the same time as the autobiography, as though there were certain things she understood about her grandfather that she could only reveal in the disguise of fiction.

The grandfather in the novel is seen through the eyes of the young boy Gard, but the memories come out of the experience of Mary: The figure of the saintly old man was for a long time associated in the child's mind with the appearance of God, "his white beard brushed out over his black coat, with his limp-covered Bible clasped to his chest as he set out Sunday afternoon for the mission . . . the half-remembered phraseology from the Old Testament readings . . . to the sound of which he so often went to sleep" (*Starry Adventure* 9).

"Grampa Gardiner's" first wife dies. Too lonely in his big house after that, he persuades his church to give him a traveling appointment, and from one of these he brings "Nettie" back, a woman his daughter thinks dreadfully wrong from the beginning. Nettie becomes dissatisfied with the limitations of a preacher's salary. She "liked pretty things; she had been attractive in a showy way, and it was all she had" (S.A. 139). "You don't know," Gard's mother explains to her questioning children, "how women run after a man like your grandfather." In her disappointment, Nettie up and leaves her husband "during one of his traveling occasions," taking money he had on hand that belonged to the church. Grampa is disgraced in the eyes of the community. "A minister," Mother says, "a Christian minister, cannot go about preaching while he is living apart from his wife, no matter how blamelessly." One's thoughts somehow turn to Grandpa Graham and the mysterious third wife, Sophia Applegate, who never appears as a member of his household. Had there been some scandal or disappointment connected with her?

In *Starry Adventure*, Gard's family has moved to New Mexico because of an invalid father's health. There Grampa, who has never heard from his missing wife, develops a friendship with one of the women at the Protestant mission who then pursues him and claims he has promised to marry her. It turns out that she is mentally unbalanced and has to be taken away by her brother from the East. The boy Gard does not understand, but he is old enough to have some sense of his grandfather's distress: "Grampa and Mother were sitting on the *banca*, and Grampa's head was in his hands, 'Oh Marian,' the boy hears him say, 'what is a man to do? It isn't as if I wanted anything that isn't right and natural. For a clergyman it is so difficult—and then the hunger of the heart, Marian!' " The conversation breaks off. That evening when Grampa reads the Bible lesson, Gard goes to him, snuggling between arm and knee, with his hand stroking his grandfather's white beard, as the child Mary may once upon a time have longed to do (S.A. 36).

When Gard begins growing up, his grandfather tries to warn him about sex:

You're a growing big boy, Gard—the fire of the flesh will begin for you, the fire and the torment and the need of the spirit of overcoming (fire and torment of the flesh hot and quaking—as it had been when Tiepolo told him things. Things like you read in the dictionary when you knew what the words said, but not what they meant. And yet somehow you did know. The meaning of them was inside you. —Sex, Grampa called it. Not just a word to be

*whispered shamefacedly. A fact that shook and twisted through you.
You couldn't help it, and yet somehow you must help it. You must
never forgive yourself if you failed, and always forgive other people
in order that you might be forgiven. Down, down at the bottom of
the pit toward which you felt yourself dragged even as Grampa
talked, you were together struggling. And yet you came through.
Grampa had come through. In that certainty it was almost as though
you had come through yourself. You had been in the pit and the
tornillo, and you were planting tomatoes with Grampa in the cool
of the garden)* (S.A. 89–90).

Later the old man tries to give his grandson another warning:

*"Gard," said his grandfather, "I've been a servant of the Lord
almost all my life. I gave myself up to Him in early youth, a year
or so older than you are. I've never regretted it. I've done my best
according to my lights. But I want to tell you—you mustn't think
—sometimes the light—fails. Sometimes when we think we have
the light we find we are walking in the desire of the flesh. And we
are punished. We are grievously punished. The desires of the flesh
are deceiving. You—we—mustn't judge each other harshly, Son"*
(S.A. 119).

There can be scarcely any doubt that Milo Graham was the
model for Grampa Gardiner, that he too had given himself up to
the Lord in his early youth and that the stern Old Testament God
had not been entirely able to suppress the kind and gentle spirit
of Milo's mother and the poetic, beauty-loving nature of his father
with which he had been born.

There are other strange facts about her grandfather's family that
Mary Austin does not reveal. According to records in a family
Bible, one of Milo's sisters had died in the state mental hospital at
Jacksonville, her trouble caused by "religious emotion and grief."
His son Otis, Susie Graham's stepbrother, died in the same insti-
tution from the consequences of what was then called "dissipation."
Was there a tendency toward emotional instability among the

Grahams that the more stolid Duggers distrusted? Did Susie Hunter have real cause to be anxious about her daughter's show of artistic temperament? Did Mary overhear too much in her childhood that was never explained, listening through thin walls or outside a closed door, like the children in two of the novels she would write years later?

Her father's disappointment in love, her mother's frustrated ambition, her grandfather's struggle against his own loving and artistic nature—these buried human emotions seem to have seeped into her to become part of the hidden experiences which she later called "ancestral" in her 1931 book *Experiences Facing Death*.

ANOTHER BABY IN THE HOUSE

Mary Austin believed that all the really important things happened, or had begun to happen, before she was five years old.

The first thing she knew, there was another baby in the house. Suddenly, mysteriously, she was transplanted out of the cradle with its comforting rocking motion and put to sleep in the imprisoning crib where she cried resentfully until Mama came and scolded and told her, "Sh! . . . she mustn't wake the baby." Waking the baby always meant waking Papa, too, for George Hunter's asthma or his bad leg bothered him at night and he had trouble sleeping. With three children on her hands and an ailing husband, Susie had little time to spend cuddling two-year-old Mary.

Susie had never been a particularly maternal type. A photograph taken in her forties suggests that her features were strong rather than tender and that her bosom might be a little hard to lean against. She had a mind of her own, too, and a brilliant one, so her Carlinville neighbors have reported. She taught in the Methodist Sunday school until for some unknown reason her husband forbade it. After his death she took it up again and continued it most of her life. When her children were old enough she never missed the Chautauqua lectures, and she took an active part in the work of the Women's Christian Temperance Union almost from its very beginning. She used to say, when other women wondered how she managed to find so much time for these activities, "I served my time at staying at home when my children were little. Now I mean to enjoy myself" (*E.H.* 177).

The new baby was another little girl. Her name was Jennie, and from the first she was as pretty as her name. All the neighbors bustled to the little house on First South Street to admire her. Mary's earliest memory was of a day when the house was full of grownup people. How lost she must have felt in that forest of aunts and uncles and cousins, for Susie Hunter belonged to a numerous tribe. Brother Jim, now four years old, would have hung about Mama proudly. No one was paying much attention to two-year-old Mary. She couldn't understand much that they said, but there is little doubt that she could sense the comparisons that were being made. All her life she had a way of knowing what was going on in the minds of the people around her.

Smothered by the folds of the aunts' long dresses and butted by the trousered legs of the uncles, she managed to find her way out of the house and halfway across the fenced yard before anyone missed her. She already felt more at home in the out-of-doors than she ever did in houses. Outdoors she could be the center of the world again. The sun shone to warm her. The leaves twinkled their shadows across her hands when she held them out. The wind ruffled her dress like a happy playmate.

All the same, it wasn't long before she thought of Papa, whose hand she usually held when she came by herself this far. Today Papa, undoubtedly proud of the way his wife's relatives were praising the fluff of soft hair, the pink-and-white coloring of his new little daughter, was not thinking much about Mary. Perhaps it is not so strange that her earliest memories always seem to have Jennie in the picture and Mary being forgotten or pushed out.

Like the other time that same summer that she recounts in *Earth Horizon:* The whole family is walking home after a Sunday visit, perhaps to let Grandma Polly see the new baby. Jim is clinging to Mama's hand and Papa is carrying Jennie. The white christening robe she is dressed in for showing off trails over his arm, dainty with tucks and ruffles. No one cares what Mary might be wearing. No one offers to hold her hand. She trudges along behind on her short little legs, getting hotter and hotter and feeling more and more deserted. The hill suddenly seems to grow so much steeper. All at once she is sure she can go no further and plants herself firmly down in the middle of the boardwalk. Papa looks around as if he were sorry. He starts to hand the baby over to Mama so he can pick up his older daughter.

"Let her alone," says Mama crossly. "She'll come when she finds she has to. Look at Jim, he's not complaining" (*E.H.* 41). Jim was bigger than Mary, of course, already past four, with a head of reddish curls and a merry look that could tease Mama out of wanting to scold him. Because he was a boy, Jim hadn't been made to feel he had to take second place when Mary came along. More and more as she grew up, Mary found that boys get their way about a lot of things that girls weren't even supposed to think of.

Before Jennie came, allowances were made for Mary, too, because she was the baby. Now, more and more, Mama expected her to keep up with Jim or else stay out of the way and not bother. When she plunked herself down on the boardwalk, Mary hadn't really expected they'd all go off and leave her. She saw the familiar figures disappear over the edge of the hill as though they were going out of her world forever. The sky spread bigger and emptier all around her. She felt herself growing smaller and smaller until she was almost nothing at all. She really must have been tired out, for when Papa came back in a very few minutes to rescue her, she'd fallen fast asleep. The moment of terror and loss left a mark that never went away.

'MAGINATION

The next thing the little girl knew they were moving a mile out of town to a small farm at the end of Plum Street. The move was made because of Captain Hunter's health. He always felt better when he could be out-of-doors. More than anything he enjoyed experimenting in the English way with growing vines and fruit trees. He had a feeling for the care of land, even though Mary liked best to think of her father as really an intellectual.

About this time Carlinville extended its city limits to take in part of the land that belonged to the farm, so Captain Hunter could hold office as city magistrate. That meant he was called "Judge," which sounded important to his children. Though the position was a minor one, perhaps it helped him feel less resentful that he had not come home from the war a general. Several of his close friends had not only become generals but had gone on to play important parts in state politics. They grew rich enough to have big houses; some of them kept fancy horses while George Hunter's family had to struggle along barely able to keep out of debt.

Mary was only two and a half when they moved, and Jennie was still a cradle baby. Jim, going on five, was old enough to have the fun of it. They let him ride on the back of the wagon with the last load of family possessions—safely settled, everyone thought, on one of the mattresses—but on the way, the horses had to tug and heave uphill through sticky spring mud and the little boy bounced off. The uncles and cousins were proud to hear how he'd scrambled back on the wagon all by himself without a cry for help to anyone.

But when Mary, feeling out of it as usual because she was little and only a girl, began to tell Jim's story exactly as though she'd been there, her mother told her to keep quiet, she couldn't possibly have seen it.

"But I did too!" said Mary. She squeezed her eyes up tight and there the old wagon was and the little boy pulling himself back up on it with mud stuck all over him, exactly like a picture in a book.

"You just imagined it," Mama said.

"What is 'magine, Mama?" Mary wanted to know.

"Thinking you see things when you don't," her mother told her (*E.H.* 42).

But how could you? [Mary wondered]. And how did you know the difference between seeing and thinking you had seen? (*E.H.* 42). Why did mother think storying was so wicked when grown-up people told stories all the time? The Hunter children had been brought up on stories since before they knew how to listen!

Like the one about "Great-Grandmother Polly being carried off by Indians" (*E.H.* 44) when she was a little girl. You couldn't possibly imagine great-grandmother being little, so it had to be yourself you saw in the story instead, and your own heart you felt beating as you lay on the ground with Mama shushing you—only it wasn't really your own mama, but great-grandma's mama long ago.

And the Civil War. By the time Mary was born, it had been over for more than three years, but she always felt as though she'd lived through it her own self. She'd stood right with her mother when the comet blazed across the sky, bright as the terrible swift sword in the hymn. She could hear with her own ears the whispers about the runaway slaves who were hidden from house to house across the Illinois farmlands on their way to Canada. She could smell the smoke of the battles and see the bayonets flashing in the sunlight, the dead strewn in the field, the flag waving victory. Well, of course she really hadn't seen a bit of it. It was just the stories she'd grown up hearing over and over at her mother's knee, in the houses of her kin, at old soldiers' reunions. It was no wonder Mary could never quite get it into her head what her mother meant when she said she guessed she'd better spank the child to keep her from growing up a storyteller.

Another thing she soon found out was that grown-up people kept things inside their heads that weren't supposed to be talked about, those "things going on in people's minds, of what they carefully weren't talking about" (E.H. 45). Mary had a way of knowing without being told what people around her really felt and thought. When Mama had company, she sometimes let Mary sit in her own little chair in the corner by the fireplace if she'd promise to be quiet and not say a single word. Mary was always being told that children were supposed to be seen and not heard, but since the moment she learned to talk, she found nothing so hard as keeping still. Words had to come out. If you kept them shut up inside too long, you felt as though you'd burst,—and burst Mary sometimes did. What she burst out with was very often what her mother's visitors were most carefully not talking about—hurt feelings, secret suspicions, or whatever the politely smiling ladies might really be thinking about one another.

Mary hadn't an idea what made it happen. It was, she said, as though a little bird hopped right onto her tongue and spoke instead of her. Mama said her friends would think Mary had overheard her talking about them behind their backs, even though no one, not even her own children, had ever heard Susanna Hunter say one unkind word about another. "I think the child is possessed," she would exclaim in pure despair (E.H. 45).

Mary hadn't a notion what being "possessed" could mean. In the Bible Grandpa Graham read aloud in his own parlor every Sunday, there were people possessed of devils—sometimes seven at a time!—and there was always a commotion going on around them trying to get the devil out. Of course, the days were long past when good Christian people believed in witches, although they hadn't quite got over the old way of speaking. If you were "possessed," it could still be said that a witch must have done it to you. Susanna Hunter had too good a mind and too much education to believe such a thing. All she knew was that there was something about this little daughter she could never quite understand. She didn't believe in Mary's little bird. Nobody ever did.

"I-MARY"

The next thing to be remembered was the coming of "I-Mary."

It must have been when she was a little past four years old, for Jim had started to go to school not many months before. That left Mary out of it again, cooped up at home, with her little mind buzzing like a hive of bees in winter and no flowers anywhere. Jennie was just a toddler, too little for games and stories. Mary missed her big brother, which surprised her, the way he always kept on being Mama's pet.

At last came a stormy day when Jim had to be kept home from school. Mama was making bread in the warm, steamy kitchen. Outside the wind howled like one of the wolves in the old settlers' stories. Needles of snow flashed against the window. Jim was sitting at one side of the table, proudly reciting the letters out of his new primer. Mary stood near him on a little stool. Mama, to keep Mary quiet, had given her bits of pinched-off dough to roll and pat on one corner of the board, but pretending to help Mama wasn't half as interesting as watching Jim say his letters, the little boy so proud of showing what he'd learned.

"A," said Jim, and "O." Mary rounded her mouth in the shape of the letter and copied him. "O, O, O," she repeated over and over. It was the same kind of fun as rolling the bits of dough into small balls when she moved her two hands back and forth.

"I," said Jim, and "Eye?" questioned Mary, pointing to her own eye like the game she sometimes played with Jennie.

"No," said Mother. "I, myself, *I* want a drink, I-Mary" (*E.H.* 46).

Something seemed to turn over inside the little girl. "The picture happened," Mary Austin writes. "There was the familiar room, the flurry of snow outside; Mama kneading bread; Jim with his molasses-colored hair 'roached' on top, so that the end of the curl fell over in the middle of his forehead; Mary in her flannel frock and blue chambray pinafore . . . how small her hand looked beside Mama's . . . the grimy bit of dough rolled out like a worm. . . And inside her, I-Mary, looking on. I-Mary, I-Mary, I-Mary!" (*E.H.* 46).

She was as clear as a picture in your mind—and yet not exactly a picture you could see. Someone who must have been there all along but never known until that minute. "I-Mary, I-Mary, *I-Mary!*"

Before she came there had always been just Mary, the Mary, one supposes, that everyone bossed around or talked about. "Mary-you," "Mary-she," "What on earth is Mary up to now?" This Mary you could see as though she were someone outside yourself, someone who had things done to and for and about her, but never before "I-Mary." "I-Mary" didn't seem to be just a little girl but someone who'd been before the Mary everyone complained about had ever been and who knew as much as there ever was to know.

At first I-Mary seemed to come mostly out of books, as though books were another world than the everyday one and as though another Mary than the one who was just one of your parents' children came to life when you looked at the printed page. As soon as ever you found out what the words meant, she was there. Was it knowing how to read that made her come? For awhile Mary kept following Jim around every chance she got and making him tell her everything he learned. He didn't seem to mind her pestering. He showed her how to put her finger under the words and say them after him. After awhile she could do it by herself, point her finger at a word and call its name. All at once something behind the word would open like a door. What a joy when you found you could read the story by your own self instead of always bothering Jim or Mama or even sometimes Papa when he seemed to be in a good mood.

It wasn't exactly as though I-Mary did the reading. It seemed to be everyday Mary who said, "I can read," just as she said, "I can button my pinafore myself." The stories were part of the world from which I-Mary came, the world of the pictures inside her mind that made Mama shake her head when she tried to tell about them.

Another thing she discovered about I-Mary: She wasn't dependent on anyone. She helped you not to feel little or afraid, not of being left alone, nor of walking a log over the brook when Jim ran ahead and wouldn't hold your hand. If you could remember I-Mary, in time you didn't mind being spanked when you did something Mama said you shouldn't, like taking your shoes and stockings off and wading in the brook after she'd told you she knew it was too cold. Mama thought you ought to feel sorry you had displeased her, but when I-Mary appeared, you knew you didn't have to feel sorry. Hadn't you put your own finger in the water and found it was as warm as ever?

Mary thought it wasn't fair of Mama not to let the children do things their own way, which was very different most of the time from the way of the grown-up world. Like when she said they could play in the meadow for an hour and then scolded them when they didn't come in at the end of it. How could children be expected to go by clock time when they were playing, no more aware of hours and minutes than wild pigeons in the wood?

Jim didn't seem to mind. When he'd been caught at anything that looked like disobedience, he'd cry and say he was sorry, as though it meant more to him to be hugged and kissed by Mama than to have fun doing what he really wanted. As for Jennie, she seemed to have been naturally born the good one. Whatever she did was what everyone loved to see her doing. She was like a tame kitten that would purr in anyone's lap and knead its little paws as softly as though they were pussy willows. But Mary, when anyone tried to hold her, seemed to be all sharp claws and bristly fur or like a slippery fish out of place in human laps.

Not that that was the way she naturally felt about herself; it was something inside her that made her act that way, like the little bird that made her say things she didn't really mean to. There was something she had to be, a kind of path of her own she meant to follow, a long journey she had to go that called her even when she was too young to understand. She couldn't ever be really content like Jennie to be held and rocked and sung to, even when she most felt she wanted to be; times when she was sick and feverish, for instance, and wanted so much to go back to being the baby;

times when she and Jim, with Jennie between them, would be sitting on the lowest step of the stairs as day darkened into summer evening, listening while their mother sang one of the wild sweet tragic melodies that the solidiers had brought back out of the South, like seeds carried in the wool of a sheep's coat.

The song, the smell of the summer dusk, the flitter of bats just outside the open door, the stir of thoughts and feelings that had no real shape or name flooded her small heart to bursting. She longed, without knowing just what it was she longed for, to have someone hold her and enfold her and keep her safe from the vast world of growing up, the beauty and pain of the world, the terror and pain of beauty. Her mother could not understand why Mary began to cry so wildly. Perhaps the child was beginning to be ill. She might almost be having some kind of a spell. Mrs. Hunter had to shake the little girl by the shoulder to bring her to her senses. Then she was sent up to bed and lay there alone in the dark, feeling very little and unwanted, as though she'd been shoved out of the family circle. Until at last, perhaps, I-Mary came, who suffered no need of being taken up and comforted, a being so wise, so firm in the conviction of her own potency and rightness that it appeared she never could be moved to tears.

THE WALNUT TREE

The Plum Street farm seemed made for the delight of little children. Insects chirped and rustled all about. Bees flew from blossom to blossom in their black-and-gold uniforms. Hop-toads stared with bright, unwinking eyes from the cool patches of earth near the rim of the cistern. A mockingbird built a nest almost low enough to peep into the spiny hedge of osage orange at the back of the house. Chipmunks scurried under the wall of the barn to be safe from the butcher bird. If the butcher bird caught one, it would most likely hang the lifeless furry body on a thorn to keep for its next meal. Tenderhearted Jennie, finding it there, would cry for Mary, who didn't mind risking scratched fingers and a torn frock to get it down. Then the two little girls would bury the limp small creature, pretending to be playing funeral. To Mary, anything you could make some kind of play out of was important. She imitated what she chose from the grown-up world without troubling herself about the pains and struggles that went with it. Most likely, it would be Jennie who, always grieved to see anyone or anything hurt, shed the real tears.

Mary was still at the age when she felt the chief purpose of parents was to make the world livable for children. They were there to tie up her hurts, to call her in to supper, to light the lamp when the dark was coming on. That they were human beings with needs and dreams of their own hardly occurred to her. They were Powers who must continually be coaxed or outwitted, escaped from or returned to. Like many imaginative children, she had a world of her own which hardly seemed to touch the grown-up world at all or which existed inside the world of reality like an aquarium full of many-colored fish. And it was this inside world that grown-ups seemed always to be yanking her out of. When she ran in to show her mother a leaf or a feather or a kicking beetle, she found Mama would rather think of something else, usually rules and duties, and why couldn't Mary ever be a good and gentle little girl like Jennie, or what must God be thinking of a parent who had not managed to teach her elder daughter to know better?

What God might be thinking seemed to be on her mother's mind a good deal of the time. He was Our-Father-in-Heaven who was always peering out to keep track of what His children were up to. Most of the time what He didn't like to see them doing were the things that seemed most fun. Especially He didn't like people to spend their time out-of-doors on Sunday, no matter how the birds were making music in the maple trees and the calves and the young colts kicking up their heels in the pastures. A little girl wasn't supposed to frisk and toss her mane of curls but must walk primly in her buttoned shoes with the rest of the family to Sunday school and church and sing hymns and think mostly about Heaven, which was the place Grandpa liked best to read about from the

Book of Revelations. Heaven had streets made of gold, and nothing seemed to grow there except one tree that wasn't very real. Everyone there went around making a lot of noise on harps; the angels were rather fierce; and there were some very peculiar and unattractive beasts. It was hard to imagine why anyone would want to spend much time there, but the reason you were supposed to be a good little girl was so sometime you could go and live "forever 'n' ever" in Heaven.

Papa never seemed to be as serious about Heaven as Mama and Grandpa and most of the aunts and uncles. Mary suspected that, like her, he'd much rather be outdoors walking among his apple trees or inspecting the budding grapevines with a careful eye. Sometimes he might even beg the children off from going to church, but that made Mama unhappy, and when she was unhappy she was likely to be more strict with them all and talk more about their Christian duty. Besides one's Christian duty, there was something called the Joy of the Lord which Mama believed in. You could feel it in her voice when she was singing hymns, but it was something she never managed to explain to Mary except that it came from having your Savior in your heart, and this could only happen when you grew old enough to be converted.

The look on Mama's face when she spoke of the Joy of the Lord was the same as Grandpa's when he sat reading aloud to them with his limp-covered Bible open on his knees. How could a lively little girl be expected to understand? All Mary could feel for herself was the scratchiness of the haircloth sofa in Grandpa's parlor that she was supposed to sit on without wriggling and a kind of magic in the sound of the words and the sentences blowing over before she had any idea of what the words meant.

Already for Mary there seemed to be two separate worlds: the world of words in books that the grown-ups were so at home in and the world of out-of-doors.

At first she did not venture very far by herself into the outdoors. She had to grow tall enough to see over the grass; then past the tangle of berry bushes; then to run among the even rows of apple trees, hither and thither, touching and tasting, like the bees that zigzagged through the sweet red clover blossoms. Patches of color would draw her further: pale spring beauties coming up through the sod in the orchard; clumps of violets around rotting stumps in the wood lot; masses of bluebells. The wind tickled her nose with different smells in every outdoor season: moist black earth in spring; the heavy, sleepy fragrance of lilacs; warm summer grass; nuts you seemed to taste at the same time you smelled them.

Beyond the orchard was an unploughed grassy meadow that sloped to the foot of a darker hill. The hill was covered with trees so closely massed that it seemed to be all in shadow. For a long time the woods remained to the child a place of mystery; no telling what might be peering out among the leaves. Not until she started to school and began to play more with other children did she venture to go there. Then it became the place where her lifelong sense of "power and personality in the wild" began to stir. Here she "could pass by way of the little animal's frisking response to bright airs and warm sun, the incentive of color, the contented hum and lively chirruping of other small creatures, so easily into the little human's appetite for handling and possessing, the delightful plunderability of forest and stream and thicket" (E.H. 78).

Alongside the impulse to seize and hold and take home to keep—at least until her mother grew tired of her collections and threw them out—was the urge just to stand very still and look, "an absorbed contemplation of the mere appearance of things for their own sake," she learned to call it later (E.H. 78). She overflowed with delight to discover the pattern of a leaf she happened to pick up, the delicate veins, the smooth or scalloped or crinkled edge, the cool or glowing colors.

Moving shadows entranced her, blue stiff-armed shadows of branches on winter snow, tinkling shadows sifted through leaves in summer. She would kneel on the damp, mold-smelling earth to peer into the miniature world of mosses and lichens, forgetting her mother's warnings about keeping her stockings clean and about not catching cold.

Her wandering eyes discovered patterns everywhere, small crooked paths in the meadow, tracks of mice and rabbits in the snow, spiderwebs delicately spun from twigs and berry bushes. These patterns spoke a language; they had something to tell her, but the telling was without words. Like most children, she felt closer to the world of plants and animals than she did to the human. If she stood very still, she could almost feel she was herself a flower opening, with a butterfly coming close.

One summer morning when she was still very small, Mary stole out of the house by herself and wandered through the cool orchard to the edge of the meadow. A lone walnut tree grew in the field, partway down the grassy slope. It was tall and gracefully balanced; its leaves hung poised on the warm air like dancers. An ancient Greek would have imagined such a tree to be the dwelling place of a dryad. The children of Joan of Arc's village of Domrémy would have hung May Day garlands on it. When the child Mary came upon the tree that summer day, something stirred in her like an old, old memory, a memory that went far back before her own life began, a memory of all that mankind has felt in the presence of special trees.

Mary Austin did not write of what happened to her under the walnut tree until she was nearly sixty years old and had been ill and surprised to find herself afraid to die. Then the memory of the tree came back to comfort her. The child she had once been was still part of the aging woman. The memory of the child and the tree became part of the half-dream she slipped into as she wrote:

I must have been between five and six when this experience happened to me. It was a summer morning and the child I was had walked down through the orchard alone and come out on the brow of a sloping hill where there were grass and a wind blowing and one tall tree reaching into infinite immensities of blueness. Quite suddenly, after a moment of quietness there, earth and sky and tree and wind-blown grass and the child in the midst of them came alive together with a pulsing light of consciousness. There was a wild foxglove at the child's feet and a bee dozing about it, and to this day I can recall the swift inclusive awareness of each for the whole—I in them and they in me and all of us enclosed in a warm lucent bubble of livingness. I remember the child looking everywhere for the source of this happy wonder, and at last she questioned—"God?"—because it was the only awesome word she knew. Deep inside, like the murmurous swinging of a bell, she heard the answer, "God, God. . . ."

How long this ineffable moment lasted I never knew. It broke like a bubble at the sudden singing of a bird, and the wind blew and the world was the same as ever—only never quite the same. (Experiences Facing Death 24–25).*

It seems rather unlikely that the child Mary could have associated the word "God" with her experience of the walnut tree when she was less than six years old. The impressions of God she had gathered from her mother's hymns and her grandfather's Bible readings and the prayers she was made to repeat would make it hard to connect Him with the delight and wonder of the outdoor world. God belonged at that time to the strict and often incomprehensible world of the grown-ups. Many years would pass before she felt sure what the word meant in the depths of her own heart. When the walnut tree vision returned toward the end of her life, God would be a part of it. For the child it was enough to be in the midst of the happening, to feel it in the same way she could feel the whisper of the wind on her cheeks, the sunlight on her fingers, the ripple of motion in her body, like the visible motion of the wind among the leaves. The search for explanations would come later.

THE FRIEND IN THE WOOD

Between the meadow and the dark wooded hill a small brook flowed, sluggish, scarely moving at most seasons. The brook was named Borough's Branch for one of Carlinville's early settlers. Most of the time, it was just called the Branch because it ran only a short way before it joined the Macoupin Creek, which itself flowed westward to the Illinois River, which emptied into the mighty Mississippi.

It was a child-sized brook. A small girl could wade there, feeling the silty mud go squish between her toes, watching the slow water scarely move over the tawny pebbles, wondering at the rippled patterns it traced, as though with a child's finger, along its sandy bed. Except at seasons of spring flood, when the whole world seemed half water, the brook was almost voiceless. In summer it spread into tiny pools where minnows swarmed so lazily they could be caught by hand and half-cooked over forbidden fires. The children used to play with the water for hours, scooping out springs, widening rills with miniature dams of twigs and pebbles. It seemed almost like a live companion.

During the eight years she lived so near the Branch, Mary knew it as the boundary of her own fairy world; "the brook that goes all about the Wood of my youth," she called it. The remembered woods, like the walnut tree and the bee in the meadow, were half real, half made of the stuff of dream and secret wishing. There was the wood that she played in with the other children and the wood she could go to only by herself. Sometimes at night when she was supposed to be asleep she would feel as though something came out of the wood and called to her. She was sure that she used to get out of bed and try to find it. If this had been only a dream, how could she feel the dew so wet on her ankles and remember afterward a chilly feeling of toads or snakes her bare feet almost stepped on? As she wrote in the unpublished essay "The Friend in the Wood,"

I must have dreamed of outdoors. . . . for years I entertained confident pictures of places in the woods about our house where I couldn't have been. In particular, there was a point from which I often set out, climbing a stream side between gnarly roots and overhanging boughs. The way to it began under three dark firs that stirred their boughs in a whispering motion . . . but there were never any firs at our house . . . nor any running water other than the placid branch between the orchard and Rinaker's Hill. . . . I suppose the picture in my mind must have been a dream extension of an illustration from a story book . . . or that I had as a child already begun visiting the Garden which for me had not yet been lost.

The Garden was the imaginary place that many children know of, "the secret place in your mind where you go when you don't like the place where you are." It became for Mary not only a place to run away to but later in her life a place where she could retreat to get in touch with memories and feelings she thought she had lost in the hard years of growing up and making her living in the world. The orchard, the meadow, the walnut tree, the woods on Rinaker's Hill were always part of it, along with the willow tree, the mesas, and springs among tumbled rocks that came much later. It was lucky for her that most of the Garden was so real or else she might have got lost in the dream world and never come back to tell us what she found there.

There was no doubt that real trees grew on Rinaker's Hill, oak trees and hazelnuts and elms and many others. Mary's father could tell her most of their names, but to the child they were at first just a general cloud of thick green that almost hid the sky completely. It was fun to step on the damp ground, to feel the moss springing under her feet, to smell the thick odors from the layers and layers of fallen leaves. Small creatures rustled through the leaves. Birds called from the upper stories of the branches.

There were other presences that no one could ever see. Sometimes when Mary was playing with the other children in the wood she would feel her skin go all prickly or a little cold wind would come creeping at the roots of her hair. A patch of darkness, a hollow tree that might hide anything or nothing, a stillness taking the place of the usual stir of leaf or wind or insect—who knows what it was that would sometimes make all the children wheel at once and run screaming out of the woods and up the hill in mimic panic? Was the panic real or was it only part of the game of pretending to be frightened when you knew there was nothing there? Or *were* you only pretending?

At first Mary was aware only of the half-dreaded, half-delightful "contagion into the ritual of flight" as she ran with the rest of the scattering children. Sometimes she felt almost like a little animal herself. She would not have been surprised to find herself knowing exactly what the red fox was thinking as it stood sniffing the wind at the edge of the wood. She could feel her own self lumbering along in the shape of the dignified old box tortoise scuffing the leaves under the oaks with his wrinkled claws.

She never found it hard to be almost anything she wanted. It was her way of finding out about the things she looked at, by getting inside them, whether they were trees or stones or a fox or a long-ago person in a story. This was a different way of knowing from being told in words or from knowing about in books. She learned to stand very still and look for a long time, until she could almost feel herself turning into a tree, roots and scratchy bark and branches and dancing leaves and all.

I would sit in the woods until my thought was as a tree, and the squirrels would take me for a tree and run over me. There would come a strange stir, and the creeping of my flesh along my spine until the Forest seemed about to speak—and suddenly a twig would snap or a jay squawk and I would be I again and the tree a tree (F. W.).

These are the words of the young Indian in a story Mary Austin would one day write, the young Indian who perhaps became part of her when she played where the woods had not forgotten the soft moccasined step of those to whom the rivers and forests of Illinois had once belonged.

Besides the animal rustlings and the invisible, faintly sensed traces of long-ago human presence, Mary found something else. Sometimes, if she could be alone and quiet enough, she would feel as though something, almost but not quite a person, were close to her, watching from among the scarcely moving leaves, something wild and shy that belonged to the woods as much as the trees and the wind and the birds, something she tried to see but never really could.

"I used to wish with all my heart to believe in fern seed," she tells us, "charms for understanding animal speech, and the power to see creatures other than my kind." What she could not manage to see with her eyes she could feel in other ways, though she could never manage to explain just how. Whether there was anything really there seemed important. The experience was real to her, and she often became quite frantic when hardly anyone seemed willing to believe her or even to listen while she tried to tell them. Was it a matter of finding the right words, she wondered? Or did it depend on finding someone else who had felt these things in the same way, someone she could talk to who would understand?

Though the experience had begun with a creepy feeling, looking back she speaks of it only as "the Friend":

It came out of the Wood. From the clearing I would be aware of it, skirting the edge of the thickets. To this day the unexpected flash of scarlet columbine between young oaks quickens in me the anticipation of companionableness. If I would be sitting quietly in the grass, the presence would grow upon me, near and personal, but never with any form or aspect. I had a finger-on-lip signal with my younger sister to notify her when it came, before the other children sensed it, and she would signal back, bright-eyed and aware. Or she pretended to awareness, for she was one of those gentle souls who always wish things to be the way other people wish them. Then I would walk apart, looking for bluer violets, or a superstitious

bird at nest, to enjoy the Friend as long as possible before I was
caught by contagion into the ritual of flight. . . .

I cannot now recall any order in which the feeling for the Friend
differentiated itself from the panic terror of the wild, nor from the
child's sense of animal kin, the brotherhood of feathered, furry
things (F.W).

Mary tried to believe later on that it was her father who had
explained to her how it was "out of this knowledge-feeling of loitering, creepy presence in the wild that all the concepts of elves,
angels and other fairy folk had grown," but it seems doubtful that
she ever had this kind of communication with her father and even
less with her hymn-singing, Sunday school-teaching mother. As
with the walnut tree moment, the explanations must have come
much later. If she had begun so young to search for explanations,
she might have lost the Friend forever, as Elsa lost Lohengrin when
she insisted that the Swan Knight tell her his true name.

SNOCKERTY

Besides the presence in the wood there was also a little demon
called Snockerty who lived in a hollow apple tree somewhere in
the orchard. Though Snockerty isn't mentioned by name in Mary
Austin's autobiography, just the barest reference to "the tree fe-
tich down by the pond" (*E.H.* 54), he plays an important part
in the early chapters of her largely autobiographical novel *A*
Woman of Genius.

"I recall perfectly," she has her heroine Olivia say, "how the
reddening blackberry leaves lay under the hoar frost in Hadley's
pasture, and the dew between the pale gold wires of the grass on
summer mornings, and the very words and rites by which we paid
observance to Snockerty. I am not sure whether Ellen McGee or I
invented him, but first and last he got us into as much trouble as
though we had not always distinctly recognized him for an invention" (*A Woman of Genius* 14).

Ellen was a wild, untidy Irish child who lived with her large family around the corner of the pasture. Her name in real life was Ellen Cogan. Her father was an Irish section boss who drank too much and sometimes abused his family. It was through him that Ellen learned the tales and the magic lore that enthralled her playmates, brought up as most of them were on pious Bible stories. Ellen "was most enviably furnished in all the signs of lucky and unlucky and what it meant if you put your stocking on wrong side out in the morning, with charms to say for warts, and scraps of Old World song. . . . Her fairy tales too had a more convincing sound, for she got them from her father, who had always known somebody who knew the human participators" (W.G. 16). "So there!" one can just hear Mary explaining to her dubious mother.

It was as though Grandpa Graham might happen to meet a man who had really been to the Heaven of Revelation and seen the angels in person. The Cogans were Catholic as well as Irish, so the saints came into the stories too. Most of the time it was hard to tell the difference between the saints and the imaginary people. Since Methodists weren't supposed to believe in either saints or fairies, Mary would have found it better to keep her mouth shut at home about what went on when she played with the Cogans in the orchard.

After being acquainted with fairyland, she was more certain than ever that she didn't want to be stuck with having to go to Heaven. The Cogans told her that Heaven could be escaped by doing the wickedest thing you could think of. The wickedest thing any of them had ever heard of was saying the Mass backward, but since she couldn't possibly be expected to do that when she didn't know it forward, Mary compromised by saying the Lord's Prayer forward while she walked backward around Snockerty's apple tree (W.G. 54). After that she felt happy to think that she positively would not be allowed in the Heaven of Revelations.

Snockerty was neither stern like the God of the Bible nor entirely friendly. He was more of a mischief maker like Puck or the Irish leprechauns. The tree he was imagined to live in had a very tempting hole in it just arm high. If you stood on tiptoe you could just push a small pebble through the hole and listen to it rattle faintly out of sight and sound. Sometimes the children tried pushing a bead or a button or a pencil or other small treasures into the tree. It began to seem as though there were something about the hole that made them do it, whether they wanted to or not. It must be Snockerty, Ellen suggested, making the name right up out of her own head, Snockerty who demanded all these offerings. In return, shouldn't the children be entitled to ask certain favors of Snockerty, as they might of a leprechaun if they ever managed to catch one? He surely had magic powers, or how could he have enticed the children into giving him so many things they really hated to part with?

They began by asking him for omens. Would they find the spring full that day? Would there be papaws in the woods? Snockerty was supposed to give his answer by rustling the leaves along the path or letting a rabbit run suddenly out of the grass. Ellen was always best at interpreting these signs. Lacking Ellen's sense of mischief and her bottomless insight into fairy lore, Mary had to contend in other ways for supremacy among the playing children. She was not happy then or ever when she had to take second place. Not long after she began going to school she developed the idea that Snockerty should have plays performed for his benefit. She made them up herself out of "scraps of school exercises, Sunday hymns, recitations" (W.G. 23) and whatever she happened to think up on the spur of the moment.

"We played at church and school in it, at scalping and Robinson Crusoe and the Three Bears. We went farther and played at High Priests and Oracles and Sacrifice" (W.G. 12). Mary not only made up the plays, she undoubtedly insisted on taking the most important parts herself. If the play were about Jacob and the Angel, she would have to be the Angel. Jim, her brother, would be given Jacob's part, and she wouldn't let him forget he was supposed to come off second best in the wrestling episode. Mary would jump all over him if he missed a single word: "Oughtn't he to say it right? It's in the Bible," spoke her character in the 1917 novel *The Ford.*

Ellen could always fall back on Snockerty as her authority. Snockerty had a will of his own, though it wasn't written in any book. Instead of issuing rules and commandments like the God of Sunday school, Snockerty just put wild thoughts into people's heads, especially into Ellen's. Ellen's imagination bubbled out of her like an Irish fairy well. She made Snockerty the excuse for more mischief than the strictly brought-up Hunter children would have been likely to contrive all by themselves. The parents never found out the cause of the mischief; not one of the children ever told on Snockerty, not even when the most priggish little boy appeared in front of his horrified mother shorn of a whole handful of his careful curls. Mary had hacked them off herself with her brother's pocketknife as a special offering. Her victim "lied like a little gentleman and said he had cut them off himself because he was tired of looking like a girl baby" (W.G. 24).

What a fierce and determined small priestess Mary must have made with her smudged pinafore, her hair tumbled loose about her face, her greenish eyes, her mouth like a witch's sulky child. Her imagination, which was frowned on at home and just as often at school, burned like a fire leaping among dry heaps of leaves when she was in company with Irish Ellen.

THE OBLIGATION OF REPUTE

As usual, the world of imagination soon came bump up against the world that parents live in. As Mary Austin has her half-fictional Olivia tell the story in *A Woman of Genius,* this is the way it happened:

> I think it must have been about the end of Snockerty's second summer that Ellen's wild humour got us all into serious trouble which resulted in my first real contact with authority.
>
> Along the west side of Hadley's pasture . . . lay the tilled fields of the Ross property, corn and pumpkins and turnips, against which

*a solemn trespass board advised us. It was that board, no doubt,
which led to our always referring to the owner of it as old man
Ross, for except as he was a tall, stooping, white-bearded, child-
less man, I do not know how he had deserved our disrespect. I
have suspected . . . that the McGees knew more of the taste of his
young turnips and roasting ears than they admitted at the time when
Snockerty announced to Ellen through the hollow of a dark, gnarly
oak at the foot of Hadley's hill, that he would be acceptably served
by a feast of green corn and turnips out of Ross's field. . . . We
were really good children in the main, but I do not think we had
any notion of disobeying. Personally I rather delighted in the idea
of being compelled to desperate enterprises. I recall the wild
freebooting dash, the scramble over the fence, the rustle of the corn
full of delicious intimations of ambush and surprise, the real fear
of coming suddenly on old man Ross among the rows . . . and
the derisive epithets which we did not spare to fling over our shoulders as we escaped into the brush with our booty. There was a
perfect little carnival of wickedness in the safe hollow where we
stripped the ears for roasting—where we dared old man Ross to
come on, gave dramatic rehearsals of what we should do to him in
that event, and revelled in forbidden manners and interdicted
words. . . . Finally . . . we all took hands in a wild dance around
the fire and over it crying, "Snockerty, Snockerty, Snockerty!" in
a sort of savage singsong (W.G. 24–26).*

After the orgy is over, Olivia with her brother and her little
sister find themselves trudging home far later than they are expected.
What will happen if Mama should insist on knowing where they
have been? Suddenly they see one another as through the eyes of
grown-ups. Their faces are smudged, their hands sticky in spite of
the washing they have tried to give them in the brook. The left-
over taste of charred corn isn't mixing too well with that of so
many indigestible raw turnips.

As though their guilty thoughts have called him up, who should
appear on their own front porch but old man Ross himself, talk-

ing furiously to Father. The children steal in by the kitchen door and huddle about their mother like chickens trying to get under the feathers of a hen when a thunderstorm appears. Mother has no idea yet what old man Ross has come about and tries to cuff the young ones out of her way as she moves briskly to and fro trying to get supper.

Father comes striding in very white and angry. Is this true what he has heard? Have his children—*his*, as if this were the worst of the matter rather than the damage they have done—actually been caught trespassing in a neighbor's field? He rounds on the three of them "through a stream of dreadful, biting things" that seem to float them "clear beyond the pale of sympathy and hope" (W.G. 29).

> *"I remember," continues Olivia, "my father walking up and down with his hands under his coat behind, a short man . . . with a kind of swing in his walk which curiously nobody but myself seems to have noticed, and a sort of electrical flash in his manner which might have come . . . from our never being brought up before him except when we had done something thoroughly exasperating: I am not sure that I did not tell Ellen McGee . . . that he rated us in full uniform, waving his sword.*
>
> *" 'Good heavens,' " he said, " 'you might have been arrested for it—my children—mine—and I thought I could have trusted you. Good heavens!' "* (W.G. 29–30).

One can see the three youngsters standing speechless before the irate man, the little sister's eyes brimming over with her blue tears; the brother hanging his head with the repentant air that could always bring Mama over to his side, but didn't seem to have much effect on father; Olivia (whom no one can help recognizing as Mary) withdrawn into herself like a turtle into its horny shell where no one can suspect how she is quivering.

Olivia starts when she suddenly hears her own name spoken. She has been keeping her eyes glued to the red-and-black table cover under the lamp, a cloth she especially enjoys hating because it is a favorite of her mother's. The more she feels disgraced in her father's eyes, the more she tries to make up for it by hating her mother.

" 'As for *you*,' " she hears her father say, turning his flashing look directly on his older daughter, 'as for you, Olivia May—I *am* surprised at you' " (*W.G.* 30).

Olivia grasps at this statement as though it could have been a form of praise. (Had it really been the closest to praise that Mary could remember ever receiving from her father, whose favorite child she had always longed to be?)

> *He had expected better of me then; he had reached beyond my surfaces and divined what I was inarticulately sure of, that I was different—no, not better—but somehow intrinsically different. He was surprised at me [She noticed he has not said so much of her brother, even though he was the eldest; he had said it was exactly what he had expected of the neighbor children.] . . . but he had had a better opinion of me. I recall a throb of exasperation at his never having told me. I might have lived up to it . . . that phrase . . . is all I have on which to hang the faith that perhaps . . . some vision had shaped on his horizon of what I might become. I was never anything to my mother, I know, but a cuckoo's egg dropped in her creditable nest. "But," said my father, "I am surprised at you"* (W.G. 30–31).

It seems a poor little crumb on which the child nourished the hope that she could have meant something special to her father. "If he hadn't up to this time affected greatly my gratitude or affections, he began to shine for me now with some of the precious quality which inheres in dreams" (*W.G.* 32). It was, as Olivia says, the beginning of "a new kind of Snockertism" (*W.G.* 28). Instead of the half-playful, half-malignant little woodland god who, in return for a certain kind of tribute, shared his knowledge of earth ways with them, there loomed, almost like an armored hero, an image of human standards to be lived up to, what the community expected of her father's daughter.

Until then, Olivia (wasn't it really Mary?) had been swimming in "my lustrous seas" (W.G. 29) of childhood, like the sea world of the little mermaid in the fairy tale. She was immersed in the "fairy wonder of the world." Now she found herself hooked like a fish, dragged up at the end of a line out of her dreamy waters. On the shore stood a new god, the god whom, for the sake of her father's approval, she must bind her life to. "I mean," Olivia explains, "the obligation of repute, the necessity of being loyal to what I found in the world because it had been founded in sincerity with pains" (W.G. 29).

But Snockerty, because he belonged to the ancient world of poetry and magic, could never entirely disappear. He continued to live at the roots of Mary's life, like the spirit imprisoned in the bottle and hidden at the roots of a great oak in the fairy tale. He belonged to the side of life from which storytelling comes and the wisdom of untamed creatures, a wisdom of patterns and omens and all that seems to happen of itself.

THE DUNCE CAP

In the spring of 1874 her mother stuck a stiff new straw hat on Mary's mop of hair, put a tin bucket of cold scraps for lunch in her hand, and sent her off on the road to school. It was April, and she was only five and a half years old. With the school year so nearly over, one wonders what the hurry was. Were there troubles at home, like a new baby for Mama to worry over? Or had Susie Hunter simply grown tired of Mary's pestering to be let go along with Jim and find out for herself about the mystery of words?

It looks as though Mary was the kind of little girl it was never easy to have around. Either you'd find her moping around the house looking for something to do or, if you had something you really wanted her to do, she'd be off out of sight behind the berry bushes or into the orchard after a bee or a bird. You couldn't teach her to be afraid of anything that crept or crawled out-of-doors. At least if she were in school you'd know where she was. And at least she'd get over having to pester poor Jim all the time to teach her reading.

School didn't turn out to be the adventure Mary expected. Instead of buzzing dizzily from word to word in a real book, she found she had to sit at a stiff desk almost all day, except when there was marching or singing or running out for recess on a bare and usually muddy playground. All she was supposed to read at first were syllables: "A–b, Ab, B–o, Bo" (*E.H.* 59), and so on. There wasn't any magic at all in just syllables, not when she felt she already knew so many words. She sat with her cousin Minnie Farrell, who'd been in first grade all year and already knew the best ways of amusing yourself without letting Teacher catch you.

When Mary was bored with looking at the chart of syllables, she read the books that Minnie brought. She hadn't guessed at first that she wasn't supposed to know how to read, so when Teacher caught her at it and asked what she was doing, she answered right up proudly, "Reading," she said, wondering why Teacher had to ask. "Oh, no Mary, you can't read; you are only in the chart class; to say you can read when you can't is a story" (*E.H.* 60). There it was again, Mary must have thought. She was being called a story-teller, and this time right in front of the whole class. Mary was already so used to defending herself that she didn't hesitate to contradict. "I can, too, Miss Snow, I *can*—" (*E.H.* 60). She knew better than to stamp her feet, but she probably had the kind of stamping sound in her voice that ruffles teachers.

Teacher couldn't let the thought come into her mind that she might be mistaken; she, too, was in front of the whole class, and it was evident that she already had her mind made up about what a little girl just started to school should be able to do. Reading wasn't possible until the teacher taught her.

"Little girls who tell fibs in school must wear the dunce cap" (*E.H.* 60).

That wasn't fair. If the dunce cap were put on your head, it meant you had been stupid, and to be thought stupid was even worse for Mary than to be called a liar. "There were two or three ways of wearing the dunce cap: with stoicism; miserably with shamed tears; or by the help of 'funny faces,' when the teacher's back was turned" (E.H. 60). Mary was never able to laugh at herself. She was determined not to show tears, and she hadn't the least idea how to go about making funny faces. There was nothing she could do except stand there with the paper cone on her head and the misery of being laughed at in her heart. What could you do but pretend you didn't care? What could you do but hold your book up in front of your face and go right on reading?

It was the story of Snow White, a picture book with easy words for little children, and the way stories seemed to do when they go along with pictures, it almost told itself. It took Mary away from where she was right into that other world. Snow White had a wicked stepmother who hated her, and she went to live in the woods with the Seven Dwarfs, who were kind. In the end the step-mother got what was coming to her. Snow White, who might even have been Mary, married the Prince and was loved and lived hap-pily ever after.

Who should come along just then instead of the Prince but the principal, whose name was Xerxes Xenophon Crum. One can imag-ine, with a name like that, he must have had some kind of sense of humor to be able to get as far as he had in the world. "What [has] the little dunce done?" he asked (E.H. 60). He couldn't have helped being secretly amused at the sight of the bigness of the paper cone and the smallness of the stolid little face under it.

"Telling a fib," Miss Snow explained in a righteous voice. "Pretending she can read . . ." Right in front of Principal she said it. It wasn't fair. Mary had to stand up for her rights. Why should Teacher get away with telling stories about *her*, she must have wondered?

"I can. I'm reading now" (E.H. 60).

Principal must have had a lot of experience in how to deal with both children and teachers. He wasn't going to ask any more ques-tions. "That's easily proved," he said, with perhaps a tiny smile at the corner of his mouth that Mary couldn't feel afraid of. "Read," he commanded. Teacher was fussed. "She probably knows it by heart," she snipped. Mr. Crum asked someone to hand Mary a first reader. The words were lots easier than any in Snow White, and Mary "simply sailed through it. With the result that Principal Crum gathered her up, with her lunch-pail, her diminutive slate, and her straw hat, and deposited her in Room Two," where she remained until the end of the term (*E. H.* 60–61). The following September, when she was legally of the beginning age, she was automatically shifted, so she says, to Room Three.

THE MAGIC OF WORDS

The best part of going to school was getting there. The school stood near the center of town and the walk was about a mile each way. The road went curving up and down, bordered with grass and trees and ever so many things to be noticed. Wildflowers splashed color through the grass in spring. In autumn, sumac flamed crimson. Scarlet leaves fluttered off the trees into heaps that made a joyful crunching sound when you scuffled your shoes. Winters when the weather was stinging cold and snowy you could stay in town all night at Grandpa's or cuddle close to the gas fire at home if you had a bad cold.

In spring, when the wild crab apples were tossing pink clouds of bloom along the gullies, when the tiny green leaves were unfurling on the maples, when the air was extra busy with birds, it was hard to find yourself shut up in a bleak brick building three stories high, with rows and rows of windows mostly kept closed or open only at the top to let out the overheated air.

Teacher complained that Mary wouldn't pay attention. Her arithmetic page was most often a scrawl; she'd be sitting at the desk with a problem barely started, staring out the open third of the window as though she didn't know where she was. The clouds drifted by. The maple leaves strained to run after them on tiptoe.

All at once she was likely to hear the exasperated voice, "Aren't you ever going to finish that problem, Mary Hunter?"

Mary would come back to earth with a start. If only Teacher hadn't spoken just at that moment she'd have flown right out the window and gone soaring among the windy treetops. She knew it could have happened the very next second, the way it does in dreams, when you tuck your feet up under you and lift and float above the muddy road.

Or she might have her face hidden in the pages of a book, one as likely as not she wasn't supposed to be reading for lessons at all. She would have gone off inside the story, like Cinderella magically finding herself away from her stepmother's kitchen and off to the royal ball. Then a bell would ring and she would be torn back to reality like poor Cinderella when her golden coach became a pumpkin. She'd hear the rest of the class go stumbling past her to recess. They would most likely be poking fun at her because she'd rather sit over an old book than come out and play. "How smart that old Mary Hunter thought she was," she might have heard them whisper, because she could read books ahead of the rest of them in class. She looked offended when Teacher called her down about her penmanship or marked lines under the spelling in her compositions. Mary could spell perfectly well out loud. All she had to do was stand with her arms folded "with the toe of one foot hooked about the other ankle, eyes half-shut, with a swaying motion [no wonder the other children laughed], she could probably spell down a whole row of columnists. . . . What nobody ever taught her was how to spell writing" (E.H. 61).

Keeping your mind on how to make the letters stand up straight, on how to spell words right when you were writing "compositions," took all the magic out. What mattered to Mary was the picture behind the words. She could be fascinated with the way one word called up another, the way images shimmered and shifted but always made some kind of pattern, patterns that formed of themselves like frost on the windowpane. You could play with these patterns the way you sometimes played with shells and pebbles "with mounds of patted dust set off by a feather or a flower," as she wrote in the novel *Outland* (45), making whole worlds out of nothing but your own imagining.

Words not only made things to be seen in the back of her mind; they crept into her ears and made moving patterns of sound. As early as Mary could remember, she was enchanted by the sound of words. Words flowing around her in rhythmic patterns drew her, she says, "as clover scent draws bees" (*E.H.* 54). When she was tiny, she used to get out of the warm bed where she'd been sent off to sleep, most likely without even a goodnight kiss, and steal across the hall to the door of the room where Mama sat up reading late to Papa when his bad leg especially pained him. The door was always left open a tiny crack so Susanna Hunter could hear if one of the children cried.

Mary would crouch as close to the door as she dared but not really close enough to hear. Often she'd fall asleep there in the trickle of lamplight, the flowing soft rain of words. If Mama discovered her curled up on the cold floor in her thin nightdress, she'd spank her awake and slap her back into bed with a warning about "catching her death" (*E.H.* 55), whatever that might mean. The sound of speech through the crack of a doorway she dares not enter, the warmth of light inside the room. One can see the little girl huddling outside, shivering and wistful like the little match girl in the fairy tale.

Mary had supposed school would be filled with the magic of words, all of them keys to open doors. Instead she found it full of stupid numbers that said nothing at all to her, hours of doing sums or copying at the blackboard, hearing the children behind her snickering right out loud because she usually did it backward. "Gogafy" (*E.H.* 61) meant lists of uninteresting facts about places to be learned by heart, though why they called it that is hard to understand, for the effort was all in the mind.

Even the stories in the readers turned out to be disappointing, and no wonder. William Holmes McGuffey, who selected all of them, was a moralist. He believed in pointing out from the first that the aim of life for a boy was to grow up to be rich and successful and patriotic or for a girl to be a pure, self-sacrificing wife and mother. Whatever happened, you must trust Providence, which knew exactly what was good for you, though its ways were hard to understand. Often it seemed that Providence would let a poor widow suffer through years of poverty until a valiant missing son showed up with a fortune in his pocket. Poverty, if not due to Providence, was certain to be caused by drink. A man who drank would end up with his face right in the gutter, sneered at by his former friends, his wife and children pointed out as sad examples.

Most of the poetry in the readers went along singsong, such as "Mary-had-a-little-lamb" or "The boy stood on the burning deck" or "Life is real, Life is earnest, and the grave is not its goal." There was hardly ever a story or poem you felt you could walk around in, the way Mary liked to do. These she found mostly in books that came from outside of school.

One day another fourth grader appeared with a copy of *Alice's Adventures in Wonderland.* Mary somehow managed to get hold of it long enough to read two or three chapters before it was snatched away. One can just hear the other child complaining, "Mary Hunter, who said you could read *my* book?" Things like this seemed always to be happening to Mary.

When she got home that evening, she found Papa in enough of a good mood that she tried to tell him about it: how the little girl called Alice had a round comb just like hers, and how she went down a rabbit hole, and she hadn't had a chance to read anymore, and "Please, Pa, couldn't I have it? Oh, *couldn't* I?" (E.H. 62). It wasn't often that Mary dared to plead. Usually she tried to just argue you into agreeing that she had a right to have what had been denied her.

Mama looked the way she did when she wanted Papa to remember how they couldn't afford things and how it was all on account of Papa's never managing to be really successful and how she didn't believe in little girls being allowed to read fairy tales. Mary argued that she had a dime of her own in the bank and that Grandpa always gave her a dime when she learned the Golden Text that was printed on cards each week for Sunday school. Papa didn't say a word. He knew better than to contradict. He took Mary up on his knee and read to her out of *Pilgrim's Progress* in words of one syllable—well, at least in easy words. Mama couldn't object to that. It didn't seem to occur to her that a lot of *Pilgrim's Progress* is very much like a fairy tale.

The next evening when Papa came home, he handed Mary, out of his pocket, "a small gray book of Alice" (*E.H.* 62). In the back of the book was a card with her own name and the stamp of the circulating library. The ticket was her own, good for two books each week. Mama said that Jim must share the ticket, but that didn't matter to Mary as long as she could keep on reading about Alice. *Alice's Adventures in Wonderland* was definitely the kind of book you could walk around in, which was another way of saying you really felt as though you were inside the story. You could feel yourself being Alice, wearing the same round comb, moving in the same matter-of-fact way among all the muddled and silly creatures of Wonderland.

What Mary liked best in school were the Friday afternoon recitations. You could select anything you wanted from one of the readers or perhaps from another collection by McGuffey called a "speaker": poetry, orations, dialogues. You had to learn your selection by heart and then say it out loud in front of the class and any visitors who happened to drop by.

She could memorize easily, and one afternoon when she was still in the fourth grade—she couldn't then have been more than eight years old, so it may have happened rather later—she chose to recite the whole of "The Lady of Shalott" (*E.H.* 63). The rest of the children started to titter. If the new principal hadn't happened to be invited into their room that day, they might even have whispered behind their hands, "What a queer faraway stare that stuck-up Mary Hunter has, and doesn't she look silly, always swaying a little as though she thought she were dancing." They'd bet she hadn't any more notion than the rest of them what the long poem was all about. She'd only chosen it so she should show off, they were probably telling one another.

They couldn't have understood that the sallow-faced little girl with the high forehead and the too-sharp nose was really enchanted by the sound and the rhythm of words, by the pictures that floated up in her mind as she read or recited. Mary was astonished to find that hardly anyone else could see them, any more than you can ever see what another person is dreaming.

For her, the fields, the winding road, the many-towered town would have really seemed to go flashing by. There was a river and in the river an island. On the island, shut in, no one knows why, among four gray walls is a weaving lady alone with her web of colors. In a book she wrote almost fifty years later, *The Land of Journeys' Ending*, Mary Austin would find herself saying "My sole purpose . . . in showing you the many-colored skein of the past limp in my hand, is that you may presently feel with me the pull of the shuttle that flies to the pattern's completion," as though the Lady of Shalott still lived on deep within her.

In the poem, the Lady is forbidden to leave her loom or a curse will come upon her. She is allowed to look at the world beyond the tower only in a mirror—shadows of the world, not the reality. She weaves the mirror's shadows into her web and does not know how she longs to be outside among the things that happen.

One day the knight, Sir Lancelot, comes riding by. She sees him like a vision flashing in her mirror, his horse, his shining armor, his helmet, and his helmet-feather

> *like one burning flame together.*
>
> . . . .
>
> *From the bank and from the river*
> *He flashed into the crystal mirror,*
> *"Tirra, lirra," by the river*
> *Sang Sir Lancelot*

Then the Lady knows that no matter what the curse may be, she must leave her loom and her mirror and try to find him.

What could a little girl only eight years old or a little more know about such things? She could only know that she loved the beauty, the moving lines, the words like the sound of the wind in the grass on the hill below the orchard, the rustle of leaves, the flicker of sunlight through the leaves, the strands of the web like the flower colors in spring. She could not know that the Knight in Shining Armor belongs to the world of dreams, the dreams we are all born with, and that many have tried to follow him away into the dream and have lost their way there. Mary, too, fell under his spell. Always afterward, no matter where the path of her life happened to take her, she was haunted by the dream, so that she never seemed quite able to put up with ordinary men.

The poem ended sadly. The Lady tries to follow where her vision leads. She "left the web, she left the loom"; she goes out of the tower and down to the stream where she finds a boat tied under a willow tree. She enters the boat. "And down the river's dim expanse, Like some bold seer in a trance, Seeing all his own mischance . . . Did she look to Camelot." The boat floats down the river; the Lady, lying down, sings as it moves, until at last, before she ever reaches the towered town, "singing in her song," she dies.

The little girl, reciting the poem, must have experienced it all, as though it were her own dream. When she finished, she awakened out of the dream-poem and saw the grubby, everyday faces gaping in front of her. The children squirmed at their desks, shuffling their feet in a hurry to get out of the stuffy classroom. Teacher was leaning down to her as though from a great height.

"And now, Mary," she heard Teacher say, "suppose you tell us what your piece means" (*E.H.* 63).

"There she had you," Mary Austin would later remember. She hadn't supposed until now that poetry was supposed to *mean* something. Poetry just *was*, the way trees are and flowers and birds and grass. She didn't know, as her teachers thought she should, that what you were supposed to do with poetry was analyze it: "resolve each sentence . . . into its elements, trace the logical and grammatical dependences of the several parts and apply thereto the rules of construction" (Newton Bateman, Report of Superintendent, Public Instruction, Illinois, 1873–74).

"Don't you think" Teacher continued (perhaps she was feeling uncomfortable because she really didn't understand the poem herself), "that when you recite a piece, you ought to know what it means?" Mary must have looked a little dazed. Then she answered with her usual air of defiance, "I learned it because I liked it" (*E.H.* 64). She heard the titter start to run around the classroom again like a rustle of dry leaves. The children loved to make fun of you when Teacher had you on the spot. She hoped they couldn't see her going red under the curls that didn't really hide her ears enough. Luckily the new principal himself came to the rescue.

"I like it too," he said, and his voice didn't stoop down to her at all like Teacher's. "Tennyson is my favorite author."

"My favorite author" (*E.H.* 64). Mary had never heard the phrase before, but it sounded very impressive, and at least it probably made Teacher shrink a little. Mary began to feel not nearly so lost and so little. She felt herself approved of, and by someone of greater authority than Teacher. She began to think of just the tone of voice in which she'd talk at home about her "favorite author" when Mama chided her for not tending to her chores.

"WILL YOU LEAVE ME ALL YOUR BOOKS, PA?"

Mary was never quite sure just when she made up her mind that she wanted to be a writer. Her mother used to claim, half in pride, half in exasperation, that the little girl began writing "as soon as she could talk" (*E.H.* 70). Stories really must have begun bubbling out of her very early. She told them to the neighbor children who tagged along with her on the way home from school. She told them on hot summer afternoons with three or four little girls perching beside her on the rim of the old rock quarry, dangling forbidden bare feet in the cool water. Winter evenings were the most perfect time for stories, along with the smell of popcorn crackling and puffing over an open fire, flames that flickered and filled the lamplighted room with shifting shadows, snow flying against the window with "a soft damping swish" (*E.H.* 72). Before long some little one would be sure to pull Mary by her skirts out of the corner where she sat hidden among her own dreams and demand that she tell a story.

It was one way she could always count on being the center of attention. It almost made up to her for being the kind who is usually left until the last in games that begin with choosing sides and who a lot of the time doesn't get invited to parties unless some mother insists. Telling stories, though, was like being able to work a kind of magic. You could make any kind of world you liked appear. You could do all kinds of things to those who listened, make them hold their breaths in wonder, make them shiver as though someone had dropped an icicle down their necks, scare them sometimes into running from a shadow. At times it seemed almost as though you could turn your listeners to stone, then with the sudden appearance of a happy ending, bring them to life again. It would have seemed especially wonderful to a little girl who felt so much of the time that she wasn't wanted.

The stories she told seemed to come up inside her, like water in a well, even when they were about the things that happen every day. She had a natural feeling for the pattern of events that make a story. Perhaps there was more of Great-grandmother Polly Dugger in her than she realized. Instead of spinning and weaving colored threads, Mary wove with words. Instead of sewing odd scraps of cloth together into patchwork quilts, Mary made stories out of the bits and pieces that went on around her. She had a born memory for whatever she heard or read, the stories her kin used to tell whenever they got together, the Bible stories she only half listened to those long Sunday mornings at Grandpa's, the stories her father sometimes read to her out of the rows and rows of books on the shelves above his desk.

Mary liked to think that her interest in writing was especially encouraged by her father. Sometimes when he was working at his big flat-topped desk, he would let Mary climb up on one corner and sit so she could watch him. She had to promise to be perfectly quiet and not say a word or else she'd be sent right off to the kitchen and what seemed to her to be her mother's far less fascinating world. She didn't mind being quiet as long as she could look at books, even before she was able to read them to herself.

The shelves way over her head held several sets of "Complete Works" (E.H. 70), Shakespeare and Burns and Ben Jonson. Ben Jonson was the set Mary liked the best because the covers were red with a tracery of gold, so much prettier than the dull schoolbooks or the finger-smudged stories from the circulating library. The books on her father's shelves made a world of their own around her, shining with color, filled with a secret life, a life very different from the outdoor world she loved so much being a part of.

Her father did more than let her feast her eyes on the books with which he seemed to be surrounded. He brought home copies of the *St. Nicholas Magazine,* beginning with the very first issue. This would have been for November 1873, when Mary was only a little past five years old and not yet in school. It may well have been *St. Nicholas* that a little later kindled her own first dream of writing. Her writing seems to grow out of reading as storytelling grows from hearing stories told.

The first time Mary talked out loud about her intention to write books was, as far as she could remember, the summer she was seven years old. It seems more likely that she was closer to being eight. Her brother George was born that August. Her mother, in the last months of another unwelcome pregnancy, had other things on her mind than keeping track of her dreamy older daughter. The little girl found herself spending more and more time among her father's books. She was able by this time to read a lot more by herself than anyone realized. The big words would not have bothered her much when she found herself on the trail of a great adventure. If she went ahead fast enough it was easy to understand the story without having to know what every word meant. Perhaps it was the little bird in the back of her mind who helped her along, the little bird who seems to have gone on being part of Mary all her life. One wonders just what she happened to be reading the day she suddenly looked up from her book and said to Pa, who didn't seem to be working at anything special just that moment or she would never have dared to interrupt him,

"Will you leave me all your books, Pa, when you die?" (E.H. 70).

It seems a strange question for a little girl not quite eight years old to ask, almost as though she were already taking it for granted that he *would* die, which he did, in fact, about two years later. Papa seemed more amused than astonished by her question.

"Well, that depends," he answered with the special twinkle Mary always loved to remember. "Why do you want them?"

"I will sell them and live on the money until I write a book my own self," replied Mary, as though this were not the first time she'd thought about it.

"Well, of course, for anything so important as that—" and one may be sure the word *important* was underlined in Mary's mind forever after. "What kind of books do you mean to write?"

"All kinds," the little girl replied airily (E.H. 70–71). She thought it a stupid sort of question. Why should anyone be satisfied with writing just one kind? She never was able to understand why people always laughed whenever her father told the story.

Years later when she was writing it down for her autobiography, Mary Austin still couldn't see what everyone thought so funny. She thought maybe they suspected her quite wrongly of being conceited. Was it conceit, she often asked herself, to believe you could do whatever you put your mind to hard enough?

A PLAY TO BE SUNG

"In her tenth year suddenly Mary began upon a serious piece of writing" (E.H. 75).

She called it "A Play to be Sung" and says she could never figure out where the idea for it could possibly have come from. Theme and story were entirely outside the dimension of her experience. She did not think that she could even have had any knowledge at that age "that there are such things as plays written to be sung" (*E.H.* 76). She couldn't remember, at the time she was writing her autobiography, that she had even heard the word "opera," which is odd, because Carlinville, like so many small towns of its time, had a building called "The Opera House." If no operas were performed there in her time, she must at least have known the meaning of the name.

She wondered if the theme of her play "might have been a half-memory . . . of something overheard on those forbidden occasions when Mary crouched outside the parents' door in her bare feet and flannel nightie" (*E.H.* 77). The setting, she supposed, must have come from a picture book. In May 1857, *St. Nicholas Magazine* printed a short story version of *Ivanhoe*, which enthralled her so much that she persuaded her father to borrow the grown-up version for her. It was part of a set that came "Complete with Footnotes and Appendix" (*E.H.* 72). There must have been castles among the illustrations, though Mary does not mention being aware of this. In her autobiography, she describes two scenes from the play that recurred to her vividly at different times of her life:

> *The setting is a castle with a conical-topped round tower at one end and a squarish . . . "keep" at the other. In the first scene the walls rise directly from the level of a garden, and from the tower window a lady leans and sings several verses about a garden, which are in reality directions for her lover, who is stealing through the park below, toward her lighted window. Every stanza ends with the refrain:*
>
> *"Come softly under my window and I will unbar to thee"* (E.H. 76).

Whether he did or she did Mary has no recollection. It is interesting to discover that in her last novel, *Starry Adventure*, written around the same time as the autobiography, Mary Austin uses the tower scene in a different setting. Had she remembered it all these years? In the novel, the tower is part of an old Spanish house in New Mexico and is called by its Spanish name, a *torreon*. This time the lover is the one who sings and the lady does indeed open the window: " . . . you stood looking at the *torreon*," she has her hero, Gard Sitwell, recall, "and the song you had been singing shaped in you and came out like the tendrils of a vine; no words, a breathy pouring cry that shook you with intensity, with scarcely any sound. Presently a thin light showed along the window-ledge, a window-frame swung back, a bright head showed and bent like a flower. You took hold of the rungs and the song, climbing in you, drew you up." It took the young man in "A Play to be Sung" a long time to reach his lady. In the novel, which was written nearly fifty years later, the lady proves false. She is using her lover only for her plaything, for what used to be called her "fancy man." The young man is bitterly hurt by her behavior. In the end, he grows up enough to put his dream aside and accept his feeling for the real and very natural girl he has known all his life.

One wonders whether Mary may have unknowingly absorbed some of her father's wordless and deeply buried disappointment in his first love. The theme of a rejected and disillusioned lover appears in more than one of her novels. In *The Lovely Lady,* written a good deal earlier than *Starry Adventure,* the cast-off lover suffers a nervous breakdown. When he has recovered, he tries to understand exactly what it was that happened to him. "The capacity for loving died in him," Peter Wetherall realizes, "with the knowledge of not being able to be loved."

Mary's own capacity for loving seems to have been blighted very early. Neither her mother nor her father were able to help her feel able to be loved. No wonder she built a kind of castle around her secret self where an inner drama of search and defense, of waiting and disappointment, went on, in spite of all her later success in the outside world.

The second scene [of "A Play to be Sung"] is in front of the same castle, with a terrace reaching the length of the house, and a lawn below; not a night scene, but still dim, as it might have been twilight or early morning. The door from the terrace is open and there is the sound of voices within. Suddenly a sword flies out of the door and a man, following rapidly, snatches it up from the turf and turns to fight another who is pursuing him, sword in hand. The two of them cross swords, and a lady comes out on the terrace and watches, with something of curiosity and cruelty on her face. . . . There is an old man in the story somewhere and a white-faced, lying woman; the whole thing utterly unaccounted for and every way inexplicable (E.H. 76–77).

It is strange that Mary does not suspect that the "whole thing" may have belonged to what she would much later call "a deeper self" (*E.H.* viii), the source of "feeling-knowledge," something much older, perhaps even wiser, than the reasoning mind. Since the scenes haunted her for so long, off and on for fifty years at least, the characters and the action may have reflected important aspects of her own inner life, as important to understanding her destiny as the arrangement of the planets at her birth might seem to an astrologer.

Is the man being pursued through the open door, one wonders, the same who in the first scene had been sung to by the enticing lady? Is the one who pursues and fights with him a rival or a defender of the castle? Who is the heartless lady who looks on? Is she perhaps the mistress of the castle, someone who lives only to triumph over men? Is she someone whom we will now and then catch glimpses of later on in Mary?

What has the "white-faced, lying woman" (*E.H.* 77) done to make her look so pale? What does she lie about? Has she opened the door of the forbidden room and seen something she must not see? Does the old man threaten the woman because she has dared to disobey him, dared to obey the impulse of her own spirit to open the last door for herself, to look with her own eyes, to look at the hidden reality in spite of all threats and warnings? Does she know she is now a prisoner in Bluebeard's castle? Will her brothers ride in time to her rescue?

Yes, there is no doubt that Mary knew the fairy tale well. In a short story called "Frustrate," written well after she was thirty, she says—and the frustrated woman is obviously herself: "All the time I kept looking out like Sister Anne in the fairy tale, and it seemed to me a great many times that I saw dust moving."

There are other fairy tales she didn't remember or was unable to see herself as part of, like those of the maidens who are locked up and given impossible tasks to perform before they can arrive at the happy ending. They must spin flax or nettles into gold or sort huge heaps of mixed-up seeds, enough to take more than a lifetime. Always some small wild creatures come to help them, ants or flocks of many kinds of birds, and so it was to be with Mary, who would turn her despised desert years into the gold of her finest writing and then abandon it all for what she felt to be the "larger life," a life of success in the outside world, a life of being noticed.

THE END OF LIFE ON PLUM STREET

Mary worked at her "A Play to be Sung" at intervals for two or three years before discarding it. She must have begun it not long before her father died. "I never knew," she says, "exactly what was the nature of my father's illness" (*E.H.* 84). Perhaps she never knew because she was shut in with her own thoughts and dreams, resenting the adult world that was pressing on her increasingly.

By the winter of 1877, Mary felt a change come over the household. The new baby, George, was only a few months old, and Susanna Hunter left him as much as she could in eight-year-old Mary's care. Mary often woke in the night to find Mama standing beside her bed with the sleeping infant in her arms. "Take care of the baby, Mary, Pa's sick" (*E.H.* 84). Later the crib was moved in beside Mary's bed. Did she and Jennie share the room together? One cannot help wondering, for Mary speaks only of herself. She "would hear, through sleep made uneasy by a sense of responsibility, the sounds of pain and restless pacing in the room across the hall." In the early morning, "thick with sleep" (*E.H.* 84), she must get up and stumble with the baby downstairs to the kitchen lest her father be wakened by his crying. Before she had anything to eat herself she must fix him a soft-boiled egg. She grew to hate the sight of soft-boiled eggs and refused to eat them herself for many years.

Summer mornings she would crumble bread into a bowl of milk for them both. If the hired man were about, the milk could be gotten warm and sweet from the cow. Then Mary would steal away with the contented baby "to the first row of orchard trees, or down between the grapevine trellises" (*E.H.* 153). There, while little George tumbled about her feet or napped, she could let herself go off again into her private world. She would be watching "the dew slip down the clover stems, or the white webby moons of spider webs made thick with diamond drops, and around her would steal a sense of innumerable bright events, of tingling and unattempted possibilities; there would be a sense of swelling, of billows coming and going, lifting and dying away—and then someone would come looking for her from the house to say that the grown-up breakfast was ready" (*E.H.* 153). She would be jostled back into the every-day world again and all the extra chores that hindered her mind from flying off on its own adventures. Unless she were prodded out of herself, her thoughts do not seem to have been involved as much with what was happening to her father as later on she wanted to believe. She was aware of the possibilities that he might die but spoke of it to no one. "It was to Jennie . . . that all Mary's confidences were made" (*E.H.* 85). It was Jennie who could always be counted on to feel for others.

Mary declares that she twice took Jennie by the hand and trudged home from school without asking permission because she had a sense of alarm, an anxiety connected with her father. She could never quite manage to cry on these occasions even though she felt it would be "the most natural way of dealing with the sense of stunned alarm" (*E.H.* 85) that dragged her homeward. So deeply buried by now were her own real feelings she seemed able to express them only when she was dramatizing. In *A Woman of Genius*, Mary Austin pictures her fictional self, Olivia, at school on the morning of her father's death. A harsh wind is blowing. The child watches "the little puffs of dust that rose between the planks of the flooring whenever the building shuddered and ground its teeth" (W.G. 34). She is "divided between an affectation of timorousness . . . as a suitable form of behaviour" (W.G. 34) and her private dramatization of the demolition of the building from which "only such occupants as I favoured should be rescued by my signal behaviour" (W.G. 35).

In the midst of this daydream, one of Olivia's uncles suddenly appears at the classroom door. He has come to take both children home. Their father has finally died. In the novel, Mary Austin alters real life enough to make the death an accidental one. She includes more detail than she does in the autobiography, but the setting is the same and so are the little girl's emotional reactions.

On the way home, Olivia begins at last to cry. The little sister "came cuddling up to me in the smother of the wind, trying to comfort me as if . . . he had been my father only and not hers at all" (W.G. 36–37). How like gentle Jennie this really seems. Mary makes her sound like the ideal little girl in the school reader who goes about "making sunshine in the house when there is none without." One wonders whether she were not sometimes a source of vexation as much as of comfort to Mary, like the sister in the fairy tale whose goodness was rewarded by having diamonds fall from her lips at every word.

When the two children come in sight of their house, the wind is still blowing, "the very smoke wrenched itself from the chimney and escaped, hurryingly upon the wind; the shrubbery wrung itself. . . . The blinds were down at the front windows, and no one came in or out" (W.G. 37).

Once inside the house, the children find their "mother sitting by the fire in a chair out of the best room, crying heartily" (W.G. 38). They fling themselves upon her, crying too. She gathers them up "in a violence of grief" (W.G. 38) and holds them to her, rocking.

"I remember getting done with my crying first," Mary has Olivia say, "and being very hot and uncomfortable . . . thinking of nothing but how I should wriggle out of her embrace and get away, anywhere, to escape from the burden of having to seem to care" (*W.G.* 39).

The house is full of neighbors and mourning relatives, weeping and quoting Scripture to the widow whose face is wan with her days and nights of watching. "The Lord giveth—" (*W.G.* 40), as though that could really make any difference to those who were left behind. The older brother, who has managed to get home ahead of his sisters, hangs awkwardly over his mother; "blubbering" is the way Mary unsympathetically puts it. He might at least have remembered he was a boy and that boys are not supposed to cry. The little sister would have found it easy to share her mother's tears as the surest means of giving comfort.

Olivia finds herself "going rather heavily upstairs and being over-taken in the middle of it by the dramatic suggestion of myself as an orphan child toiling through the world—" She catches herself acting this out with great effect. "I dare say I had read something like that recently—and carrying out the suggestion with an immense effect on Uncle Alva, who happened to be coming down at that moment. And then the insidious spread through all my soul of cold disaster, out of which I found myself unable to rise even to the appearance of how much I cared" (*W.G.* 39).

The version in the autobiography omits the fantasy of the orphan child, which most likely came straight out of one of McGuffey's readers. "Then there was I-Mary, and Uncle Otis with his arm around her, and she hiding her face against him lest somebody should see that she had no tears and think she did not care" (*E.H.* 86).

One wonders whether she cared too much or not enough. At the time she wrote her autobiography, Mary Austin was very much concerned with what posterity would think of her, and she works hard to give the impression of a child who has been overwhelmed by her own grief. "For once Mary had nothing to say; she laid herself dumbly against the sharp edge of sorrow, fearful that she would miss . . . the least aching instant of loss" (*E.H.* 86).

In the novel, written so many years earlier, the realization of loss does not come to the little girl until the evening after the funeral:

> *The room had been set in order while we were away at the ceme-*
> *tery; the lamp was lit and there was a red glow on everything from*
> *the deep heart of the base burner. [A neighbor woman has set a*
> *meal on the table for the bereaved family.] Under the lamp there*
> *was a great bowl of quince marmalade which she had brought . . . ;*
> *the colour of it played through the clear glass like a stain upon the*
> *white cloth. [It had been a favorite dish of the child's father. Almost*
> *automatically, she finds herself getting a small dish from the cup-*
> *board and starting to set aside a special portion as she used to do*
> *for him.]*
>
> *All at once it came over me . . . the meaning of bereavement;*
> *that there was nobody to be done for tenderly; the loss of it . . .*
> *the need of the heart for all its offices of loving . . . and the un-*
> *availing pain" (W.G. 43).*

The months that followed were a blur for Mary. Susanna Hunter had never had any particular love for the Plum Street farm, but there was still "livestock to be looked after" (*E.H.* 86) and debts and accounts to settle. The small family stayed on at the farm through the winter. It was the last place that would really feel like home to Mary until she built her long dreamed-of house in New Mexico almost half a century later. Even there the house itself was never as much a joy as the landscape she looked out on. In the same way, it had been the Branch, the woods, and the myste-rious presences in the woods that her heart remembered from childhood.

With the cold autumn days coming on, the trees bare of their leaves, she was shut away from the outdoor world. It appears that, with the realization of her father's death, Mary began sinking into one of the depressions that she was subject to at periods of crisis all her life. Once again, as on the day when she had watched Papa vanish, with the infant Jennie on his arm, over the curve of the steep hill, she knew the terror of abandonment. Her mother had little time to pay attention to what was going on within her unusually silent elder daughter. After all, Mary was now ten years old, the same age Susie Graham had been when her own mother died, and Susie had managed to grow up enough to take care of the younger children until the arrival of her stepmother. "She'll come when she finds she has to" (*E.H.* 41), was what Susanna Hunter still must have thought of Mary.

Early in December, Mary came down with a severe sore throat, but this was nothing unusual for her. In those days, no one thought of sending for the doctor unless there was a real emergency. Only Jennie seemed to realize how ill her big sister really was. At night when Mary's "throat ached chokingly, Jennie would put her arms about Mary, stroking her face" (*E.H.* 86) as though she longed to help.

After Mary recovered from her sickness, Jennie came down with it. She would sit in her little corner by the fireplace looking desperately ill but still trying not to be a bother. "There came a day when she could neither swallow nor speak" (*E.H.* 86). By the time the doctor was sent for and diphtheria diagnosed, it was too late.

Sunny-haired Jennie was buried beside her father in the graveyard, close to the little babies who had died before her. The oak trees that had spread such a rich shade in summer were cold and leafless on that winter day. The gravestones could no longer remind anyone of the walls of a fairy city. Mary found herself turning toward her mother with a small human gesture of comfort. Was it a blind effort to do as her little sister might have done? Now that Jennie was gone, could Mary perhaps take her place as the beloved and loving one?

But the mother's thoughts at that moment were only of her loss. She turned away from her daughter's awkward touch and gave way to her own grief. To Mary, it would seem that she had been again rejected. That night, according to Dr. Helen McKnight Doyle, who came to know Mary Austin years later in California, Mary heard her mother say to Aunt Effie, "Why couldn't it have been Mary?"

It is hard to believe that a fine Christian woman like Susanna Hunter could really have spoken such cruel words. Mary Austin does not record them in her autobiography. She tries hard enough to give an unsympathetic picture of her mother but admits that "never in my life did I hear her speak of any person with envy or malice or the color of ill nature" (E.H. 221).

Is it possible that Mary only imagined what she thought she heard? Might it have been she herself who wished, on the day of the funeral, deep inside herself, that it could have been Mary instead of Jennie who had died? Thoughts sometimes lurk in the back of a child's mind that are too dreadful to be allowed into the light. How often she may have caught herself hating Jennie, then hating herself for being so unlike Jennie.

Why, she must have wondered, were the princesses in the fairy tales always golden-haired, blue-eyed, and rosy-lipped? Why was it that the way you looked seemed to matter so much when it came to being loved? She made herself pretend that it didn't matter, that it was, in fact, much better to be thought clever. I-Mary must have backed her up in this. The trouble was that I-Mary didn't always come around when she was needed. At the time of Jennie's death, and for a long time after, she didn't come at all. What must have made it worse was the thought that Mary's own unresisted longing for tenderness had perhaps caused Jennie's death. If only she hadn't let Jennie creep so comfortingly close; if she hadn't longed so for the touch of her little sister's hands. . . .

"The loss of her is never cold in me, tears start freshly at the mere mention of her name," Mary Austin writes years later. "And I would not have it otherwise. She was the only one who ever unselfishly loved me. She is the only one who stays" (E.H. 87).

She stayed, perhaps, as the reflection of Mary's own lost ability to love, shut away in her heart like Snow White in the glass coffin, whose stepmother poisoned her for being too beautiful.

Austin notes in her autobiography, "From that moment on the hillside under the leafless oaks above my father's grave, and my mother thrusting me away to throw herself upon it, I have no instant of recovered recollection until early the next spring when, as we were about to leave the farm to a tenant, the livestock and farming implements were put up for sale, which marks the end of the life on Plum Street" (*E.H.* 86–87).

GOING ON ELEVEN

The house the Hunter family moved to on Second South Street seemed cramped and unlovely to Mary after the childhood years on the Plum Street farm. Gone were the imaginative excursions on the way to school, the dreaming adventures under the apple tree and by the Branch, the wistful hours among her father's books. She was going on eleven years old, and everyone expected her to be a big girl now and a real help to her mother.

For the first few years, before her husband's pension was allowed, Susanna Hunter went out nursing to earn a living. Whenever she was away from home, Mary was the one who was expected to look after things. She writes that "she would hurry home from school, collect Georgie from the woman who, for a pittance, took care of him during the day, 'clean up,' cook supper, sleep with one ear awake toward the child . . . scramble through breakfast, put up lunch for herself and Jim, deliver her young charge, and, if anything went wrong, be held responsible" (*E.H.* 92).

One suspects that Mary rather enjoyed dramatizing herself in the part of the only daughter of a widowed mother, like one of those pathetic but virtuous children the McGuffey readers were so full of. In reality, Susanna Hunter seems not to have found widowhood as hard as her daughter likes to make out. Once she got used to her loss, it would have been a relief from the years of bearing and taking care of children, as well as of her ailing husband.

Susie always enjoyed being among people. The house on Second South Street was near some of her kinfolk, Uncle Billy and Aunt

Sophia Farrell. Uncle Billy kept a hardware store in Carlinville. He and Aunt Sophia had five children. Two of them, Minnie and John, were "bosom companions" (E.H. 92) of Mary and Jim. The Hunters spent a lot of time at the Farrells the year they moved into town. The Farrells were musical, and Uncle Billy loved nothing better than a family program. The young folks, all but Mary (who, for all her sense of rhythm and for the sound of words, just could not carry a tune), joined in singing or accompanying on the triangle or the drum. Instead of joining in games like Authors or Old Maid, she listened in on the conversations of her elders. She seems always to have been a great one for listening in on conversations, and the children in at least two of her novels take after her.

With the Farrell cousins so near, Mary's responsibilities for her brothers and the many household duties couldn't have weighed on her as hard as she tries to make us believe. Besides, there was Grandpa Graham, who, as long as he lived, which was until Mary was almost sixteen, kept a kindly eye on his elder daughter and her children. The first summer of Susie's widowhood he sent her, along with Mary and three-year-old Georgie, to visit Aunt Mary Peter on the farm in Kansas.

This Aunt Mary was Susie's sister Mary Ann, she whose indulgent father had once allowed her to go tilting off to church in her wide hoopskirt, she of the "snapping black eyes and the ruddy color, that . . . after the birth of thirteen children, had not yet washed away" (E.H. 24) Things must have changed considerably for Mary Ann after she married Uncle Peter, who was, though Mary Austin does not mention this, her second husband. Her first had died in the Civil War, leaving her a very young widow with one child to begin her eventual "garland of thirteen" (E.H. 25). Uncle Peter was a tall, impressive man, a homesteader, a crossroads blacksmith, and an ordained "Free Methodist" (E.H. 95) minister. The Free Methodists were much more strict than the Carlinville Duggers' kind. Uncle Peter had insisted that his wife strip herself of "the vanities of dress" (E.H. 95), even to leaving off her wedding ring. This didn't seem to trouble Mary Ann nearly as much as it did Susie.

No one knows just why Uncle Peter should have said one day to Mary's mother, with Mary as usual overhearing, "If you are bringing up your children to think that their father has any other lot in the Hereafter than that of eternal damnation, you are bringing them up to a lie." Susie cried at that, and Mary talked right back to Uncle Peter. "I guess my father wouldn't want to be anywhere with people who thought that sort of thing, anyway!" (*E.H.* 96).

It seems odd that what Susie scolded her daughter for was talking back rather than for thinking her father might prefer Hell to being in Uncle Peter's Heaven. She made Mary apologize to her uncle. If there was anything Mary hated all her life it was apologizing. Why did you have to, when you always knew that you were right? Since she had managed to escape Heaven for herself in the Snockerty days, she couldn't really take Hell seriously, could she? At least she could never admit to herself that she did. She must have pushed all the frightening images from church and Sunday school, from *Pilgrim's Progress*, from the illustrations in *Paradise Lost* far down into the darkest depths of her mind. She pretended to herself that they didn't exist, yet all her life she would struggle almost frantically to find out what she really believed happens after death. Although she sounded very brave when she talked back to Uncle Peter, there was something within her that must have been very much afraid. The incident made a mark that never entirely left her, or why should she remember it so long and think it an important thing to tell about herself?

Most of that summer she seems to have been happy enough and as carefree as one ever finds her. She had laid her books and her writing things away for the time being. Her brother Jim wasn't there to compete with. He had stayed in Carlinville to help on one of his uncle's farms. There were plenty of Aunt Mary Ann's young ones about for Georgie to tag along with, so Mary could shed for a while the burden of responsibility for her little brother.

"I remember everything that happened at Aunt Mary's," she writes in her autobiography, "the vast roll of the prairies like the suspended breathing of a huge earth creature . . . the rhythmic sweeping movement of the wind-break in the perpetual wind, the strange flowers, our playhouse in the young peach orchard, and the rattlesnake we found sunning there. I remember taking turn and turn riding double with the other children, guarding Uncle Peter's stock grazing on governmental land; watching the dark menacing whirl of a small cyclone that veered off and left us in a dead calm; watching at night the running prairie fires and going next day to see in their black wake the little calcined skeletons of wild things overtaken in mid-flight" (E.H. 95–96).

Mary absorbed all these sensations into herself almost without knowing. Buried within her, they became part of the same experience of the American landscape which was to be so important to her later on and which she tried in so many ways to put into words. This would always be her best way of knowing: not the knowledge that came to her out of books in schools and libraries but the knowledge that sifted in through all her senses, through eyes and ears and fingers—patterns in sound and color that became part of her, the rise and fall of wind, the far-off horizon, "the incalculable blue ring of sky meeting earth" (E.H. 33) and herself at the center of it all, a small child, as she would be a grown woman, forever wondering.

This was the same summer that Mary, as she declares, "left off playing with dolls" (E.H. 94). Someone had given her a doll, she says, for Christmas—the Christmas that came so soon after Jennie died. The doll was "a wax beauty with open-and-shut eyes. She did not really play with it except when younger children visited her, but it was a treasured fetish of that lost romance of little-girlhood, and she liked, nights her mother was from home, to think that it kept all night its large cow-like, cerulean gaze upon her" (E.H. 94). The doll may have reminded Mary in some way of her lost little sister or of the golden-haired charmer she always wished she herself could have been. She gave it the lovely name of Angela Catherine—as different as possible from plain Mary.

It was a sharp end to childhood the day Mary watched one of her playmates step squarely on Angela Catherine's face out under the apple tree. Mary makes it obvious that she felt it was done out of meanness. She carried the doll into the house where her mother was entertaining callers. She was hoping for sympathy, she says, though it would have been more like her to have wanted justice. However it was, nobody paid any attention. After all, why should they? Everyone must have thought her much too big a girl to need comforting about a broken doll. Besides, why should she need a doll with Georgie to mind? How could anyone understand that looking after one's little brother wasn't at all the same as having a doll to tell yourself stories about, as though she were yourself. So Mary went off to her room and laid the broken treasure away in the back of the bureau drawer. And that, she says, was that.

A different version of this story has come down through Anna Burns, one of Aunt Mary Peter's children. This little girl, grown up, told the story to her daughter, who remembers only that after the Hunter cousins left the farm that summer, her mother's own cherished doll was missing. Later it turned up in Mary's house. Mary seems to have coveted the doll from the moment she first saw it. The two little girls used to fight over it and pull each other's hair. Could it be that Mary really hid Angela Catherine in the bottom of the bureau drawer because she was afraid of having to give her up?

THE OLD RED SANDSTONE

Mary was twelve years old in September of 1880 and beginning the eighth grade. School, as usual, didn't interest her very much except for reading. She floundered through arithmetic without ever learning what it was all about. Geography was just a list of dull facts to be remembered, the capitals of states, the names of rivers, what was manufactured in different cities, nothing that kindled a spark of interest in her mind the way poetry did when it spoke of fields and rivers. How she felt about history she would explain many years later in a pamphlet that summarized her career as a feminist: "The immediate concern of youth is not to know what emperors died or made die, but whether there is a soul in life" (*The Young Woman Citizen* 35). That was something she would spend a lifetime trying to find out for herself.

She read lots of Longfellow that year, *Tales of a Wayside Inn* and *Evangeline*. (She already knew much of *Hiawatha* by heart.) The "magic of words" carried Mary swimmingly much of the way through Milton's *Paradise Lost*, long before she could really understand the story. "Like watching a thunderstorm at sunset," she called it (*E.H.* 105). Why bother with stupid arithmetic problems that you could never get right when you could escape right out of the everyday world on the wavelike surges of poetry?

The best books always seemed to be the ones she read out of school, the ones she just happened to come across and then suddenly found herself carried away by. Usually these were books, she says, that everyone, especially her mother, thought she was too young to read. Like *The Old Red Sandstone*, for instance, by the Scottish geologist Hugh Miller. The book fell into Mary's hands because some of the Carlinville ladies were taking the Chautauqua home-study course in geology that year. Young Mrs. Keplinger, the wife of the Methodist Sunday school superintendent, who had come to live next door to the yellow house the Hunters were living in on Second South Street, was an ardent Chautauquan, and the Literary and Scientific Circle often met at her house. In spite of her busy life, it is said that Susanna Hunter never missed a meeting. Mary would no doubt be listening in whenever she could, poking her inquisitive nose into every book she could lay her hands on.

The title *Old Red Sandstone*, she tells us, had "a calling sound" (*E.H.* 104). It was to be often that way for Mary. Small things that seemed hardly worth paying attention to would call her, the way it often happens in fairy tales—the little magic bottle labeled "Drink Me," or sometimes a plant or a stone or a small animal that suddenly for no reason insists on being noticed. In her later years, Mary Austin wrote of watching fish from a glass-bottomed boat off the California coast. She saw "the lovely fairy shapes glide up from under ferny weed and mottled stone, to hang quiveringly about [a bit of bait the boatman had let down. They seemed to tremble with recognition of] something to be delightedly absorbed, made part of itself. . . . *Recognition!* Intuitive certainty of absolute rightness. . . . Leaning far over not to disturb the rapture of little fishes, it dawned upon me that this, of course, was what happened to me and to the Indians when anything wordlessly 'spoke' to us" (*E.F.D.* 254–255).

It was typical of Mary to remember all her life the effect of Hugh Miller's book upon her and nothing in detail about it, not even the correct wording of the title. It should be THE *Old Red Sandstone,* for it is an account of the many different forms of fossil life that are found in one of the most famous sandstone formations that fill many of the valleys of Scotland and parts of England.

There is no wonder Mary was impressed, for in Hugh Miller she must have found for the first time in her life a truly kindred spirit. Hugh Miller was more than a scientist. He was a poet, a lover of his country's folklore, a deeply religious man who managed to combine a literal belief in the Bible account of creation with an infinite capacity for wonder and for the kind of knowledge that grows out of wonder. In the beginning, like Mary herself, he had scarcely known that such a science as geology existed. Born in the north of Scotland to ordinary working-class parents, he tells how he set out without much enthusiasm when he was a young man of about nineteen or twenty to earn his living as a quarryman in the wild shire of Cromarty, where he had grown up. A great reader himself, he knew that Robert Burns had referred to quarrying as the most disagreeable of all employments and dreaded the loss of his young days of freedom. "It was twenty years last February since I set out, a little before sunrise to make my first acquaintance with a life of labour and restraint," Hugh Miller writes, "and I have rarely had a heavier heart than on the morning. I was but a slim, loose-joined boy at the time, fond of the pretty intangibilities of romance and of dreaming when broad awake." How

Mary's heart must have leapt in recognition! The dreamer in her that her teachers were only vexed by stirred and began to see itself reflected. After that, no matter how many times her mother may have called her, she could hardly have been able to lay the book down. Says Miller:

> *The portion of my life which had already been gone by had been happy beyond the common lot. I had been a wanderer among rocks and woods, a reader of curious books when I could get them, a gleaner of old traditionary stories, and now I was going to exchange all my day dreams and amusements for the kind of life in which men toil every day that they may be enabled to eat.*

Mary was already beginning to find out what it was to exchange her daydreams and amusements for the hard necessity of growing up. She would have known just how Hugh Miller felt. There was a part of her that had been born to be the same kind of person, something that had come to life in her when she was a child on the Plum Street farm, and that now, when her childhood was beginning to disappear, seemed to be disappearing too. It would reappear again when she found herself "a wanderer among rocks and woods" in a very different part of the country, faced as Hugh Miller had been during his days of quarrying with marvels she could find no one to explain.

Hugh Miller's first day as a common laborer breaking up stone in a quarry turned out to be full of surprises. He discovered how much there was to learn about the proper way of handling pick and shovel; he had never seen gunpowder used for blasting and enjoyed the sense of risk and adventure connected with it. Marvel of marvels, as the first shot blew a piece of the rock cliff to fragments, out of a cleft in the rock fell two dead birds. They must have taken shelter from a storm and been trapped in one of the rock hollows. Young Miller examined them with a precise eye for color and detail. "The one was a pretty cock goldfinch, with its hood of vermillion, and its wings inlaid with the gold to which it owes its name, as unsoiled and smooth as if it had been preserved for a museum. The other, a somewhat rarer bird of the woodpecker tribe, was variegated with light blue and greyish yellow." The young quarryman found himself "thinking of the contrast between the warmth and jollity of their green summer haunts, and the cold and darkness of their last retreat." It is evident that Hugh Miller knew how to look with his heart as well as with his mind.

Each day at the quarry brought something more to wonder at. As the blocks of stone were moved away, he found himself gazing on the fossil shells of creatures that had once lived in vanished seas. For a long time he had no one to tell him the meaning of what he saw. "Without guide or vocabulary I had to grope my way as best I might and find out all the wonders for myself."

Mary had most likely forgotten these words by the time she went to live in California, yet there is much in her writing that resembles no one's work as it does Hugh Miller's. Though she liked to think she had been born with "noticing eyes," it may have been Miller's words that first taught her about the power of language. "Learn to make a right use of your eyes," he advised the young Scottish workingmen for whom his book was written. "The commonest things are worth looking at—even stones and weeds and familiar animals." It was through doing just that that Mary Austin would be able to write what everyone agrees is her finest book, *The Land of Little Rain*, as well as the best parts of many that came later.

No wonder that *The Old Red Sandstone* was the first book she bought with her own scanty pocket money. Being a girl, she couldn't earn for herself the way Jim did and had to make do with the little her mother could allow her, so it took a long time. During her college years, the book disappeared from the family shelves, but the door it opened for Mary never entirely closed.

"I remember the very look of the pages, the easy, illustrative charts, the feel of the author behind the book, the feel of the purposeful earth," she says in her autobiography (*E.H.* 104). She read it, she says, out-of-doors, perched in her favorite seat in the cherry tree. As she read, the familiar landscape of her childhood days—

Rinaker's Hill, the Branch, the old rock quarry—began to shine for her in a new way: "the earth itself became transparent, molten, glowing" (*E.H.* 104).

At the end of her life, alone among the mountains of New Mexico, the geological pages of the past would sometimes open and turn again. The mountains would seem for a moment to be illumined "by such self-generated light as first shone" (*E.H.* 105) for her from the pages of *The Old Red Sandstone*.

THE PAINS OF GROWING UP

Around this time Mary found herself taken hard with the pains of growing up. The first outward sign of it was having her skirts lengthened halfway to the tops of her high-buttoned shoes. With her skirts that much longer, she was supposed to be too old to read *St. Nicholas*, so the subscription was given up. Yet when it came to reading *The Old Red Sandstone*, her mother had said she was too young. Too old one minute, not old enough the next. How were you supposed to know? Like Olivia in *A Woman of Genius*, it seemed to Mary as though she kept bumping into things she was too old for and then caromed to the things for which she was quite too young.

Toward the end of her thirteenth year, seeking for "an appreciable rule to live by," she joined the Methodist church. The church presented her with "a criterion of conduct" (*W.G.* 57) that left no room for question. She writes in *A Woman of Genius*, "You attended morning and evening service; . . . you taught in Sunday school; you waited on table at oyster suppers designed for the raising of the minister's salary, and if you had any talent for it you sang in the choir or recited things at the church sociables" (*W.G.* 57). "If you were careful about reading the Bible and doing good to people—that is, persuading them to go to church and to leave off swearing—all the more serious details such as making a living, marrying and having children would take care of themselves" (*W.G.* 63).

As though the rules were not enough, the church "provided a chart for all the by-lanes of behaviour" (*W.G.* 58). The evangelists who first addressed the young converts told them that they were never to go anywhere that they could not take their Savior with them.

A Savior, as Mary knew him at thirteen, was a solemn presence that ran in her mind with "the bleakness of plain, whitewashed walls and hard benches and a general hush, a vague sensation of your chest being too tight for you, and little of the feeling you had when you had gone to call at the Allinghams and had forgotten to wipe your feet . . . it was manifest if you took that incubus everywhere you went you wouldn't have any fun" (*W.G.* 58).

Fun was something you apparently had to give up in the process of becoming a young lady. There were all sorts of things your mother kept warning you you mustn't do. You weren't supposed to wander off into the woods by yourself anymore. You mustn't talk appreciatively about landscapes and flowers and the habits of little animals and birds to boys because they didn't like it. Boys weren't interested in *you* but only in the pleasant, usually stuck-up way you could make them feel. You had to pretend to be helpless so they could feel important and protective. If a boy took you walking, you should be interested in what *he* wanted to talk about, not in telling him your own ideas. You mustn't quote, especially things like poetry and Thoreau. Susanna Hunter kept calling Mary's attention to a book that Great-aunt Mary Dugger had treasured through her own youth. According to this book, "the Lady must be sufficiently well read to be able to introduce aptly the most fruitful topics," but she was not to express an opinion on them. "The gentleman will tell the lady what to think" (*E.H.* 113).

"Not Mary, they wouldn't," she decided. "They would have to be spry about it or Mary would end by telling them" (*E.H.* 113).

Her mother said she mustn't argue with boys or older people the way she always argued with her brother. "Jim was extremely fond of an argument, rather fancied himself in forensic attitudes, and it had to be admitted that none of the girls he knew, and few of the young men, provided him with such satisfying occasions for it as his sister Mary. They argued about everything from Herbert Spencer to why pearls occur in oysters, and it was extremely good for them" (*E.H.* 130).

About this time Mary happened to pick up a copy of Ruskin's *Seven Lamps of Architecture.* The illustrations almost literally enchanted her. The buildings might have come out of her own secret world, columns and arches marvelously carved with "strange and lovely whorls and intricate lacings and vinelike twistings of forms in stone" (*E.H.* 132). Something in Mary was deeply stirred and even somehow troubled. "She read and read, not always understandingly, sick, genuinely sick for someone to talk to about it" (*E.H.* 132). She wanted to read this book with her mother, the way Mother and Jim were always reading books together, the way they were just now reading Roosevelt's *Winning of the West,* which they seemed to think was ever so much more important than anything in Ruskin.

Susie was disturbed by Mary's wild, emotional reaction to the book. She clouded her daughter's yearning enthusiasm with morals. It was "all right to read Ruskin; but not until you were older. And not to make it seem so important. It was all right after you had attended to the real things of life, to have a little of this sort of thing thrown in for sauce; but to read things like 'Seven Lamps,' before you could understand them, was what made you queer, so that people didn't like you" (*E.H.* 132–133). To be odd, to be different from the others—this was something that most people in Mary's day thought must at all costs be avoided. Had Susie suffered enough through the "queer birds" in Milo Graham's family that she was sincerely worried about Mary? Just going off by yourself to read so much was enough to get yourself suspected, let alone wanting to write.

At the time she came into conflict with her mother over reading Ruskin, Mary does not seem to have dreamed of becoming a genius or to have given the appearance of being one, except perhaps through her oddity. As she wrote in her story "Frustrate," she was aware only of some kind of "shifty, glittering flood; . . . a beautiful kind of life deep down inside her singing and burning blue and red and gold as it sang." It was an urge for life that found no way to exist in the midst of what her mother called "the real things" (*E.H.* 133).

Mary learned to shove these feelings more and more deeply down, never to let them show if she could help it. She developed a kind of outward behavior that her mother called "not taking an interest." This could have been instead an intense preoccupation with her own inner self, "the veil of withdrawal behind which . . . she had concealed both her sensitivity and that absorbed, selfless attention which she gave the external world, the product," she insists, "of an intensity of interest which had the unfortunate effect of making her appear uninterested" (*E.H.* 171).

The explanation couldn't have made any sense to Susie, who was such a different type of person. Susanna Hunter's thoughts and energies were entirely engaged with the external world, the world where "real things" happened. She was an extrovert who enjoyed nothing so much as activities among people, "a life of seeing and hearing, of social participation," as her daughter herself understood it (*E.H.* 177). Mary was chiefly concerned with what was going on within herself. She had to take the external world into her inner being before she could understand it. Eventually, sometimes not until years later, she would give it back again, transformed by the mysterious alchemy of the creative spirit. No wonder she turned out so difficult to teach. She learned to defend herself against accusations of stupidity by a display of arrogance.

HER MOTHER'S HOUSE

The new house on Johnson Street was about as far from Ruskin as you could get. The Hunters moved into it sometime in 1881, and thirteen-year-old Mary hated it from the first moment she saw it, as she felt bound to dislike most things connected with her mother. Susie had built the house with money she received from the sale of the Plum Street farm. Her pension had at last been allowed, along with officer's back pay. This meant she no longer had to go out nursing except when she wanted to help some neighbor through a time of trouble.

Everyone in the Carlinville community must have been happy to see valiant Susie Hunter settled into just the kind of house she'd always wanted. Everyone, that is, except her daughter Mary. "We lived there about seven years, and Mary was never at home in it at all," she complains. "At that time nobody ever thought of inquiring what Mary thought of anything, so nobody found out" (*E.H.* 107). She bottled up her feelings inside her and went glumly about from room to room, her "budding instinct for beauty" chafed, like Olivia's in *A Woman of Genius*, by a thousand inharmonies against which she pushed out "a kind of shell, hung within with the glittering stuff of dreams."

The parlor, she thought, was the worst. The furniture, except for the piano, was new and ugly. The blinds at the undraped windows were a dark chocolate color; the carpet and upholstery had been chosen of reds and greens that were supposed to "set each other off" (*E.H.* 110). The two fireplaces for burning coal had imitation black marble mantels, and the woodwork in the two front rooms had been grained to take on the look of an expensive hardwood finish. Susie was extremely pleased with it all. Mary, though she didn't know why, hated imitation materials. Even if she didn't come right out and say so, she must have found other ways of making her opinions felt. "The conviction that was pressed upon her from every side," she says, "that any dissatisfaction she might have

121

felt was inherently of herself, that she was queer and ungrateful and insensitive to the finer aspects of existence" (E.H. 108).

Well, why did you have to like the same things as everybody else? Why wasn't there even one corner in this dreary house that you could fix up your own way, so that it looked as though it belonged just to you and not to the whole family? Why did your mother think that being clean and tidy was the most important? There were other things a girl liked to think of than turning and pressing her clothes so she could look neat and trim, as Susie always did. Why should everyone laugh when Mary complained that the house was so bare of decoration it didn't even have a Whatnot?

A Whatnot (E.H. 111) was an old-fashioned piece of furniture with three-cornered shelves that could hold the most improbable assortment of objects collected from every corner of the country: Indian arrowheads, a tropical shell with the Lord's Prayer engraved minutely on it, a glass paperweight with tiny glass flowers inside alongside a stuffed bird, perhaps, or a polished buffalo horn, curious mineral specimens from California.

For Mary, the items on a Whatnot would have been keys that unlocked her tingling imagination. It was not the buffalo horn but the buffalo in his snorting reality she would behold; not only the arrowhead, but the arrow aimed by an Indian youth of long ago. The stuffed bird could tell stories of the forests through which it once had flown, the way Mary Austin would one day have the stuffed animals in the glass cases at the Museum of Natural History tell their adventures to the little boy Oliver in her collection of stories for children called *The Trail Book*.

Oliver, whose father is a night watchman in the museum, is sitting in front of the buffalo case, wondering what might be at the end of the trail. He has always felt sure that the great animals could come alive again if they wished. All at once, the glass case seems to disappear:

> *He could see the tops of the grasses stirring like the hair on the old Buffalo's coat, and the ripple of water on the beaver pool which*

THE EARLY LIFE OF MARY AUSTIN

was just opposite and yet somehow only to be reached after long travel through the Buffalo Country. The wind moved on the grass, on the surface of the water, and the young leaves of the alders, and over all the animals came the start and the stir of life.

When she began to write these stories, Mary Austin was living in New York and was very lonely. The staff of the museum would allow her entrance at night, and she was given free reign to explore the contents of the cases. The little girl who found it so hard to grow out of her childhood in Carlinville was still very much alive in the fifty-year-old woman, though Mary would not have liked to admit that about herself. As for the collection of stories, it did not sell very well. Austin claimed that the stories were meant to be factual, that the publishers had failed to understand her intent. By this time she was determined to be accepted as an authority on history rather than an imaginative writer. How hurt she must have been when she expressed her longing for a Whatnot, for Susie could hardly have missed the chance to warn her again about her childish daydreaming and the danger of being labeled queer.

Susie wasn't much for having art of any kind around. Her Methodist convictions were probably responsible for this. Grampa Graham, for all his artistic inclinations, had only two sentimental prints that Mary could remember—*Fast Asleep* and *Wide Awake*, they were called—and a black-and-white copy of Landseer's *Stag at Bay*. The walls of the Johnson Street house were bare at first, except for a few family photographs. "Later a lithograph of the martyred Garfield adorned one wall and a cheap papier-maché 'placque' of Lily Langtry another" (*E.H.* 110).

One can hardly conceive the glamorous "Jersey Lily" to be a subject with which Susanna Hunter would choose to decorate her parlor. Could the plaque possibly have come from Milo Graham's home, he whom we know to have had an eye for beautiful women? Grampa Graham died in 1884 when the Hunters had been living for three years on Johnson Street, a gentle patriarch, as Mary preferred to see him; his daughter Susie might have cherished Lily's likeness for her loving and lovable father's sake, though it does seem improbable.

The beautiful English actress was already famous when she arrived in America in the autumn of 1882. Her charm and her unconventional life were headlined in all the newspapers, for she had a knack for getting herself involved in interesting scandals. She was a friend of Albert, Prince of Wales, as well as of Oscar Wilde and of that fabulous American character, Diamond Jim Brady, who arranged for the special train and luxurious parlor car in which she made her first theatrical tours. These took her in the beginning to such cities as Boston, Philadelphia, Chicago, and Cincinnati, in addition to the regular New York season. In January 1883, she was as close to Carlinville as St. Louis. There Fred Gebhardt, who was her constant and much-talked-about escort, challenged one of the editors of the St. Louis *Globe-Democrat* to a duel because of a sensational article that had been published about Lily and Freddie. Though the duel didn't come off, there is little doubt that the hometown papers were full of all the latest gossip about Lily.

It would have been hard for a girl like Mary, then in her early adolescence, not to have her dreams stirred up. Lily Langtry was the beauty all girls longed to be. When she appeared at her first social occasion in London, the painter John Everett Millais exclaimed to his hostess, "Ah Madam, you have a goddess among your guests!" (quoted in *The Jersey Lily* by Pierre Sichel, 1958). Goddesses would not have been very well thought of among Mary's Methodist relations, let alone one with the shady reputation of an actress. Who but Mary could have argued Susie Hunter into hanging such a likeness in her home, "neat and hard and squared up," as Mary claims it was, "with a purely objective domesticity within which it was not possible even to imagine any other sort of life"? (*E.H.* 108).

To imagine another sort of life was exactly what came easiest for Mary, in spite of what, looking back, she wanted to believe. With her novel *A Woman of Genius*, she dramatized her struggle with the people of Carlinville. In the novel, Olivia puts herself at odds with the Taylorvillians:

> *It was as if, being required to produce a character, I found myself with samples of a great many sorts on my hands which I kept offering, hopeful that they might be found to match with the acceptable article, which, I must say here, they never did . . . the most I got by it was the suspicion of insincerity and affectation. I sensitively suffered the more from it as I was conscious of the veering of this inward direction, without being able to prove what I was sure of, its relevance to the Shining Destiny toward which I moved* (W.G. 47–48).

There must always have been a suppressed actress inside Mary, among all those other characters. She would go on acting her own life out to the end. She would even work her way into the Little Theater movement for a time, convincing herself that she was the founder of it.

Who can say that a large part of the life she gives herself as Olivia was not spun in the scorned Johnson Street house under her mother's bewildered nose? Behind her "veil of withdrawal" (*E.H.* 171), she may have been imagining herself into the beautiful Lily's place on the parlor wall and thence off into her own "looking glass world" as fast as Alice.

THE HORRID APPETITES OF HUSBANDS

"Mary was never much taken with the wish of many girls of her acquaintance that they had been boys. She thought there might be a great deal to be got out of being a woman" (*E.H.* 157), at least if you weren't being made all the time to feel that just being female made you inferior.

What gave brothers the right to oversee their younger sisters' behavior? she wanted to know. Why did they always feel it their duty to tell on you at home, pretending they only did it to keep you from getting into trouble? Didn't a sister have any rights at all? Why Mother and Jim both made a fuss simply because she wanted her egg boiled four minutes instead of three Mary could not understand.

She was perplexed by her mother's relegation of brother Jim to the position as head of the family before he'd even outgrown being a gangling boy. "At times when I felt this going on in our house, there rose up like a wisp of fog between me and the glittering promise of the future, a kind of horror of the destiny of women. . . . I could be abased, I should be delighted to be imposed upon, but if I paid out self-immolation I wanted something for my money, and I didn't consider I was getting it with my brother for whom I smuggled notes and copied compositions" (*W.G.* 75).

Mary got the impression that it was to be for Jim "as nearly as possible as it had been when the whole affectional and practical interest of the family had centered on Father having what he wanted and being pleased by it" (*E.H.* 128). She didn't think it odd that in Father's case she hadn't exactly minded. She even claimed to have felt deprived, at his death, of all the items that make a place a home, "the community of interest, family ritual, the dramatic climax of Father's daily return, the praise, the blame, the evenings around the lamp" (*E.H.* 91). As she has Olivia say in *Women of Genius*, "My life was at loose ends for the loss out of it of a man's point of view, and the appreciable standards which grow out of his relation to the community."

Her life was even more at a loss because there was no real father at this time in her life who might have treated his daughter tenderly as a developing young woman. Without an understanding father, with the memory of a father whose own emotional life had been severely blighted, with a mother who seemed only too happy to have been relieved of her marital "duties" and to have for the "head of the house" a son who offered only filial affection, how could this growing girl have wakened to any secure knowledge of the living relationship between adult men and women?

Although Mary likes to picture herself in constant rebellion against her mother, she could not help being influenced by the pattern of her mother's life. Any girl is part of her mother long after she is born. She is, Mary would come to realize much later, a branch of the same tree. It is through their common root that most girls become aware of what it is to be a woman. Not from anything Susie told her directly but from her half-understood aware-ness of her mother's buried frustrations, Mary came to feel that being a woman was full of disadvantages, in spite of the protests she makes to the contrary. All a woman had to look forward to was marrying some man and having babies one after the other the way her mother had—and Susie's own mother before her, who had died trying to deliver her seventh child.

There was something mysterious about having babies which Mary could never exactly find out. She knew her mother had not wanted all of hers. Those times when she used to lie curled up in her nightie outside the door of her parents' room to listen to reading out loud, there seem to have been other sounds, sounds like those that years later she has the boy Kenneth Brent overhear in her novel The Ford. Kenneth is disturbed as much by the tone of voice as he is by the words. Through the thin walls of his bedroom he hears "the fretful sound of hopeless chiding . . . issuing from his mother's room at night, the sharp, reiterated protest and the patient low rejoinder, 'It's too much, Steven . . . it's too much.' " Ken-neth would pull the bedclothes over his head and lie "rigid with misery," as Mary herself may have done when she was far too little to understand what the troubled grown-ups were talking about.

During Susanna Hunter's married life, there had been almost always another baby on the way, an increasing burden on a mother who had never cared much for domestic life to begin with, who had been brought up to have a horror of debt, and whose husband had never been strong enough to earn a comfortable living, much less make any kind of real success of his life. What had Susie's husband been, in fact, but "just another child, an ailing and not very resigned child," as Mary Austin has Laura remind Gard about their father in her novel Starry Adventure.

It was most likely Susie that Mary was thinking of when she has Olivia say in *A Woman of Genius*, "I think it probable that my mother had, in the country phrase, 'never seen a well day' and what was meant to be the joy of loving was utterly swamped for her in its accompanying dread."

Susie Hunter's sympathy with the overburdened mothers of too many children must have been what drew her, even more than her Methodist prejudice against alcohol, into the work of the Women's Christian Temperance Union, her beloved WCTU. She joined it "probably the first time she heard of it" (*E.H.* 142), which would have been around the time Mary was six years old. Without stretching the truth too much, Mary could claim that she was "practically born and brought up on the temperance platform" ("Amorousness and Alcohol," *The Nation*, June 23, 1926).

"How the women of our town, an important minority of them, loved that organization," comments Austin in her autobiography. "With what sacred pride they wore its inconspicuous white ribbon; with what pure and single-minded ardor they gave themselves to learn to serve it, legal technicalities, statistics, Roberts's Rules of Order, the whole ritual of public procedure" (*E.H.* 142–143).

Whatever Mary was supposed to have been learning during her years of high school (and she says very little about it), she appears to have been far more deeply impressed by the ideas she absorbed sitting through all these meetings and temperance speeches in company with her mother.

It was no surprise to her to be told that the saloon was the great threat to American womanhood. She had known about the evils of drink almost as soon as she began to go to school. The McGuffey readers were full of stories about how drunkards were the ruin both of themselves and of their families. Coming and going on her schoolgirl errands, she experienced the town saloon as "a place of sour, stale smells, of loud, foolish laughter, a laughter such as accompanies things not said in the presence of women, raucous, quarreling voices. It was a place from which might issue at any moment people you knew, other girls' fathers, forcible ejections of sodden and bleary men who proceeded to be violently sick on the sidewalk as a prelude to going to sleep there, or at best mouthed obscenely their sense of irreparable injury . . . there was always a stench coming out of saloons in the eighties, stale beer, hot whiskey breaths, the smell of vomit, the faint unmistakable odor of male-ness on the loose" (*E.H.* 139–140).

"Maleness on the loose." It was the opposite of everything in Mary's mind that her father stood for, uprightness, success, intel-lectual aspiration, the "obligation of repute" (*W.G.* 29) that had come to replace the spontaneous and forgotten joy of her Snockerty days. There was a side of men she had always dimly known women must be afraid of, an earthy untamed side that could be released by alcohol and that threatened everything that had been built up by the careful industry of her own forebears who had "driven out the wild tribes and subdued the wilderness."

What sank into her most deeply was a fearful idea of the harm a drunken husband—or even just an ordinary husband—might inflict upon his unborn children. If a man drank, Mary learned, he couldn't control his impulses. What was known as "hard liquor" begat violence in drinkers. The father of the young Cogans had been that way, he from whom all those wonderful fairy stories used to come in the days when Mary and Ellen invented Snockerty.

From the things her mother left unsaid, from conversations half overheard, then suddenly hushed, from the WCTU pamphlets she would find from time to time left without explanation on her bureau, Mary learned to dread something called "the horrid appe-tites of husbands" (*E.H.* 163). Husbands, she gathered, were apt to have the most horrid appetites when they were drunk. When men drank, it made them "amorous," and from amorousness came babies, mostly unwanted babies. What was worse, the children of hard-drinking men were more likely than not to be born defective, deaf, blind, or even idiot. What could be more tragic than going through what was always referred to as "the perils of child-bearing" (*E.H.* 141) and then to have your child turn out to be an idiot? Apparently it would be all your husband's fault, either because he drank or because he concealed from you the fact that there was a "defective strain" (E.H. 163) in his family background. This was an idea that Mary could never quite get out of her mind and that would one day drive her to make bitter accusations against her own husband, though she admitted he never drank at all, when their own child turned out to have been born, as it was thought, defective.

"I remember," she says, "the first woman who was allowed to speak in our church on the right of women to refuse to bear children to habitual drunkards, and my mother putting her arm across my knees and taking my hand in one of the few natural gestures of a community of woman interest she ever made toward me" (E.H. 142). It seems a rather strange "community of woman interest" for a young girl to find herself sharing with her mother. Not once, in those days, would anyone have dared venture to suggest that "women are passionately endowed even as men are" and that men's "appetites" were not entirely "horrid" (E.H. 163).

A LIKENESS OF FRANCES WILLARD

"And then," says Mary almost in the same breath, "I remember Frances Willard" (E.H. 142).

It would not have been at all surprising to find a likeness of Frances Willard hanging in the parlor of the Johnson Street house rather than the one of Lily Langtry. No two women in the world could have stood at such opposite poles. They had only one thing in common: their delight in standing before an audience.

In 1883, when Mrs. Langtry made her famous and widely reported visit to St. Louis, Willard, the national president of the WCTU, set forth on another kind of tour. With one companion she would travel thirty thousand miles through every state and territory and to every town of any size west of the Missouri, even including an eighty-mile journey up the Snake River to Lewiston, Idaho, on what the two ladies called their "Temperance Round-up." The Union was sprouting buds on the barest possible twigs of interest. The newspapers would not have covered Willard's travels with the same enthusiasm they broadcast the reports of Mrs. Langtry's. There is no doubt, though, that the Methodist ladies of Carlinville heard all about it, even if they had to wait for the full account to filter down from the national convention of the WCTU, which was held in Detroit that autumn.

Willard must have spoken in Carlinville on more than one occasion, and there could have been no one whom Susie Hunter more admired, which may explain why "the influence of Frances Willard in Mary's life was more informing than almost any other of that time" (E.H. 147). Mary saw her as "slight and pretty, full of patience and tact unending and great charm for women. There is no woman of her time Mary would have regretted more to miss; notwithstanding that her manner, her method with her public, her moral sentiments and religious convictions were cross-gartered to Mary's own" (E.H. 142)—at least to what Mary's became in the public phase of her adult life.

What Mary came to resent in Frances Willard was "her continual expenditure of charm in the pursuit of her social goal. . . . Given a clear perception of intellectual soundness in her claim, woman should be able to dispense with charm, should rest upon the proved rightness of her cause" (E.H. 144). So speaks Mary's opinionated mind, the weapon she came to use against the instinctive woman in herself and in everyone else.

Frances Willard did not rely on arguing and reasoning like a man. She was skillful at playing upon the feelings of her audience, the hopes and fears and frustrations of a multitude of women too long suppressed by the age-old masculine conviction of female inferiority. Sitting with her mother at Frances Willard's feet, this frail-appearing woman, unswervable in purpose as a spider at the center of its web, as a bird building a nest in which to rear its young, Mary must have been as spellbound by the charm as anyone.

Mary wrote, "I do not mean . . . that Miss Willard posed her charm; she produced it; she was the charm itself, the key woman of her time. She had a verse of Scripture for every type of spiritual aspiration and knew when to work it and on what souls, to their complete enchantment" (*E.H.* 144). For Susie Hunter, Willard's magic verse had been, "Though ye have lain among the pots, yet your wings shall be covered with silver, and your feathers with fine gold" (*E.H.* 144).

How could Susie have helped rising to such enticement? She had never been content with her life among the pots. None knew better than Mary that Susie had never liked, had genuinely revolted against, the routine of housework. It was only for love's sake that she found these things possible, and even that love may have been obedience to the stereotype of what was expected of a wife and mother.

There was a new spirit stirring among women of Susie Hunter's day, rising, for some of them, out of their pre–Civil War experience in working for the liberation of black slaves. Something within them, hardly as yet understood, was struggling to free itself, to emerge from the dark season of unconscious submissiveness into the brightness and creative challenge of the daytime world. There were slumbering powers in woman, powers of ingenuity and invention, which traditional attitudes were not allowing her to use. Times were changing. The business of ordering the large pioneer household had dwindled to a petty housemaid's round, nothing to satisfy an intelligent woman's sense of her own worth.

"When I remember with what energy of concentration my mother would work through her daily routine in order that she might free her hands and time for the spiritually releasing labor of her church and her beloved W.C.T.U., I seem to see what was going on in most of her contemporaries," says Mary in *Earth Horizon*. "And when Frances Willard, with her marvelous penetration into the precise dimensions of the task that irked, came whispering her magic scriptures at their ears, it was like having the sacred haruspices opened before them for a sign" (*E.H.* 145).

As often happened, Mary was a little confused about the meaning of her big word. "Haruspices" were priests in ancient Rome who predicted the future through examining the entrails of sacrificed animals, a practice that doesn't come exactly under the heading of magic. Mary intuitively felt something about Willard's effect on an audience that was hard to find the right words for. "Without her really remarkable psychological divination of approach, Frances Willard would have got nowhere with the American women of her own time," wrote Austin (E.H. 144). She was the haruspex herself, who instead of revealing the entrails of a slain animal revealed to women what was hidden in their own collective hearts. She was the first, perhaps, to be aware of the collective woman in all women.

Identification with such a power can make a woman feel much more than her own insignificant self. Frances Willard was obviously carried away by the pleasant sensation. "To be widely known, to be widely helpful and beloved, that was my idea. . . . Every life has its master passion, and this—to be one on whom the multitude would lean and love and believe in—is mine," she confessed (E.H. 278).

Mary Austin is sharply critical of this attitude. She had read Willard's autobiography by the time she came to write her own and knew that Frances Willard observed the social conventions of long hair and voluminous starched skirts in order to win even the most conventional to her cause. Mary thought she should have been strong enough to renounce the power to please, as Mary herself would do when her own time came. Mary also felt critical of the element of salesmanship in Willard's approach.

The day would come—had already come by the time she was expressing this opinion in her autobiography—when Mary Austin quite openly prided herself on her ability as a "publicist." In a letter to her publishers at Houghton Mifflin, dated July 18, 1920, she declares, "I speak as a publicist accustomed to selling the American people ideas that they do not want, to which they are often hostile." The poet in Mary was not fond of the publicist. She may have seen the salesman in herself, the woman who enjoyed more than anything her own power over an audience, reflected in Frances Willard, and attacked blindly what she would not dare admit as her own weakness.

Great as Frances Willard's influence was on Susie Hunter's daughter, "more informing than almost any other of that time," Mary instinctively felt something about her that was hostile to her inner self (*E.H.* 147). As she explains, "It was Miss Willard's exemption . . . from any understanding whatsoever of the creative life, that, although it did not remove Mary from the circle of her activities, cut sharply off any possibility of her being drawn into the sphere of her personal influence. Ardently concerned as Miss Willard was to create for women a new scope and medium of expression, she missed so far as could be the faintest realizing sense of the province of the creative Arts" (*E.H.* 149–150).

To the end of her life, Mary would be furious with her mother for taking a poem out of the wastebasket and asking Willard's judgment on it. Without Mary's knowledge or consent, the poem was printed in the *Union Signal*, the organ of the WCTU. Susie Hunter undoubtedly felt that her daughter would be pleased. Instead, she was insulted. Even as an awkward beginner, she seems to have felt that poetry belonged to the most private and personal side of her life. Mary herself didn't understand the fierceness of her reaction. Instinctively, she realized that the sources of poetry belonged to a different world than the one on which Frances Willard was so determined to make her mark. She could not have suspected that poetry and the drunkenness that Frances Willard and Susie Hunter were doing so much to combat both had roots in a side of human nature that the "good" women of her day were most determined to suppress.

BREAKDOWN

There could have been an element of sour grapes in Mary's resentment of Frances Willard's desire to "react upon the world." Mary so far had been unable to do much reacting on anyone. Outwardly, during her teens, she appeared to live pretty much in the shadow of her capable mother, teaching, like her, in Sunday school, going about with her to the temperance meetings, carefully building the shell of conformity from which, in the words of Olivia, "afterward to burst was the bitter wound of life" (*W.G.* 58).

Then, in the autumn of 1884 when Mary entered Blackburn College, she found herself in danger of being overshadowed by her brother Jim. In spite of the difference in their ages and the fact that she was a girl—even more *because* she was a girl and felt compelled to prove her superiority—she had always struggled to get ahead of him. Since the day when she watched Jim reading his primer in the kitchen of the Plum Street farm and suddenly became aware of the element in herself she calls "I-Mary," she had felt a surge of power that came to her from words, words in books, words as women such as Frances Willard could use them to kindle an audience to her own purposes.

This was part of the atmosphere of the times. The president of the Southern Illinois Normal School proclaimed in his inaugural address in the early 1870s that "speech is power. The great aim of education ought to be to confer this power, the most useful, the most delightful, the most admirable of human requirements." Blackburn, like other educational institutions of its kind, paid "constant attention to composition and elocution in all departments and courses of study" (*History of Macoupin County*). The college, with an enrollment of around one hundred, had been founded by Presbyterians but was nonsectarian in its outlook. It was unusually enlightened for its time, admitting male and female students equally to all activities. The men's and women's literary societies included oratory and debating in their programs, though meetings and activities were not shared. Mary became a member of the girls' society, the OIO (Oioparthenian), in October 1884. The Blackburn catalog for 1884–85 lists her as a sophomore in the science course, junior college department, a somewhat mystifying classification, but the case nonetheless.

During her sophomore year, Austin's full-time studies were interrupted by illness. However, she continued to attend the college for the rest of the year as a special student in the Art Department. Apparently she was allowed to continue taking part in OIO activities. The college magazine, the *Blackburnian*, notes that on February 20 she upheld the negative in a debate, "Resolved that Political Economy should be taught in the Public Schools in Preference to the Languages." The affirmative won.

To find herself on the losing side in a debate would have been particularly frustrating, for "the phase of college life in which Jim shone was debate and oratory," she tells us (*E.H.* 134). She then goes on to suggest that it was she who was really responsible for Jim's success. Oratory was "an enterprise which was peculiarly susceptible of outside aid," she remarks. Susie put all she had into coaching her son, and we know that Susie herself was an accomplished public speaker. "Susie had power with an audience; sweetness and sincerity shone forth in her, an aura of spiritual integrity and some degree of social divination," Mary says in one of the few compliments she ever pays her mother (*E.H.* 145). Mary doesn't exactly say she had a hand in writing her brother's speeches but implies that it was exactly the kind of thing she was quite capable of doing.

Moreover, she prides herself on having had lessons in elocution from a professor of the art. Her teacher "must have been genuinely good, since she . . . makes use successfully of what he taught her. That was how it was that when Jim decided to go in for the Oratorical Contest, he put himself into his sister's hands" (*E.H.* 134). The Oratorical Contest "would begin with a competition among the small College Literary Societies, from which the winners would go on to the Inter-Collegiates, and from that to the State and Inter-State contests, so that once a young man's feet were set on that ladder, a long brilliant prospect glittered before him" (*E.H.* 134–135).

About the time of Mary's comedown in the OIO debate, the young men of the college held a Longfellow's birthday celebration in which they debated, "Resolved that American Poetry has been a more Powerful Agent in Civilization than American Statesmanship." The *Blackburnian* comments that "James M. Hunter upheld the negative with a set speech, most of which he read." One can't help suspecting Mary of having had a hand in the speech, at least in having badgered Jim with what she always considered her superior knowledge.

She was at loose ends and no doubt restless with her own unadmitted sense of failure. Jim, in his third year in college, was flourishing. He and W. E. Andrews were chosen business managers of the *Blackburnian*. He was president of one of the two men's literary societies, the Orthopatetic, for that term. In May, his oration, "Our Need," won primary honors in the Oratorical Contest, although for some reason this oration was criticized in the *Blackburnian* as "lacking in gracefulness." He delivered the same oration in June in the Junior Exhibition, which was held according to custom in Carlinville's massively imposing courthouse.

Mary's chronology becomes somewhat obscure at this point. She tries to take credit for Jim's success in the spring of 1885. In the fall, due to continued poor health, it was decided that she would attend the State Normal School at Bloomington to prepare her for earning a living as a teacher. This was Jim's last year in college, and Susie may have thought it best, for the sake of her son's success, to have Mary out of the way.

> *That was how it happened that when Jim was preparing for the Inter-Collegiate, Mary was out of reach. The first informative news she had of it was that he had taken the lowest place. As all the reports made a point of his forced and awkward delivery, she grieved privately, suspecting that she might have prevented the disaster. When she had to go home herself a month or two later, she confidently expected that something would be said about it, such as "If you had been here, Sis . . ." —anything that would have admitted her to the community of her family interest. But nobody so much as mentioned it* (E.H. 135).

Mary had returned home from Bloomington due to the onset of a nervous breakdown. For the second time, she found herself unable to carry on a required course of study. "The breakdown," she tries to explain, "was supposed to have been caused by overwork. . . .

What did for Mary, however, wasn't the amount of work expected of her, the hours and the mark set, but the unremitting fixation of attention on objective detail, not of true learning, but of pedagogical method. . . . At the normal school she was simply redriven over the curricula of public school grades with immense and boring particularity; spelling, punctuation, phonetics, arithmetical devices; history reduced to a precise allocation of names and places, middle initials of unimportant generals, dates of undecisive battles; reading reduced to the rendering of the content of literature in the most explicit rather than the most expressive verbal terms" (E.H. 151–152)—everything that Mary had always found most difficult to cope with and would never consider worth the effort of mastery. Her creative spirit was a wild Pegasus who resisted being put to bridle and saddle, a winged energy, preferring to soar among the clouds of fantasy rather than plodding the stony trails of earth.

> Along this trail you were nagged and lashed with the utmost efficiency of regimentation, and the least allowance made for individual variation. After five months, combined with cold weather and the stuffy diet of a period in which green vegetables were unattainable at any price, and bad colds not admitted to the category of excuses, Mary was sent home in a condition which old Dr. Hankins looked grave over, and suspected that it might have something to do with the natural incapacity of the female mind for intellectual achievement (E.H. 152).

Mary instinctively knew that masculine and feminine ways of learning are very different. At least the inarticulate woman in her knew. When she speaks, as she does more than once at this point, of the "natural motions of her own mind" (E.H. 152), one catches oneself thinking of motions in nature, tidal motions, rhythms of night and day, of growth and bloom and leaf fall. "Women have times," she would say, explaining the divergence in viewpoint between herself and her husband many years later.

The trouble seems to have been that Dr. Hankins couldn't help thinking of Mary's femaleness as a weakness, and she herself believed the "motions of her own mind" were too superior to accept the real discipline of thought.

ALL THE KNOWLEDGE IN THE WORLD

Mary had not yet begun to find words for what she would later come to call the "Dweller in the Core of her Mind" and the "Middle Place of the Mind" (E. H. 154) and her "Sacred Middle" (F. W.). Through the dweller in this middle place, an entity seemingly apart from herself, she felt herself connected with all the knowledge in the world. It came up *inside* her, she was uplifted with it, rocked upon it, like a child, one can hardly help feeling, effortlessly rocked at its mother's breast. It sounds like a rather dangerous state of mind for a young woman like Mary whose relations with the outer world were so insecure, who was so sure she was unloved and so afraid to open herself to love lest she be either rejected or violated.

Every now and then, one of the young people who sought Mary's society confessed to her, half shamefacedly, that they had experiences when it seemed to them that she knew everything in the world. Feeling that all the knowledge in the world was hers, no wonder Mary was impatient with the dull routine of study. Her teachers must have found her appearance of arrogance inexcusable. Why did so many candidates for teacher training lack the most elemental qualifications, the harassed instructors at the Normal School often wondered. Some instructors observed that students could not control their bodies in sitting or standing or walking nor control their hands in writing, their minds in study, or their powers in speech or writing. They seemed merely to have learned a few facts from their textbooks, and to have done that very imperfectly.

Not all these shortcomings would have applied to Mary; the ones that did she couldn't possibly admit were her own fault. Instead of accepting the fact of her own failure, she tried to believe that she could have prevented Jim's—if only she were not so far away from home.

In the interval of convalescence, Mary not only failed to be prop-
erly humbled by her misadventure, she began definitely to realize
that the breakdown represented for her the need of a quicker intel-
lectual tempo, a more expansive and varied rhythm. She began
privately in her own way to plot and plan to secure it for herself
(E.H. 156–157).

At least this is the way she sees it herself, looking back, pushing out of her mind as far as she can the recollection of her failure. I-Mary is not mentioned during this period of Mary's life, but
it is easy to recognize her influence at work. Who but I-Mary,
that glorified manifestation of a more-than-human ego, could have
come to the humiliated girl's rescue, assuring her of her real, if
unappreciated, superiority to her elder brother?

This was the time when she swallowed her hurt because Jim had
failed to realize the contribution she had been willing to make to
his oratorical success. . . . She had long suspected that a slightly
posed level of emotional restraint, which was generally described
as "self-control," was no such thing, but . . . simply due to his
being not so quick on the up-take. . . . It was not that he . . .
had all the instant flashes of enthusiasm, indignation, whimsy,
humor, counter-fact and unrationalized rejection, and suppressed
them; he simply didn't have them (E.H. 157).

By implication, of course, Mary did. "She meant not to remit a
single flash of wit, anger, or imagination. She had no idea of what,
in her time, such a determination would entail. She was but dimly
aware of something within herself, competent, self-directive; she
meant to trust it" (E.H. 157–158). This something in herself was
rather different from I-Mary; it worked always beneath the level of
thought, like a bee's instinct for finding its proper flower or a cat's
for rolling in catnip.

Mary's instinct for curing herself was surprisingly sound. After
a month or two at home, she began to paint again and to write
poetry. She explains that these were her means of achieving

"subjective coördination" (*E.H.* 159), which could be another way of saying that they were her way of getting in touch again with her creative inner self. She paid attention to some of the baffling urges within her by keeping three or four diaries in fictitious characters. In one of these, she found herself impersonating "a man who must have been sired by Edgar Allan Poe upon the author of 'St. Elmo,' with Ralph Waldo Emerson at the baptismal font, and yet showing, here and there, the explicit, uncompromising outlook of Mary-by-herself" (*E.H.* 159). This sounds as though she were getting her own character a little mixed. Surely she must have been thinking of I-Mary.

She got permission to attend classes again at the university (Blackburn College, founded in 1837, had been chartered as a university in 1857) in botany and rhetoric. Busy with interests that satisfied her own particular hungers, she seems to have given up the struggle to compete with Jim, whose orations continued to appear in the *Blackburnian* during his senior year.

As a final step in her recovery, Mary was sent to spend the summer in Missouri, at the edge of the Ozarks, with Uncle Sam Dugger and Aunt Eliza. (In her autobiography, she gives the year as 1885, but it could only have been the summer of 1886.) Mary's beloved Grandfather Graham, who had always kept such a kindly eye on Susie and her children, had died two years before. He never quite disappeared for Mary the way her father had. For many years, perhaps until she managed to write him into her novel *Starry Adventure*, he remained "always about in a shy faint friendliness, enclosed in a dimension I could not pass, wisely smiling and close at hand."

In Uncle Sam, who had "helped to carry Lincoln to his grave" (*E.H.* 160), Mary found what she most needed at this time of conflict between the demands of the outer world and the effort to discover what she was meant to be within. Uncle Sam was a large, slow, venerable man who kept a general store and managed a railroad station and a post office in a small community whose few inhabitants had long ago given up the struggle for "progress" and "success," settling down to a poverty of stimulation.

In Uncle Sam, she found someone she could talk to without trying to show off. She renewed the art of listening that the schools of her time had quenched by too much emphasis on argument and debate, where one listens only in order to plan what one must say to overcome an opponent rather than for the delight of hearing and understanding.

Uncle Sam was "now come to the time of life when he had pleasure in remembering and re-living the backward-rolling scroll of pioneer life in Illinois" (E.H. 160). Mary seems already to have begun keeping the notebooks that she was to make such good use of in her years in the California desert. Much of the material for the earlier part of her autobiography she heard from Uncle Sam. He had a feeling for the land, the dry, native wit of the Duggers, and was the last of the family, she remembered, to eat sugar on his lettuce! He had a humorous insight into the ordinary people he lived among. When the railroad first reached Macoupin County, he told Mary, "People would drive miles to take little trips on it, trying it out as a spider tries the stays of his web, timorously, and then go home subtly altered, somehow, by the certainty that now they were bound at last to the great web of world affairs" (E.H. 160). He was the one who told Mary about the possible strain of Indian blood in the family into which the first Daguerre had married in Virginia, but though Mary in later years longed to believe that her interest in Indian life came to her through the bloodstream, this could never be proved. There seems no doubt that through her contact with Uncle Sam in the summer just before her eighteenth birthday, something of her Dugger heritage woke in her, a plain and solid person at her core that kept her balanced in spite of all intellectual pretension.

AT THE AGE OF EIGHTEEN

Mary came home from the Ozarks, greatly improved in health, to make a new attempt at college. What else was there for a girl to do unless she got married? Neither Susie Hunter nor Mary would have liked to see that happen, at least not for a while. It didn't look as though it would be easy for Mary to "catch a husband" even if she had a mind to. She didn't seem to have the slightest feminine instinct for drawing people to her. "And what would I do with the people after I have drawn them to me?" (E.H. 171), she would ask tartly when Susie tried to discuss the importance of certain social graces.

"I do not recall now that I ever had any particular instruction as to how to conduct myself toward young men except that they were never on any account to take liberties," Mary has Olivia say (W.G. 87). It would be hard to conceive of the young man who would dream of "taking liberties" with Mary. There was something stiff and standoffish about her, and her appearance, of course, was rather against her.

She was, at the age of eighteen, "rather under the average height, not well filled out, with the slightly sallow pallor of the malaria country" (E.H. 170), with bluish shadows under her eyes and a mass of too-heavy brown hair. The hair fell below her knees when it was loose, but what girl in those days would dream of letting herself be seen in public with her hair down? The fashion was to have the front hair cropped in a bang right to the eyebrows and the rest "somewhat clumsily disposed in braids about the back of the head and neck—a style popularized a few years earlier by the famous Jersey Lily" (E.H. 170), the Liz Taylor of her day.

The clothes of that period couldn't have been worse designed for such a straight up-and-down immature figure; impossible bustles of wire and buckram over which the skirts were draped, the glove-tight corsets drawn in to make the waist unnaturally tiny. In Lily Langtry, the effect was of grace and elegance. In Mary—well, it would have hardly been worth trying, even if she hadn't hated the awkward contraptions. What the real girl looked like inside her layers and layers of clothing would have been hard for any young man to imagine. It would vex Mary all her days that men were apparently more interested in "the looking and the seeming" than in a girl's inner self or in the qualities of her mind, which might very well be superior to their own.

The struggle to get through college was partly in order to equip Mary to make a living, and even so, most of Susie Hunter's contemporaries shook their heads over the widow's determination to secure a college education for her daughter. "What a waste," they said. "[Girls will] only get married as soon as they're out" (E.H. 162), as though marriage was the inevitable destiny of every female. The girls Mary associated with most closely during her Blackburn years talked constantly of careers. Most of them quite frankly admitted the expectation of marriage, but there were a few who were also determined to "do something with our educations" (E.H. 174), as their teachers and monitors were constantly advising. Nine of the girls formed a secret society of their own with the mystic initials NMS, a code never explicated. At their first meeting, the young ladies wrote out their life programs and entrusted them to Mary, who was very likely the secretary. Mary's plan was to teach, "preferably natural science, and then 'to write novels and other books' " (E.H. 175).

It was lucky for Mary that a college like Blackburn was available in her own hometown. The enrollment was small, the administration enlightened, and the rates of tuition from twenty to fifty or even, because of scholarships, a hundred percent lower than in other similar institutions, which explains how a widow like Susanna Hunter could afford to give both her elder son and her far more difficult daughter a higher education.

Blackburn was situated on the northeast side of Carlinville within easy walking distance of the Hunters' Johnson Street house. It was set in a magnificent campus of some eighty acres, with plantings of many varieties of stately deciduous trees at the front and in back, toward the east, an undulating natural park of great beauty, "a sort of wildwood" principally composed of native oaks. How Mary must have pined for all this verdure when she found herself only a few short months after graduation in the barren San Joaquin Valley of California.

The campus was entered by means of a stile over a fence that enclosed it. One visualizes the young ladies in their clumsy skirts being helped modestly over the stile by a modest swain who would hardly, in those days, have dared to steal a glance in hopes of a dainty ankle. If one did, he would have found the vision unrewarding. "Shoes were high," comments Effie Vancil Jordan, a classmate of Jim Hunter's, "laced or buttoned at the side over black cotton, sometimes woolen stockings." In a letter to her mother, she wrote, "I bought some new stockings and they should be good for I paid 25 cents a pair for them."

Mary was piqued throughout her life at the idea that men seemed especially interested in a woman's ankles. Her own were thick. "She was one of those women whose legs were too short for her top side," Mabel Dodge Luhan would write of her in later life. At the time Mabel knew her, her torso had thickened and her bosom sagged, which must have contributed to her top-heavy look. In her college years, she secretly lamented her lack of feminine contours. "Mary had too little figure to draw in effectively, and as she always constitutionally despised the wire 'dress forms' with which worldly minded young women concealed their lack of womanly endowment, it happened that the only really attractive feature that nobody denied her was a pair of shapely, expressive hands. Her arms, too, were graceful, but that was a matter nobody was allowed to discover" (E.H. 170).

Young couples, if their relations were sufficiently approved, must have held hands, though Mrs. Jordan declares, "Believe it or not there was no necking; all tender contacts were termed spooning. . . . We were taught, and observation strengthens the belief that 'familiarity breeds contempt'. . . . For a social evening our crowd would gather about a piano in a home and sing; sit on sofas and look at plush-covered albums or stereopticon views; or if warm, swing in hammocks, or stroll on the board walks in the moon-light. . . . There were not autos, couples went riding if buggies were available. . . . A request for a girl's company was formal. Among my keepsakes is this written on note paper and enclosed in an envelope: 'Miss Vancil. . . . If agreeable to you may I have the pleasure of your company Sunday night to church!" (Mary Austin Collection, Huntington Library).

Convinced of her own unattractiveness—the comparison with her lost little sister's beauty still seemed to be festering—Mary took little part in the social life of the college young folk. Sere-nading was in vogue; the boys sang under the windows of the girls who lived in town, old sentimental songs such as "My Bonnie Lies over the Ocean" and "Come Where My Love Lies Dreaming."

Jim had graduated in June of 1886, the year that Mary began her junior year at Blackburn, and was immediately faced with the problem of what to do for a living. Mary claims that he would have liked to study medicine if the family finances had made it possible. What he really wanted, she says, would have been the life of a country doctor. "To be close to people, in everybody's confidence, helpful and important, to be out along the country roads, noting the earliest tapping of the flicker in the woodlot, the seldom flash along the creek of the scarlet tanager, farming a few acres, maintaining a favorite team, with an occasional ven-ture into fancy stock, experimenting a little in horticulture as his father had done—that would have suited my brother admirably" (E.H. 176).

These are almost the kindest words Mary has to say of Jim. Under-neath her habitual barbed reaction there lurked a real affection for her brother that she usually found it impossible to give in to. It is interesting that two of her most successful novels, *The Ford* and *Starry Adventure,* are concerned with the understanding between a brother and sister as they grow from a childhood cama-raderie into their adult lives.

Both of the fictional young men have a sensitive, almost mysti-cal, love of the land and of the farmer's relation to the land he

146

ploughs. "Land was to be cherished, to be made productive," not used for men's greed and profit. The sister in each book helps make her brother aware of where his true feeling lies. "[Jim] would have liked to own a farm and work it" (*E.H.* 175) was what Mary really understood about her brother.

"I have improved my time and made a little money in the past six months," Jim would write to his beloved Effie Vancil after moving to California, "and have now found a good chance to carry out what has always been my inclination, viz: to be a farmer and stock raiser. . . . Ever since I came to California I have been watching for a chance to get hold of land enough for a farm."

In the meantime, Jim was doing what lay closest at hand, teaching a small country school not far from Carlinville, which at least removed him as a source of competition to Mary in her efforts to find her own niche in the college scene. However, without her brother to fall back on, she was faced with the problem of finding an escort to the various social functions. Aloof as she liked to think herself by preference, she did not enjoy being left out of things —hayrides, sleigh rides, Halloween parties, entertainments at the old Opera House, nutting parties to Coops Indian mound, as well as a surprising number of lectures by the faculty on their travels to other parts of the world. It wasn't so much being left out as the humiliation that would have bothered Mary, the appearance of not seeming to be popular. "As a measure of self-protection she had to have an assured companion to be 'going with' " (*E.H.* 172).

At the beginning of her junior year, Mary drifted into accepting for a regular escort the best of the youthful Divinity students whom Susie Hunter liked most to entertain. "He had for Mary the special attractiveness of offering no resistance to her accustomed way of thought, and making few demands on his own account. . . . His steady regard, his natural honesty and sweetness of disposition enabled her to get through the next two years with complete relief from other social complications," she writes in her autobiography (*E.H.* 173–174). Though it sounds as though it were I-Mary rather than human Mary who chose the escort, he had enough pleasure in her company to ask her by mail, a year or two after she had moved to California, to marry him. Mary, even though her own situation at the time was somewhat desperate, was as much in love with her dream of a literary career as ever and could hardly have helped refusing.

Every young girl carries somewhere within her inner recesses an image of man that is the opposite of the dignified man of authority or the dragon-slaying hero she has been brought up to admire. This image contains all the animal wildness that has been lost or suppressed from human nature in the course of civilization. It is part not only of every man but of every woman, no matter how deeply hidden. Invisible, belonging to the realm of the unconscious, she can behold it only in dreams or reflected in the figures of folktale and poetry. Sometimes it seems to look out from the eyes of an actual man, but in fact he only wears the mask, for a while, of one of the characters of that ancient dream that inhabits us all.

Mary Austin may never have been aware that this image was part of herself as definitely as that of her father, the father who would always have understood her, or the political hero, or the enterprising mining engineer, or the unscrupulous but clever speculator with his genius for manipulating land and human lives to his own profit; all those who were types of the living folklore out of which her novels came to be constructed.

In her strange work *Outland*, the fantasy novel she wrote with George Sterling and published pseudonymously, meaning can be derived only from examining Austin's own mysterious inner world. The central character surely belongs to those lost remnants of a pagan world that today are glimpsed only by children or visionary artists:

> I saw that around his body was a sort of sash of green cloth wrapped several times, and stuck through the folds of it, various tools of the cruder sort of silversmiths. Also, though his figure was young, the skin of his face was drawn in fine wrinkles. He had a thin, high nose with a slightly mobile tip that seemed to twitch a little with

distrust as he looked at me. The mouth below it was full and curved,
his eyes bluish black, opaque and velvet-looking; windows out of
which came and looked boldness, cunning and power, and the
wistfulness of the wild creature questioning its kinship with man.

Such a figure within themselves can entice women away from
their existence in the world of human reality; it can, with its aura
of ancient magic, make mere mortal husbands seem dull. On the
other hand, it can often connect a woman with the source of what
is called genius—the spontaneous flow of images that is always
going on in the depths of what it is no longer fashionable to call
the soul. Snockerty may have been a manifestation of this spirit.
Perhaps it emerged again for Mary in the pages of Ruskin, for the
"vinelike twistings of forms in stone" (*E.H.* 132) are echoes of
the Dionysian side of life of which the Greeks were uneasily aware.
Driven into still deeper recesses of her inner being by the strict
efforts of the WCTU to suppress all spontaneous and joyful impulses
associated in their minds only with drunkenness, in college it
could only exist far out of sight, bricked up by walls partly of
Mary's own making, as she tried to prove that she could lead as
normal a life as anyone. The wild spirit that was part of her
nature emerged only now and then through a secret cranny.

Though with an almost heartless rationality she chose an ame-
nable Divinity student for her steady escort, she admits that "in
the spring after returning from normal school," she had rather liked
"a young man . . . who wore bright neckties and smoked cigars"
(*E.H.* 172). Because her mother had not encouraged him, the relationship didn't get very far. "Years after, when Mary acccidentally
ran across him, when they were both married to someone else, he
told her that he hadn't exactly known whether he was in love with
her; she had had for him the same sort of attraction, in her admitted oddity and reputation for intellectuality, that a girl touched
with the rumor of witchcraft might have had in New England times.
But her mother's preference for Divinity students had daunted him"
(*E.H.* 172).

The image of a young man with the cigar and the bright neckties plays a much larger part in the novel *A Woman of Genius*. In fact, he becomes the romantic hero of the novel. It is Olivia, rather than her mother, who discourages the young man the second time she sees him. At their first meeting, he had kissed her, unknowingly in front of the whole school picnic, and she still remembered the "little snigger of laughter" (*W.G.* 100) that had snatched her out of her moment of happiness. The following Sunday as Olivia is walking to church with her mother and two of her small Sunday school pupils, the young man with the bright necktie greets her as he drives past behind a team of fast horses. Hardly realizing what she is doing, Olivia pretends not to see him, and he apparently passes out of her life. They meet after many years and carry on a secret and impassioned love affair. In the end, Olivia refuses to marry him because he will not give up his own career as a mining engineer to "marry" her career as an actress. The young man haunts Olivia's dream world throughout the book, as he must have haunted Mary's:

> When I found sleep at last, it was to dream . . . of Helmuth Garrett. I was made aware of him first by a sense of fulness about my heart, and then I came upon him looking as he had looked last in the Willesden woods, writing at a table, a pale blur about him of the causeless light of dreams. . . . I stood and read over his shoulder what he wrote, and though the words escaped me, the meaning of them put all straight between us. He turned as he wrote and looked at me with a look that set us back in the wrapt intimacy of the flaming forest. . . . The sense of a vital readjustment remained with me all that day; there had been after all, in the common phrase, "something between us" (W.G. 145–146).

THE HABIT OF OBSERVATION

Though Mary Austin claims that "singularly little deserving of special mention stands out of the crowded two years of college" (*E.H.* 166), they appear to have been among the happiest years of her life. "Happy and important seeming" (*E.H.* 175), she admits they were, yet for some reason she feels called on to belittle their influence on the important person she liked to feel she had become, little thanks to her family or her teachers.

"I think she had a sense of individuality and superiority and separateness from the first, and to the end of her life," says Harriet Stoddard, who grew up, in a later generation, on the Plum Street farm and taught at Blackburn for forty-three years. Through her own relation to the same environment and her lifelong experience in teaching literature to young women of Mary's age, as well as from acquaintance with her writing, Stoddard has gained insight into Mary's nature during her Carlinville years and especially the years at Blackburn:

> I see her from the beginning as living a life within herself—seeking for her own identity—"who am I?" to use the current jargon. . . .
> More than most women she had the desire and determination to accomplish, to create—jellies or books—to break out of bonds or bounds—to be different. As a student, as a teacher, the pattern is neurotic, irregular, self-dominated from the beginning. And she had in some degree an actress-like desire for attention. . . . Women were beginning to do things other than housekeeping. . . . Hints of the revolt of feminism were already stirring in the 1890s. . . . Her husband and child were cast aside by the stronger drive in her own direction. . . . Success through her writing brought self-fulfillment she could never have found otherwise, woman though she was. And it brought attention (Harriet Stoddard correspondence, PPC Papers).

Mary declares that everyone who knew her was astonished when she elected to major in science rather than in English. Susie

Hunter couldn't see the connection between science and writing, and Mary claims that for once she could reasonably explain it. "The relation of science to what she wished to do was a thing felt rather than rationalized" (*E.H.* 167).

The "reasons" do not seem as obscure as Mary tries to make out. Stoddard observes that "the college records are alive with emphasis on science from 1884–'88." An interest in teaching the natural sciences at the grade school level had begun to smolder and then to flame among Illinois educators a decade before Mary entered college. In his report for 1877–78, Newton Bateman, superintendent of public instruction for the State of Illinois, himself pointed out the connection between science and writing. In arguing that the study of natural history was particularly important in developing the habit of observation, he asks, "How do we learn English or Orthography? Is the habit of observation unaided by the sense of sight, or are keen vision and cultivated perceptive faculties the element of success in acquiring a knowledge of our multilingual language? And why must every branch of education invariably have so clearly a practical turn? Why must it be made at once available in dollars and cents? Is it nothing to educate the child to note the design, everywhere, on the unfolded book of nature?"

Mary could have had no knowledge of these words. She was only ten when Bateman's report was issued. It included responses from more than twenty teachers in the county schools on their experiences under the new law requiring that natural history be taught in addition to the three Rs and the usual doses of patriotic history and geography. More than half the teachers were surprised and delighted at the results. They found themselves learning much they themselves had not known, and the children had brightened up and taken a keener interest in all their subjects.

The topic must have been discussed among both educators and parents during most of Mary's school years. Some of her instructors at Blackburn may even have spoken in terms similar to Mr. Bateman's, stressing the "habit of observation" and the "design" in nature, so that unconsciously these ideas slipped into the current of Mary's mind until she came to feel they were her own. There was also the deeply imbedded influence of Hugh Miller, his "learn to make a right use of your eyes," hidden away like the unsuspected treasure in the nut the wise old woman gives the questing maiden to be opened in the moment of her greatest need. Beyond all this was Mary's inward likeness to her grandfather Milo Graham and his father Jarrot, those Scots who had loved the beauty of nature and delighted in using their eyes for looking. Strange that Mary seems never to have suspected a connection between her interest in science and her grandfather's delight in experimenting "with unusual varieties in flowers and plants."

Instead, she singles out as a major influence one of the Blackburn instructors, Charles Robertson, a botanist and something of an eccentric, in whom even before she began attending the college she imagined she might find a kindred spirit. She "used to see him occasionally setting out with insect net and botany case, or coming home evenings happily mired as to boots, smelling of meadowsweet. He was the one person in Carlinville whom Mary heartily envied, and would have given much to meet" (E.H. 112–113). Robertson's specialty was the adaptation of flowers and insects, an interest that may have been partly responsible for Mary's lifelong fascination with the adaptations not only of desert plants but of human beings to their desert environment.

Robertson does not appear to have been one of her teachers at Blackburn but came in occasionally to lecture to one of her classes. "[One] day when, spring being well on and the orchards blossoming, nobody else came, and Mary had the whole hour with him and his subject. It was a thin little trail Charles Robertson showed her, broadening as it went," so that to the end of her days "her happiest relaxation from the world of human reality is to leave everything else and walk in it" (E.H. 166–167).

Another teacher whom she mentions with special admiration —even a rare suggestion of affection—was Professor William Andrews, listed in the catalogue as an instructor in biology. He was the only one, she says, who "seemed likely he would achieve

literary success for himself; he was the only one who could talk
intelligently about the professional literary procedure" (E.H. 166).
Later in her autobiography, Mary, with typical inconsistency, would
deny having ever been given a knowledge of such procedures. As
one of the excuses for uprooting her young husband of ten months
from their farm near Bakersfield, she would declare that at the time
it would have been impossible to overestimate her ignorance of the
professional procedure of writing.

Of even more importance in her mind, Professor Andrews had
been the one to introduce "the modern method of science teaching" (E.H. 166) that relied on direct observation and experiment.
No other method contributed so consistently to the education of
Mary Austin.

This was what she wanted to believe, yet it seems as though she
would always confuse the meaning of objective "experiment" with
her own subjective "experience." A scientific experiment must
be capable of repetition by many others before its conclusions can
be considered valid. Subjective experience is individual and never
twice the same. "The *felt experience* of life," Austin would write in
her *Experiences Facing Death*, "must, in any conclusion of mine,
always take precedence of the orthodoxies of science. . . . I make
this rule for myself out of a profound experience of my own that
the *method* of consciousness . . . is not the method of the scientist, but of the creative artist" (E.F.D. 273).

In an earlier book, *Everyman's Genius*, which contains flashes
of magnificent insight embedded in paragraphs of half-digested theories stated as though they were edicts from on high, Mary Austin
defines *experience* as the power of entering into different phases of
the environment and collecting something from that contact. . . .
"Thus one man has the power to enter intimately into the nature
of matter and brings back knowledge of the mode of the experiences of matter, which we call physics. Another man enters into
the experiences of plant life, and the enrichment of our knowledge thus gained is called botany . . . while others enter into personal experience and record the knowledge gained in fiction and

poetry." This statement would be sure to infuriate the scientists she longed, for some inexplicable reason, to class herself among. The poet in her felt the world in quite a different way from the would-be scientist; she herself recognized the difference, but a stubborn element in her nature made her try over and over to repudiate the poet. A letter to her publishers, Houghton Mifflin, written in 1905, is especially revealing:

> I am naturally gratified by the reviews of "Isidro" which you have sent me—but I wish they would not insist so much upon my style. All I have concerned myself with is to find out exactly how things are, and having said so as nearly as possible at every step. . . . Sometime ago I spent several summers satisfying myself at considerable personal risk that the thunder shock is the immediate cause of the shattering of the Sierra crest and only lately an unripe literary critic has taken me to task for a "pardonably beautiful poetic license." And the phrase he had in mind was my own proved scientifically exact "thunder-splintered." It may well be that literary style consists in telling things exactly the way they are, but they have no business to call it poetry.

One might just as well argue that she had no business to call it science! *Isidro* was Mary Austin's first novel, written shortly after her first and finest book, *The Land of Little Rain,* so the struggle between the "scientist" and the poet began very early and continued throughout her life. One of her most sympathetic editors, Dr. Henry Seidel Canby, whom she chose as her literary executor, would say some years after her death, "I wanted her to go on as an interpreter and imaginative artist; she felt that her career, broadly speaking, was in science" (Hoagland Memorial 1947).

Whatever others wanted her to do was just what Mary would usually feel called on to set her mind most obstinately against. Why did she have to be so insistent that science was her real field or that her subjective and poetic way of looking at things was really objective and scientific? Did she hide behind a mask because she was inwardly very much afraid of what she was or because of that "obligation of repute" that had become so deeply ingrained during her most susceptible years?

It is odd that Mary makes no mention at all of the Taylor Museum of Natural History, which occupied the second floor of Robertson Hall at Blackburn. The museum had been set up to house the rare collection of Indian relics, fossils, modern shells, and corals that had been given to the college by Dr. Julius S. Taylor, a venerable friend of Agassiz, the naturalist, and director of the museum during Mary's senior year. Twenty-five thousand fossils and eight thousand minerals had been classified and were displayed in glass cases. Mary surely attended classes in Robertson Hall. Besides the science laboratories, it contained an art studio described as "elegant." Mary's interest in both science and art would have taken her into the building frequently. One would have thought that anyone inspired by reading Hugh Miller, who had once made her own youthful collection of fossil crinoids, and who had been so enchanted by the miscellaneous objects displayed on an ordinary Whatnot could hardly have helped having her sense of the "purposeful earth" rekindled by this treasure.

Perhaps it was the "classification" that put her off. Laborious detail always interfered with the sudden surges of her imagination. She only got through mathematics by the skin of her teeth in spite of the vague fascination she insisted the subject always had for her. "Even those propositions which she could only master sufficiently to make a passable recitation set up in her a spiritual goingness, an awareness of space as one of the dimensions of reality, the dance of time throughout its varying dimensions" (*E.H.* 168). (She had been reading Dunne's *Experiment with Time* when she was working on the autobiography and could have been confusing her present state of mind with the past she was trying to describe.) "In the midst of problems but half-apprehended she would be seized with a sudden dazzle of the spirit . . . sensibility for which there is no intelligible speech" (*E.H.* 168), which must have made her a little hard for her teachers to pin down (Mary Austin Collection, Huntington Library).

156

FOLKLORE

Mary says almost nothing about the poetry she was writing during her final two years at Blackburn. "The notices of her public occasions in 'The Blackburnian' seldom fail to do justice to her literary reputation, and she was elected Class Poet. I spare you mercifully all quotations" (*E.H.* 167). In these two sentences, she hurries us past a door that she seems to think not worth opening. Is something hidden there of which she does not wish to be reminded or which she would rather we would not see? Perhaps the stumbling rhythms of these early poems proved too disillusioning to her established writer's eye. Perhaps the determination to be considered an authority in the eyes of the world, the "obligation of repute" she attributed to her heroine Olivia, had overwhelmed the poet by the time the autobiography came to be written.

Peering at Mary through the lines in which she tells us about herself, one catches glimpses of other Marys. There is not only the rather insufferable I-Mary and the Mary who walks in the shadow of her mother, in yearning recollections of her father, in sullen envy of her long-dead little sister, in despair of affirmation by her brother (and perhaps the rest of the male world), there are aspects of Mary kept hidden away or still invisible in the bud, like leaves on a winter branch. Some of them perhaps even Mary herself did not recognize. There were Marys who seemed able to exist only when they were mirrored back from someone else's eyes or as they were reflected to her from a character in a poem or a storybook; fragments of herself inhabiting her dreams or that childhood dreaming of mankind that we call folklore, which always had an uncanny fascination for Mary Austin, even though she would try to convince herself that her interest was entirely "scholarly."

"There is a trick man has," she writes in *Experiences Facing Death,*

of turning his insides outside, which if it were presented to a race of beings wholly without the instinct for story-telling, would appear the most incredible of human performances. Man everywhere has

157

*a habit of creating out of scraps of his own experience, out of rag-
tags of observation, out of a curious usage such things have of turning into something which is neither one of them, which, nevertheless,
has in it enough of the stuff of human reality to serve as a sort of
pattern reflection. The stuff that goes into these stories is not all of
the sort we call actuality; some of it is the stuff of dreams, of wishful
thinking, of unmeasured desires and ambitions. Much, very much
of it is drawn from patterns made on the immediate consciousness
by the unpremeditated motions of man's Sacred Middle; things going
on so deep down in him, that he is aware only of the fact that they
are going on and that they are important. . . . One sees the sense
of pattern in behavior exteriorating itself in the string games developed by Esquimaux in the long Arctic nights, in the patterns of
sticks and bones thrown in a gambling basket as an index of fortu-
nate adventure, in the disposition of man to seek for patterns as
auguries, in the entrails of his kill, in the flight of birds, the throw
of cards. If you were to sit down with me to shuffle and throw any
four- or six-parted deck of playing cards, I could tell you a pattern
of your own personal activities which . . . would surprise you with
its suggestion of veracity. And that not because there is anything
mystic in myself or magic in the cards, but because, being an accomplished storyteller, I know that the patterns of the cards, the "dark
lady," the "person in authority," the "undeserved good fortune,"
the "peril of accident," were all patterns in the mind of man before
ever they were extroverted in carved bones or reduced to painted
figures on bits of pasteboard. And being by natural constitution a
story-teller, it amuses me more to play with my folklore than to write
articles upon it for encyclopedias, although I can do that too, on
occasion* (E.F.D 74–77).

Oddly enough, she says, there was not a word about folklore in
any of the subjects she either chose or was made to study at Blackburn; the word did not come into general use where Mary was
concerned until later. The stuff of folklore, however, lay all about
her, and Mary seems to have absorbed more of it than she real-

ized. "There was a book of classic myths, which was a handbook to Latinity, and in ancient history, subsidiary to battle notes, small-print paragraphs about lost religions. . . . Mary in particular followed the growing popular interest in Egyptology in the writings of Flinders Petrie" (*E.H.* 169). (She has already mentioned in connection with her breakdown at Normal School that the "Dweller in the Core of Her Mind" [*E.H.* 154] had a special appetite for Egyptology and Oriental literature.)

Though she claims that as far as possible she avoided the college English courses, she was obviously reading a great deal of English literature on her own. She must have recognized the classic allusions in her books as having their roots in folklore and in the great biblical narratives that she had heard read aloud throughout the half-dream of her childhood and now expounded upon aridly as doctrine in a course labeled "natural theology."

The poetry she herself was writing—at least the samples that appear in the *Blackburnian*—is full of allusions to her mythological reading, applied in often awkward ways to her own inner experiences. Of the "observation of nature" that could have resulted from the natural history courses there is little trace. She has not yet begun to look closely at the living world about her and seek the exact phrase. There is a feeling for nature, but it tends to be muffled in abstractions, a hangover, perhaps, from all that training in rhetoric and debate. Her essay "The Man and the Place," which appeared in the January issue of the *Blackburnian*, resounds in windy praise of Daniel Webster and reads like the kind of thing she supposed would have won her brother's oratorical contests for him if he had only been willing to let her teach him!

In the same month of January, Mary must have been happy to see a poem of hers printed in one of the hometown newspapers, the *Carlinville Democrat*. Titled "Bring Him Home," she had written it in tribute to General John A. Logan, a senator from Illinois who had died suddenly in Washington, D.C. Many believed that because of the senator's distinguished service to his country, he should be buried in the nation's capital. Illinois citizens naturally claimed that the native son should be buried in the state where he had been born, and Mary upheld that opinion.

> He will need no marble column
> Punctured shaft or sculptured dome
> In our hearts we'll write his praises
> When they bring our hero home.

There seems no reason why Mary should have a special interest in General Logan, who never lived in Carlinville. It would have meant nothing to her had she known that this same Senator Logan, only a year before his death, had succeeded in having the gifted young ethnologist Frank Hamilton Cushing dismissed from his position at the New Mexico Indian Pueblo of Zuni because Cushing had interfered, on the Indians' behalf, with a landgrab in which Logan's son-in-law was involved. Mary Austin would one day write an introduction to a reissue of Cushing's *Zuni Folk Tales*.

Though she never met Cushing, who died not long after Senator Logan's disastrous interference with his career, his writing would greatly influence her own. She saw in him a personality at the opposite pole, it seems, from that of Senator Logan, the hero of her youth. "Perhaps," she would write, "he was in fact a changeling, a throwback to the mysterious little people, traces of whose life, so close to the earth, make a network of folklore over ancestral Europe."

THE GLORIOUS DESTINY

Outwardly, Mary's life at Blackburn seems at first to have followed a rather conventional pattern. She was listed as corresponding secretary for the YWCA during her junior year and was musician for the OIO at its meeting reported for December 1886.

In 1887, something of the recognition she had always longed for began to come her way, as though one of the submerged Marys was breaking forth into the light of day at last. The *Blackburnian* for February carried the name of Mary Hunter on its masthead as literary editor. The editor was a senior named J. E. McClure, who is not mentioned in Mary's autobiography. However, from a few of Mary's poems that were printed that year, usually signed only with her initials, M.H., and from one or two unsigned editorial comments on her work, one suspects that young McClure may have played a part in Mary's inner drama that he probably never was aware of.

In the *Blackburnian* for March 1887, we find a poem called "Endymion," signed M.H. and written in a very different tone of voice from that of any of the Marys who have appeared on the stage before.

> *Soft as the moonlight dropping down*
> *Over the autumn meadows brown,*
> *Fair Dian, stooping from above*
> *Wakes with a kiss to life and love*
>   *The youth Endymion.*
>
> *So oft like Dian's kiss, unsought*
> *Some careless word of yours, some thought*
> *Half-uttered, falling on my heart*
> *Wakens new impulses that start*
>   *Suddenly into life.*
>
> *Visions of things that are to be,*
> *Glimpses of a glorious destiny.*
> *And as beneath the summer showers*
> *The meadows blossom out with flowers*
>   *My thoughts arise in song.*

The poem is curiously mixed as to gender. It is very feminine in some respects, more feminine than any aspect of herself Mary has yet revealed or seemed to be aware of. There is the presence of moonlight, of summer showers followed by blossoming flowers. This theme—a sudden blossoming after a period of sterility and depression—will occur and recur like the flash of a secret bird, a motif in music, throughout Mary Austin's autobiographical writings.

Someone, Mary does not suggest who, has wakened a dream in this discouraged young girl's heart, a vision of herself, perhaps, as she had always longed to be, in contrast to the unloved and unlovable person she had grown to feel she was. There is the magic of a kiss, fair Dian's kiss (it seems that Mary must have been reading Keats, who names the moon goddess in his poem "Diana" the Roman Artemis, although Endymion in the original tale was Greek and the moon's name Selene). The kiss, in Mary's comparison, wakens Endymion to life and love. In the myth, the shepherd Endymion, after being kissed by the moon in his dream, begs Zeus to let him sleep on and on and never waken. He will never reenter daily human life but exists forever in the embrace of his lovely goddess. Some say that Selene bore fifty daughters to Endymion through these encounters while he slept!

The Endymion in Mary's poem, however, wakes, and wakes like a young hero, not under the spell of a kiss but through the fertilizing power of a word. It is not a maiden, as one might expect, but the youth, the young man in herself, that wakens to "Visions of things that are to be,/Glimpses of a glorious destiny"—hardly the instinctive ambition of an ordinary woman.

Mary has always been aware of something extraordinary in herself, or perhaps among her many selves, some kind of force or spirit that seized upon her, shaping her to its own purposes. She came to name this special power within "genius." "If I know anything of genius," she has Olivia say, "it is wholly extraneous, derived, impersonal, flowing through and by. I cannot tell you what it is, but I hope to show you a little of how I was seized of it, shaped; what resistances opposed to it; what surrenders. . . . When it refers to myself you must not understand me to speak as of a peculiar merit, like the faculty for presiding at a woman's club or baking sixteen pies of a morning . . . rather as a seizure, a possession" (W.G. 4–6). So men have sometimes spoken of the Muse; so Keats may have experienced the poet in himself as Endymion and the moon as the muse who cast her spell upon him.

Where, as is often claimed, a man needs a real woman to play the part of his inspiring muse, Mary seemed often to need a man to call forth the creative powers in her own nature, not in the conventional sense of a sexual affair but in the sense of a lighting up of spirit, the kindling of a fire. She herself, in "Frustrate," used the phrase of matches needing to be struck upon a box.

Could it have been through her casual association with young McClure that Mary first began to think of herself as possessing—or being possessed by—genius? "I think the child is possessed" (*E.H.* 45), her mother had sometimes lamented long ago, but if whatever possessed you could be called genius, something that rose in you from the "source of selfness" (*E.H.* viii), would this not be enough to justify all your condemned behaviors, rid you, as Mary would write in the introduction to *Earth Horizon*, "of the onus of responsibility for those that failed to coincide with the current standards of success" (*E.H.* viii)? It was, of course, a serious temptation to make such a claim, and Mary would walk the fine line all the rest of her life between humility toward the creative powers and the most outrageous identification of her own human ego with them.

The May 1887 issue of the *Blackburnian* contains a long poem of Mary's called "Oak Leaves." In the first stanza, the writer expresses her longing to partake in the life of nature as though she were a tree:

> Hope, despair and exaltation
> Sweeping in swift alternation
> Weary me, and I would rest,
> Mother nature, on thy breast.
> Leave for all time, earth's ceaseless toil,
> Strike my roots deep in thy soil,
> With each returning spring to feel
> The life sap through my branches steal,
> And as each twig new strength receives
> Laugh my joy in a thousand leaves . . .

With no other toil than this,
The tree's epitome of bliss,
As the seasons circle by,
But grow, and reproduce, and die.

In the second stanza, the poet hears "the woodsman's stroke." The tree is cut down by the activity of man. The poet becomes aware of her human, perhaps her share of masculine, nature:

My little brood of hopes flocked home.
The old longing and desire,
Embers of Promethean fire,
The secret hopes and silent yearning,
Deep within our hearts still burning.
We cannot fuse into the tree
The spirit of humanity. . . .
Gone thy spell, O sacred tree,
My soul shakes off its lethargy
And feels once more, with secret awe,
Its symmetry with nature's law.

She has yielded—how much was Mary ever aware of what was happening?—to the thought of her "glorious destiny" and seems to renounce the contact, the identification with nature, from which the Endymion side must always draw its inspiration:

. . . the green-robed priest of the forest lies
Bound low to earth with iron ties
Where the revolving wheels of trade
For themselves a path have made,
Through the forest's very heart
Commerce treads, and cities start . . .
Ever the rebellious Pan
Must resign his way to man . . .

In Mary Austin's collection of folk tales, *One Smoke Stories*, there is a haunting and bitter tale called "Lone Tree." The lone tree grows on a ledge of rock above a dripping desert spring, "as unrelated to the vast empty land as a woman would have been." Hogan, a would-be prospector, working for a pittance at one of the mining camps, hates the tree, perhaps because of its feminine delicacy and rootedness. The day he finishes his job and is free to go his way, some malice makes him strike his pick into the tree, giving it a pull that almost drags it from its roots. Two years later, on his way with his pockets full of ore, to file on a claim "that left him giddy with its promise," the prospector loses his way in a sandstorm. He remembers the spring with the lone tree beside it and manages to drag himself toward it. "When he came the last hundred yards, creeping at the bottom of the yellow murk, he found the roots that held the rock had been torn away by the falling tree, so that it had dropped into the sources of the spring. Across the sand-choked basin lay the withered stock of the lone tree, but it was three years before anybody came that way to find the bones of Hogan mixed with the stark branches" (*One Smoke Stories* 25–26).

How strangely like the theme of "Lone Tree" is that of "Oak Leaves," but with what a different twist! Did Mary Austin know that this story, too, was a reflection of the drama of her own inner life, or did only the wise old storyteller in her know, leaving it to whoever can to recognize its likeness?

J. E. McClure, Mary's companion editor, was impressed by the poem "Oak Leaves." It seems safe to assume that it was he who contributed the unsigned remarks under the masthead in the same issue of the *Blackburnian:*

> *In this issue is published a poem from the pen of our literary editor, Miss Mary Hunter. A careful perusal of it reveals the fact that it is the work of a genius, and one destined in the near future to be recognized in the literary world. She is well known in some literary circles and her reputation is constantly widening. The Blackburn college is to be congratulated upon having such an able writer among its editors.*

What manna it must have been for Mary to find herself publicly announced as a "genius." Here at last was someone who recognized her true worth. She, the sullen-looking girl whom no one had ever really appreciated, who had "grown up as the least important member of the family" (E.H. 171), clearly "destined in the near future to be recognized in the literary world"! One remembers the experience with her father that Mary Austin attributes to the child Olivia in A Woman of Genius: "He had expected better of me then; he had reached beyond my surfaces and divined what I was inarticulately sure of, that I was different—no, not better—but somehow intrinsically different" (W.G. 30).

No matter how haughty and self-assured Mary would appear most of her life, there was something in her that always hungered for affirmation, especially from anyone of prominence. Young McClure could have been scarcely as old as her brother Jim, yet he was the senior class editor and someone of status and popularity on the campus. One likes to hazard the guess that Mary unconsciously found in him, projecting her own longings, some elements of the "young man . . . [who] wore bright neckties" (E.H. 172), at least a young man different from the usual run, who must have liked poetry and appreciated her efforts. In her novel, this young man, coming upon Olivia in the woods dancing and reciting passages from Shakespeare (Perdita's lines, as a matter of fact, from A Winter's Tale), calls her "you beauty, you wonder" (W.G. 100).

All that we really know about J. E. McClure was that he liked Mary's work and encouraged her. It could have taken no more than that to release the image of the young hero that slumbers in every woman's heart, part of herself, part of her own active nature which is always urging her to free herself from bondage to her exclusive biological destiny.

In the final issue of the Blackburnian for 1887, there is a note on "The Alumni Banquet" that is unsigned but that had most likely been written by the editor. "I suspect this is from the same J. E. McClure," says Harriet Stoddard in a personal communication, though she goes on to suggest that Mary might have written it herself, a possibility, of course, for one who could keep diaries under many different names, but rather unlikely. The senior editor could hardly have let her get away with it:

> *One of the best essays of the evening was by Miss Mary Hunter, Carlinville, upon the subject, "American Elements in Literature." Miss Mary has quite a reputation as a literary character and much was expected of her. But she was equal to the occasion. The cry is often raised that we have no American literature. European writers were not confined by geographical boundaries and may we not have books that even though they do not bear the tracks of the great American eagle upon their pages, may have as distinct a national character as do these. Examples were cited from such authors as Emerson, Hawthorne and Longfellow, in a manner that showed familiarity with their works. Miss Hunter read her essay in an easy, graceful manner and was loudly applauded.*

In the June issue of the *Blackburnian* for 1887, the same that contains these unsigned words of praise for Mary's essay, the opening feature is an also unsigned poem addressed "To J. E. McClure." According to Harriet Stoddard, the poem was definitely written by Mary. Stoddard had the assurance from her father, who had known many of Mary's contemporaries at Blackburn and learned that the poem was indeed hers. Young McClure was about to graduate and would leave the editorship of the monthly journal upon which he and Mary had worked together for at least five months. In her poem, the author wishes to offer a tribute of honor and praise "to crown your labors, a friend of mine," and selects a "garland of evergreen pine" as more appropriate for this hero than the "lowly laurel."

> *Deep-rooted and firm, but with head toward the sky*
> *Growing up to the light with a purpose divine*
> *And this be your emblem, the evergreen pine.*

These lines may have described the young hero within herself as well as her opinion of her friend.

It seems to have been a case of mutual admiration, and one is even more puzzled to know why Mary left any mention of the friendship out of her autobiography, unless it was out of her habitual reluctance to acknowledge a debt. McClure's editorial praise may have unintentionally kindled a spark that would go on smoldering in the undergrowth of her life to burst into flame in what became Mary Austin's later preoccupation with the American scene, especially the effect of the environment, the "landscape line," the rhythm of winds and waters, and of men's daily occupations, upon their poetry, both primitive and modern.

GRADUATION PORTRAIT

In the fall of her senior year, Mary was listed as "Associate Literary Editor" of the *Blackburnian*. By March 1888, her name no longer appeared on the masthead. Various unsigned essays may have been hers, but otherwise she ceased to be a contributor. No doubt she needed to concentrate on finishing her academic work. In June, her class poem appeared, based on the Greek legend of Tithonous, another young man loved, like Endymion, by a goddess, this time Aurora, the goddess of the dawn.

Aurora begs the boon of eternal life for her beloved but forgot to ask also for eternal youth, "So when life came to be a burden, death came not to set him free from his most cruel immortality." It is hard to figure out just how Mary manages to apply this legend to the situation of young men and women leaving college except that she charges her classmates to maintain their high ideals and not give way to "lust or greed or fame." If they do, "Old age will bring . . ./Impotent grief, remorseful memory/And in the thoughts of immortality/There can no comfort lie/To one who longs for death/Yet fears to die."

> We have left our youth within the walls
> Of these old college halls,
> Laid with our books away

With flowers and tokens of commencement day,
But still keep young, although our heads are gray
And back to God we go
With hearts pure as he gave them long ago.

The comparisons are confused, the poem far from equal even to Mary's schoolgirl beat. We can see her laboring on it, rather desperately, through the last anxious weeks before graduation. The weather would have been hot and humid. She would have undoubtedly been straining to uphold her reputation for being a genius with little real inspiration for it. There would have been all the pressure of the last day's traditional ceremonies. Effie Vancil Jordan recalls that "at the close of our Junior year we were required to write an essay or oration and deliver it before an always crowded Court House. And that was an ordeal. . . . And when at the close of our senior year this was repeated it was serious."

There had to be special dresses both for junior and senior exercises. Effie's graduating dress was "white, thin wool trimmed with white velvet, tight-fitting bodice, stiff and hot." One of her classmates swore that her own dress had twenty yards of silk in it. In 1886, the young ladies were wearing their hair in a pompadour with the aid of a wire rat, and a Psyche knot behind, or in a single braid down the back; bangs were no longer stylish.

Mary's graduation portrait in 1888 shows her head and shoulders in profile. Her hair is drawn back from her high forehead in a becoming and natural wave, leaving her ears bare, and is pinned into two thick coils at the back of her head. A few untidy strands have escaped at the nape of her neck and straggle over the dainty but rather prickly looking lace collar, which fills in the V neck of her dress. Her eyes have a faraway look, though one sees only the right eye full; it is the left one that is usually supposed to be the dreamer. Her nose seems too large at the tip; a deep shadow under the nostril gives the unfortunate suggestion of a proboscis.

Indeed, in later years there was something greedy about Mary, as though her animal nature, too strenuously denied, showed through the mask of the intellectual woman. On the other hand, is it not the despised animal in the fairy tales that often turns out to be the prince whom a wicked witch has enchanted and who must wear this form until a loving human being is willing to embrace him?

The angle of Mary's lower jaw is heavy. Her lips turn downward only a little; the lower lip is full, with a faint suggestion of a pout or the look of one who has been given bitter medicine instead of the sweet that had been promised. A child longs for affection but is held in check by some relentless force within it. There is the determination to go one's own way in spite of everyone, and also the shadow of dread, the reluctance to leave the shelter and safety of the known, the companionship of those who are content to be part of the unadventurous flock. Already there is a little of the look in this face of the "maverick, leaderless, lost from the main herd" that Mary Austin would become.

One wonders whether at the time she posed for this portrait Mary was aware of her mother's decision to take her daughter and her younger brother, George, to California where Jim had been for almost a year now. After his first year in the small county school, Jim had realized that teaching would never satisfy him. Other young men in his situation were scattering west. A few of the Dugger tribe had already joined the general migration, and letters had been coming back to Carlinville from Cousin George Dugger, who was impressed with Southern California's promise of expansion.

In the spring of 1886, a rate war between the two great railroads, the Southern Pacific and the Santa Fe, had reduced the price of tickets from points as far east as the Mississippi to $15 or less. Land was cheap and speculators were holding out enticing promises. It began to sound as though no one could really afford not to go west. At the end of his teaching term in 1887, Jim Hunter had left to seek his fortune in Pasadena, where Cousin George had happily located.

Mary says she does not know just when the plan developed for the rest of the family to join him "as soon as Mary was through college" (E.H. 176). No one had bothered to consult her, she complains, yet almost in the same breath she tells how her mother would read Jim's letters "over and over to anybody who would listen" (E.H. 176). On the sixteenth of May, Jim wrote a special letter to his sweetheart, Effie Vancil, giving her news that he had surely already shared with his mother:

> . . . I have begun this letter in the store [he was working there as a druggist's assistant]. Business is dull now, so I won't have many interruptions though I am all alone, the proprietor having gone to Los Angeles today. Well, Effie, I have at last determined what shall be my calling, at least for several years to come. You know I did not go into the drug business with any fixed idea of staying, but simply took it because it was the most profitable and suited my tastes until I could get what I really wanted. I have improved my time and made a little money in the past six months, and have now found a good chance to carry out what has always been my inclination, viz; to be a farmer and stock raiser. Are you surprised? Ever since I came to Cal I have been watching for a chance to get hold of land enough for a farm.
>
> Town lots or little vegetable gardens weren't to my taste but now I have gotten a start. . . . I heard of a township of fine government land in the San Joachin [sic] valley that has just been thrown open to settlers, went to look at it, found it splendid and filed a homestead claim and have my receipt from the U.S. land office for 160 acres of as fine land as may be found anywhere. I have 6 mos. before going onto the land and must then live on it 6 mos. of the year for 5 years and get a title. I shall probably stay in the store until time to sow wheat and barley this Fall and will then get a team, go out and put up a small house and begin permanent improvements. If I receive the proper authority from Mother in time I will file a claim for her adjoining mine and will have Mary come out and also file near me. If you have a good map of Cal. you can find right where I will be. It is in Kern Co. 20 miles south of Bakersfield right at the head of the great San Joachin [sic] valley.

The Sierras are on two sides about 4 miles back, at the mouth of the Tejon Pass are the ruins of an old Spanish fort—a little lower down nearer my land is Rose's station, a station on the stage line from Los Angeles to San Francisco. A R. R. is being built through Tejon Pass which will come right by my land.

Its chief attraction for me is that it is right in the heart of a fine stock country, 20,000 head of cattle grazing over the land now while on a ranch near are 5000 head of horses. . . . (Mary Austin Collection, Huntington Library).

It seems impossible that Mary could have heard nothing about all this—unless her head was buried too deeply in the laborious composition of the class poem. Yet she maintains that all she knew of California came of reading Bret Harte and Helen Hunt Jackson. Considering Jim's letters and the articles that were appearing in most of the national magazines (an article on Southern California by James M. Hunter himself had even appeared in the *Blackburnian* for January), she could hardly have been as uninformed as she makes out.

"The opposition she raised to her mother's plan did not arise from any preference of her own" (*E.H.* 177). This implies that she knew enough about the plan to take a stand against it. Mary would have been convinced that as usual she knew what was best for her mother and for Jim. "It would be better for Jim to have a life of his own, better for her mother to keep to the life and society she had grown into, the house she had built, the useful place she had made for herself" (*E.H.* 177). One suspects that Mary dreaded losing the importance she had managed to feel in Jim's absence. Now the mother would be able to concentrate on her favorite son again. Jim would be head of the family more than he had ever been. Who would there be in California who would recognize Mary the genius? She could hardly have been aware that Destiny was working in its own mysterious way to set her reluctant feet upon a special trail.

"Against all advice our home was dismantled, our goods sold or shipped, tenants found for the house. Within a week or two of Mary's graduation in June, we were on our way" (*E.H.* 177).

ONE HUNDRED MILES ON HORSEBACK

"It was down this way Mary came, riding a buckskin horse" (*E.H.* 190) into the drought-parched San Joaquin Valley of Southern California on a hot afternoon in September 1888.

It was the last part of a long journey, a journey that had exhausted her body and was erasing all familiar patterns from her mind. The sidesaddle twisted her muscles, and the jolting gait of the wiry little horse, endured day after day for a hundred miles, had jarred through every bone. After nearly eight days on the road, her long full skirt was stained and dust-covered. She must have felt as though her hair would never be clean again. Loose strands escaped from the coil in which she tried to pin it tightly. Her face was sallow and sticky with heat, and the corners of her mouth drooped as though she had long ago given up expecting to be happy. Her eyes were weary with looking. Ahead, the road that had wound dizzily through steep canyons and crumpled mountains suddenly came out into the flat valley that stretched on and on as though it had no end.

A short distance behind on the long grade lurched and rumbled the battered "prairie schooner" in which Mary's mother and two brothers had traveled. The wagon was most likely driven by the professional mover who owned it, a noncommital man who made a business of transporting the "Easterners" who were coming in such droves to take up land in California. It was filled with camping gear for the journey, kettles and pans and bedding, and with the few possessions the Hunters had been able to bring with them from Illinois.

Carlinville was two thousand miles away. Susanna Hunter and Mary and small George had come by railroad as far as San Francisco; from there, two seasick days by coastwise boat to Los Angeles. There had been days and days of visiting on the way—Denver, San Francisco, San Diego, and finally Los Angeles. It seemed as though all America was heading west, with the Carlinville kin among them. Eight days ago, relatives and old friends had been left behind, and here the Hunters were, facing the unknown adventure of homesteading, with brother Jim the only man of the family, twenty-two years old and still pretty much of a tenderfoot. As for Mary herself, she was just twenty. When her mother was that age, she had already taught school a year, married, and knew what it was to lose her firstborn. Her daughter knew nothing about life except what she found in her dreams or had read in books. Neither dreams nor books had prepared her to be cast away in a wordless wilderness.

She had always believed, if she ever left Carlinville, she would go east, east to New England where everything, as on an earlier visit to Uncle Charles and Aunt Mary Lane, had seemed so familiar. She already felt as though she knew everything about Massachusetts from her reading—the seasons, the names of the plants that grew there, "blueberry, bayberry, partridge berry, and ground pine" (E.H. 97). Her school days had filled her with the literature and lore of New England; she knew much of Longfellow by heart and had absorbed Hawthorne's recounting of old Greek legend, his tales of Puritan austerity. In her college days only three months away, but that now seemed years behind, Mary had been steeped in Emerson, who was not so full of atmosphere as of ideas, ideas which had seemed to bring her father closer, since she found books by Emerson in his library. Thoreau she had loved. He too made New England seem a place she knew.

There was no resemblance to Thoreau in the bare landscape she now saw all around her. Bret Harte's stories may have prepared her a little, and she had read Helen Hunt Jackson's *Ramona* for the sake of an English theme. She was too used to the lush green of Illinois to make much of the scenic descriptions in *Ramona*. There were too many names she hadn't known how to pronounce, like Jacinta and San Juan—the J's not a J at all but an *h* sound, like the blowing out of a candle. Now they were approaching this unknown stretch of desolation called San Joaquin (Hwa-keen, her brother informed her was the way it should be said).

Nothing she saw between Carlinville and California reminded her of *Ramona,* much less of New England. The vastness of the American earth had somehow stunned her. The serene woods of Illinois withdrew. The plains spread flat without interruption until the Rocky Mountains heaved themselves up out of nowhere against the sky. Beyond the mountains the desert began. Acres of sage-brush flats, then glittering sandy wastes on to which naked hills appeared to have been flung down, as though by giants playing at making scenery.

Mary, with her cheek pressed to the window, had been both repelled and attracted by the landscape flowing past in all its monotony. Yet even now she began to feel, she says, "a realization of presence . . . not the warm tingling presence of wooded hills and winding creeks, but something brooding and aloof, charged with a dire indifference, of which she was never for an instant afraid" (*E.H.* 182). Or if she felt a twinge of fear, she buried it deep or refused to admit it even to herself. Her resolute ego could admit frustration but never fear.

She had fallen in love with San Francisco, as almost everyone in those days did. Her cousin George Lane, son of her father's sister Mary and Uncle Charlie, the mining engineer, had squired her around on Sundays and occasional afternoons off from his job in a broker's office. He showed her the famous views of the bay, "gray and white houses like huddled sea birds, wet blue strips of woodland, fawn, and silver streaks of dunes" (*E.H.* 184). He introduced her to "good eating" places (*E.H.* 183) and made her aware of the haunts of artists and writers. There were places that had been frequented by Robert Louis Stevenson. Mary began to realize that the whole literary existence of America didn't necessarily center in New England. All her days in the desert she would especially hanker for San Francisco and escape to it now and then for the sake of the intellectual contacts she always longed for. Eventually, she would tear herself free to build a home in Carmel, at that time an undiscovered dream world some eighty miles down the coast.

In contrast, the outskirts of Los Angeles appalled her. "She was daunted by the wrack of the lately 'busted' boom" (E.H. 186)—the real estate boom of 1887, when it seemed the whole population of Southern California had gone quite mad with greed, buying and selling property, making and losing fortunes, blighting the landscape with jerry-built bungalows. Mary saw abandoned avenues of unwatered palms that had, it seemed to her (at least in retrospect), "a hurt but courageous look, as of young wives when they first suspect that their marriages may be turning out badly" (E.H. 186). Writing this description toward the end of her life, Mary may have been drawing the simile from her own experiences, four years away, then mercifully not yet guessed at.

The absence of taste, of any feeling for beauty, the mindless hodgepodge that was becoming Los Angeles appalled her. The Johnson Street house she had hated so in Carlinville shone by comparison. "What have I come to?" Mary asked herself. "What if this thing should catch me?" (E.H. 186). All at once she felt a real anxiety to reach the Tejon. Whatever it might be, she knew it was not a boomtown.

The family from Carlinville had met Jim at last in Monrovia, a little foothill "half-town" (E.H. 184) where he had been working in a drugstore until he could make money enough to acquire some land and fulfill his dream of becoming a farmer. There was still government land in California to be had merely for the cost of living on it and doing some improvement. In May, Jim had filed on three sections at the head of the San Joaquin Valley, one in his own name and one each in the names of his mother and sister, which would give them 480 acres altogether. He must have had his first sight of the property in April, the month when California is still green from the winter rains, and his mind was full of visions: little streams coming out of the mountains and spreading over the land; rows of vineyards to be planted; fruit trees; perhaps alfalfa

176

—everyone was saying alfalfa would be a real moneymaker; it wouldn't be long before he could acquire a few cattle—no telling where a dream like this might end in this land of abundant promise!

They were eight days and seven nights on the road, out past the shoddy houses, the half-built towns abandoned where the collapse of the boom had left them, "past acres of neglected orchard and vineyards being retaken by the wild" (E.H. 187). The season itself was like nothing they were used to. Peach and apricot trees were already sheddding their leaves but with no hint of color. Mary shared with her mother a pang of longing for the crimson and golden splendors of the Illinois hills in autumn.

The second day, they traveled through a sere brown landscape. There were long stretches where nothing grew but tangles of brown prickly brush called chaparral, stabbing blades of yucca, masses of spiny cactus. There seemed to be no singing birds. In place of streams, there were dry stony washes where lizards both sleek and horny blinked and rustled.

What had become of the fairy wonder of the world? Where was the feeling of gentle presence Mary had felt as a little girl under the walnut tree? There was something hostile about this land, so bare and unwatered; the tumble and spread of stones telling of angry and fruitless storms; the skulk and slither of creatures like diminished relics of an age of dragons.

"There was something else," Mary says, remembering years later, "a lurking, evasive Something, wistful, cruel, ardent; something that rustled and ran, that hung half-remotely insistent on being noticed, fled from pursuit, and when you turned from it, leaped suddenly and fastened on your vitals . . . beauty-in-the-wild, yearning to be made human" (E.H. 187).

Silently she soaked up her impressions. There was no one she could talk to. Neither her commonsense mother nor her earnest brother Jim would have understood. George, not yet eleven, most likely had his mind on what they were going to eat next or when they were going to get there. "Aren't we almost there?" he would have kept on asking.

It is doubtful if even Mary could have put into words all that she was feeling, all that was happening inside her at the time. The words "beauty-in-the-wild, yearning to be made human," came much later. Perhaps what she thought she saw in those waste places was partly a reflection of something in her own nature, a spirit, a longing that had been closed in since the days of her earliest childhood because the world she lived in had no use for it.

The fairy tales she had loved so much to read had wakened in her the ancient world of legend, of myth that lives deep in all of us, especially when we are children, the sense of invisible life in nature out of which the Greeks made nymphs and dryads, fauns and satyrs, "the ultimate Pan" (E.H. 187), as Mary herself called it, god of fields and forests, wild animals, flocks and shepherds. Out of this invisible life, Mary's own English, Scottish, and Irish ancestors had spun their tales of fairy folk in the greenwood, goblins and leprechauns and elves, pots of gold and magic swords. Nature for them was a kind of stage that imagination filled with dramas woven from the invisible fears and joys and hungers of the heart.

Hugh Miller, author of *Old Red Sandstone,* the geology book that had so charmed Mary in her early teens, in addition to being a student of nature was a man of imagination who delighted in fairy tales and folklore and collected legends of the Scottish countryside with as much delight as he collected his rock specimens. He mixed his scientific observations with enchanting tales of the little folk who once danced about the glens and burns of Cromarty. He saw the sudden fountaining forth of an artesian well as the birth of a naiad—or, as he put it, "what a Greek poet would have described as the birth of a naiad."

The arid California landscape through which the Hunters were now traveling had no fountains, no green grass, no tinkling leaves. Later Mary would write in one of her poems for children,

> There are no fairy folk in our Southwest.
> The cactus spines would tear their filmy wings,
> There's no dew anywhere for them to drink
> And no green grass to make them fairy rings . . .

178

By that time, she would have learned to see that the desert lands had a magic of their own; the Indian inhabitants had peopled it with imaginary beings whose names were as full of poetry as any race of European gods and goddesses. The same poem mentions several of those that are found in New Mexico—the Flute Player, the Turquoise Horse, the Rainbow Boy.

Just now as she found herself toiling on the tired little buckskin horse up and over what seemed range after range of rumpled mountains, the earth so dry and dusty, the road full of chuckholes over which the wagon rumbled and jounced, she felt more and more an exile from the lost world of childhood. Several times the road was swallowed in narrow canyons. The rocks exposed in the canyon walls writhed and twisted and folded back upon themselves. Mary could hardly conceive, she says, "of a force that could throw the elements of earth into such confusion." Because she was one who made herself part of everything she saw, she felt as though she herself were undergoing the stresses and upheavals, as though her past life were being wrenched and contorted and thrown back upon itself.

One night the party camped by a spring where they found the first bit of natural green grass since they entered California. By this time, Mary's spirit felt as sere and withered as the landscape. That night they tossed in their blankets, the boys on the ground, the women in the stifling wagon. Coyotes howled and growled and barked around them all night long. Mary had heard nothing in her life half so demonic. The night was hideous with noise that seemed to come from all directions. Another night when even Susie had consented to spread her blankets on the ground under a sheltering oak, a bear came lumbering heavily out of the brush and frightened the horses. Mary and Jim took "turns lying awake" (E.H. 189) until daybreak to reassure their mother.

No one seemed to inhabit these wild regions but a few Mexican or Indian families who had built their huts of mud or reed wherever a side canyon opened into a larger one. Mary noticed that each had a few grapevines and usually a hive of bees. The little huts seemed "overflowing with dogs and children in dirty but picturesque confusion." Sometimes, a little distance from the house, a small white wooden cross and a mound of earth would mark a burial. The tiny graves stirred Mary's first feeling of sympathy. These wild-looking people were human, then; they too knew what it was to suffer loss. Later, when she came to know them, she counted both Mexicans and Indians among her special friends. She found them to be filled, not as she was, with book knowledge, but with knowledge of the earth, the lore of the land they lived in, its seasons and its weathers.

If the journey to the San Joaquin was erasing the familiar patterns of Mary's life, new ones were already beginning to take form within her. At first these were barely discernible, but like the pattern of a leaf still hidden in the seed, they would come forth in their time and form the recognizable theme of much of her nature writing.

In the introduction to her autobiography Mary Austin declares that her life's pattern was set for her, "the main lines of it clearly indicated" (E.H. vii), before she had lived the first third of her life, the stage she had only just reached. In a later passage, she admits that her months on the homestead altered her to an extent that nothing she wrote ever fully expressed. The alteration, whether she was aware of it or not, must surely have begun on that hundred-mile horseback ride when she first became aware of the yearning for words of "beauty-in-the-wild."

On the afternoon of that last day of her journey westward—where we now leave her—she sat stiffly on the little horse, staring with unbelieving eyes over the vast dim oval of the San Joaquin Valley. She did not know that the barren wilderness had its eye on her and would use her for its own purposes.

❧

IV
THE FRIEND IN THE WOOD

☙

Mary Austin

Austin's "wick-i-up," her Carmel writing retreat.
Courtesy of The Huntington Library, San Marino, California.

182

First there was the presence in the Wood.

It would come upon us in the midst of playing, making a silence filled with the certainty of more than could be seen or heard. Or if we strayed beyond our usual playing place at the bottom of Orchard Hill, it would be lurking, peering. Out of the hush of our childish adventure it would swell suddenly to the dimensions of panic. In an instant there would be the other children fleeing between shivers and laughter in the sudden drama of ancient fear. That is how the others remember it, panic observed not so much as the reality of terror, but as a rite. But for me it was always the Friend. It came out of the Wood. From the clearing I would be aware of it, skirting the edge of the thickets. To this day the unexpected flash of scarlet columbine between young oaks quickens in me the anticipation of companionableness. If I would be sitting quietly in the grass, the presence would grow upon me, near and personal, but never with any form or aspect. I had a finger-on-lip signal with my younger sister to notify her when it came, before the other children sensed it, and she would signal back, bright eyed and aware. Or she pretended to awareness, for she was one of those gentle souls who always wish things to be the way other people wish them. Then I would walk apart, looking for bluer violets, or a superstitious bird at nest, to enjoy the Friend as long as possible before I was caught by contagion into the ritual of flight.

In every congery of children who play habitually together there are always inveterate fear tasters who will be at great pains to manufacture occasions out of wind and waving shadow and the mysteriousness of hollow trees, or coal holes and city basements, for the drama of flight. It was this half realized element of ritual in our panic that led us to locate the presence in a particular hollow appletree, and to pay it votive tribute with posies of wild flowers and valued small possessions dropped down the hollow. With these went a wish, for which an augury was taken from anything that happened immediately afterward, a sudden bird song, or an unexpected ruffling of the wind. We named the presence Snockerty, but it was I who was most fertile in inventions by which his cult was imposed on all our plays. I recall as one of the rules of the Snockerty game, that the finding of a hollow tree anywhere in the wood conferred for that occasion, the office of augur on the discoverer. But when I walked in the wood alone, invention fell away before the veritable presence of the Friend.

As I recall now, the Friend was seldom experienced anywhere but in our own particular wood, from the bottom of the orchard down past the hazel thicket where there was a spring and every season a cat-bird's nest, and on up Rinaker's Hill. Summer nights when the moon was full it would come up through the orchard to the edge of the house garden and call. Several times I got myself suspected of sleep-walking by going out to it, but that couldn't have been the case, because I have distinct recollections of wet grass about my ankles and quite definite timidities about snakes and hop-toads underfoot. And how else could I remember, as I do to this day, how the orchard looked, sentient and communica-

184

tive, and the lifting cymes of the older flowers and dew on the teary jewel weeds. But I must have favored the sleep-walking supposition because if I had admitted going out at night on my own account, I should have been spanked.

This was before I was ten, for we moved away from the wood about that time. I must have dreamed of outdoors much more often than anybody realized, because for years I entertained confident pictures of places in the woods about our house where I couldn't have been. In particular, there was a point from which I often set out, climbing a stream side between gnarly roots and overhanging boughs. The way to it began under three dark firs that stirred their boughs in a whispering motion . . . but there were never any firs at our house—except as I discovered them later on the way to the Garden,—nor any running water other than the placid branch between the orchard and Rinaker's Hill. Years later in the Austrian Tyrol I came upon a rushing stream so like the one on the way to the Wood that I suppose the picture in my mind must have been a dream extension of an illustration from a story book . . . or that I had as a child already begun visiting the Garden which for me had not yet been lost.

I cannot now recall any order in which the feeling for the Friend differentiated itself from the panic terror of the wild, nor from the child's sense of animal kin, the brotherhood of feathered, furry things. They must have kept along close together at first, for I recall occasions when the presence took on such sharp reality that I wouldn't have been surprised to catch it as a fox, which was the seldom seen, most important wild inhabitant of our woods. And once I was so close upon it that it escaped me only by turning into a box-tortoise, walking sedately between the young oaks on Rinaker's Hill. I recall hanging about for the rest of the afternoon, hoping to catch it turning into the Friend, which it never did. For even in those days I had no capacity for visual pretense. I used to wish with all my heart to believe in fern seed, charms for understanding animal speech, and the power to see creatures other than my kind; but there was never anything walked in the wood with me but the veritable animal people and the Friend. Probably I was saved by an early assurance—it must have been given me by my father, though I have no recollection of the actual telling—that it was out of this knowledge-feeling of loitering, creepy presence in the wild that all the concepts of elves, angels and other fairy folk had grown. My father was the only one accessible to my youth who was wise enough to have known my need for such teaching, and as he died when I was ten, it is scarcely reasonable to suppose that I could have read it for myself at that age. And for several years after my father died, I had little opportunity for imagining it anything more than a friendly presence, for we moved to town after that, and walks in the woods for a girl alone were not approved. Then it was that I began to go in dreams through the familiar wood to the Garden and failed to distinguish one from the other.

It was in that interval of its being seldom encountered that the experience of the Friend altered subtly away from the myths of fairy folk and the animal helper and became at once more personal and less personalized; more sharply mine as I discovered it to be the common possession of contemporary adolescence. We talked of it, other girls and I, as a presence natural to outdoors of which we were variously aware, and some of them a little afraid. Although we scarcely expressed it so, the creature feeling was identified with appreciations of beauty: beauty of the wild, of moonlit groves and budding gardens, with the hot color of the maples in October, the lilies at ease on the placid water of Beaver Lake. And by degrees it passed for the others—but never for me—into a nameless urge that demanded presence for its fulfillment. As if the Friend having withdrawn, left an image of emptiness, never in my case to be filled by blurred presentiments of "a boy I know."

I think I must have gone through a period of pretense that for me, also, beauty in the wild was the mysterious foreshadowing of the mate as it was for my companions. It would have been so natural a way for the mate to come, all the way out of childhood, foreknown as Beauty and so certified to be the absolute One. It may be that in the life before we lived this life, before the Garden was lost by the crossing of the fourth river by which Beauty ceases to be known as significance and becomes a fact, that was the way the mate did come . . . beauty as its speech and advertisement . . . beauty in the flower . . . the bright wing, the shining coat and tossing antler . . . beauty not apprehended but felt. But for me beauty in the wild took no appeasement from the mate. Never at all the mate!

With a puzzled sense of desertion I saw the Presence withdraw itself from my companions, saw the wild empty itself for them to the mere dimension of line and color and association. This was one of the sharp way-marks of growing up, that you got to know one by one as your friends married—and even though you became engaged yourself—when you could no longer talk to them of the Friend in the wood, and guardedly of the wood itself. . . . Americans generally, though they wish it known that they approve of fine landscape, do not care for discussions of it, or of beauty as an item by itself. Women, I suspect, withdraw themselves from the appeal of the Wild because it distracts them from that compacted rounding of themselves which is indispensable to the feminine achievement.

So then I married and was too busy to go to the wood for a long time, and grew restless in the night and walked about under the weeping willow and up along the stream side, and knew at last that what I looked for was the Friend who had come and looked in at the window pane and called.

And if not the mate, who came and walked with me in the woods, what then? Let who will walk in the wild long enough to lose the feel of conventional securities and he will begin to go stilly, with vague apprisals of unease along the back of the neck and between the shoulders, to sleep with an unspecified sense awake, and all the others, hearing, sight and smell-raised to forgotten levels of sensitivity. As if in every cell of man there is

a latent life of knowingness left over from whatever animal ancestor contributed it, which, given occasion, wakes to the need and
warns of weather changes, of the approach of friend or enemy, of
unanticipated dangers. In mountain men sometimes the very likeness of the animal ancestor awakes and looks out of their counte-
nances, vulpine, wolfish or merely sly and evasive. Among sheep
herders and rangers, frequenters of the wild who are neither hunters nor hunted, ancestral alertness pools, as it were, in the half
conscious centers of self-expression so that they dispose themselves,
wherever they are, according to that law of protective mimicry by
which creatures that live by inknowing rather than by intelligence,
are assimilated to their environment. As if between all forms of
Life there spread a more subtle medium even than the ether that
runs between the worlds, upon which the sharp suggestion of the
thrush in attack runs apprisingly to the happy fiddler on the maple
bough, or from the swooping hawk and the sharp nosed creeper in
the grass; . . . as if so subtly and so swiftly the thrush's doubt
whether it wore insect or dead leaf, the hawk's question, Is it field
mouse or field stone? so far out ran the snap of bill and beak that
it stiffened the quarry to the protective likeness before the deadly
stroke could take him. Everywhere, at all times, to the frequenter
of the wild, such apprisals delicately arrive and incite him to the
animal habit of awareness, all the more certainly when he is not
too much occupied with the business of being intelligent. To Our
Ancients in whom intelligence did not burgeon so rapidly as animal sensitivity diminished, out of this multitudinous impact on
the failing sense, the impression of entities from whom it might
proceed would easily arise and be projected into figures of faun
and nymph and satyr, great Pan himself. Such as these were rationalizations of beginning-man for the experiences which he could
only conceive as proceeding toward him from beings similar to
himself. But this occurred surprisingly, for one rationalizer, that
when nymph and faun and satyr had vanished out of the wild, the
Friend remained, the subtle peerer between tree boles, the Presence walking in the meadows, the caller in the night. This, for

the people in whom pride of intellect has long since overthrown the inknowing consciousness, called for new rationalizations, which have latterly been built up out of the expectation of the mate, the sole other experience which is still ardently charged with associations of the wild, out of the long time in which the wild was man's only environment. Thus to move the mate over to the place left vacant by lost sensitivity, might answer for those who find the end of life in its creature fulfillment. But how shall it answer for those to whom the mate has arrived and the experience of the Friend remains. Wouldn't it rather leave the rationalists as a last resort, the final explanation of the Presence in the wild as reality, as ghosts, perhaps, as the Irish insist they have seen it, the irrefutable Little People.

But for me there was always this persisting experience, removing itself steadfastly out of the shadow of any other human experience by which for the moment it might have been separated.

It was this stubborn quality of experience, its persistent aloofness from my wish that sustained for me the importance of the Friendliness in the Wood, unaffected by any weather of my soul as by blowing wind or falling rain. On Kearsarge, under the yellow pines, by little grass of Parnassus and Prince's Pine, at Sur across the thousand year leaf-litter of redwoods, between flecked shadows of the cypresses on Lobos, it came walking, as once between the young oaks and hickories on Rinaker's Hill. On Superstition Mountain between the tall saguaros it shone for me as a candle burning through the light of the sun. It was the Friend-in-the-Wood and answered to no other name. Always it could be found anywhere beyond the house infested places; sometimes it called from these insistently and had no appeasement until I left my work and all, and went apart where it could find me. In an unanticipated moment it would be there, off to one side, gathered together in the midst of a thicket, lurking just beyond eye reach under the marching pines, or, suddenly it would be all around me, friendly, exultant, clamorous.

Now and then I met people willing to discuss the Friend as having occurred to the Greeks or Cro-Magnon man, but never to us, never by any possibility *to us.* Or shyly, others might attempt to identify it with Immanent divinity, subjectively experienced, objectively conceived. But for me divinity does not wait only in the wood, it has no place nor times. It might be that the Friend is the stuff of which gods have been made, but never God. The two experiences are as distinct as that: divinity the sun, and the Friend-in-the-Wood the candle burning. But the figure of the flame is too explicit; the Friend is neither form nor symbol; it is the substance of experience.

Of Fear, which was so natural and even enjoyable, an item of early recognitions of the Friend, and the swift passage of it into panic, there was for me, too little to fix attention. If I thought at all of why I never suffered panic with the other children except by contagion, running when they ran, the question was baffled by the judgment of my parents that, as a child, I was abnormally insensitive to fear. Played around by the exasperated cry "Will that child never learn to be afraid!" as by a protectiving flame, panic passed me by. So it was a great surprise to me at last to be seized upon by fear in its worst, its viewless form, fear of nothing whatever that could be named.

There was one special time of its coming that stands as the type of all terror. That was after I had left the pleasant middle-western wood where I began, and had come to the desert outposts of the eastern slope of the high Sierras. There, astonishingly, with cold sickness fear had come to me in flashes. Walking or riding, out of utter desuetude, instantly the land would bare its teeth at me, crouch, tighten for the spring, and before the sweat of terror was dried, fall into desuetude again. It was never associated, this sudden qualm of fright, with the sense of the Friend. Rather with his absence, or, especially, with that impress of sentient personality which mountains give, and the snapping of the too long suffered tension of their brooding calm. Startling as such flashes were, they had been too brief to have any more significance than the vertigo which attacks many people in the presence of great height, or the mountain terror which is attendant upon the realization of human helplessness which occasionally overtakes houseliving people. So that when the viewless fear finally caught me in its claws, it was without any preparation.

There were three of us making camp in one of the desert cañons of the east sloping Sierras. There it became necessary for me to be left alone with my baby for practically the whole of one day; not in itself an occasion of terror. No objective danger was to be feared, nor was there anything in my experience to suggest any other terror. Uneasiness began about mid-morning with the growing sense of personality in the grey ribbed hills and the rushing water under the cottonwoods. Slowly at first, and then menacingly, the mountains came alive, they swelled with unappeasable insistence that filled the cañon like a tide. I fought the onslaught for a while, with wave on wave of succumbing in which the one strange point of sanity was the baby, cooing and unaware. It was my fear, my inescapable piled up terror, before which presently I dropped my gun—for this was no instinctive animal warning of avoidable danger, such as I had had, times enough, in the open—and tying my baby around my neck, as I suppose my fore-mothers had done in the grip of original fright, I climbed into a sizeable tree. I was only twenty-two, and I had never known fear before; and what can one do when the friendly earth denies you! I remember tying the baby's blanket, hammock-wise, safely into the horizontal boughs, as though it were the last thing I was to do, and giving myself up to being overwhelmingly sick with the sickness of a house-bred dog when it comes unexpectedly on the spoor of a wolf. From where I clung in the middle branches of my tree, I could see no sky, and was partly screened by leafage from the menace of the naked mountain walls; so as I pressed against the trunk of the tree and made with my body a little answering warmth, assurance began to creep up to me with the sap. I was able at last to bring my will to bear on the threatening wild, to compel it back to its normal state of earth and stone again. I did not know then what the Indians afterward taught me, of the measures for exorcising this most ancient terror of the Earth-will, but by degrees, measured by sharp recurrences of paralyzing fright, I felt the earth spell subside. Presently resentment came to reinforce such courge as I had,—for how can one know much of courage, either who has been unfamiliar with fear—the resentment of the Sacred Middle against the insubordinate earth it is predestined to subdue.

I can sympathize now with my parent's wish that I should have learned to be afraid as other children are. Taking all one's terror in a lump might easily be an irrevocable experience. Though I came back from it, altered and sane, I did not come down from my tree until late afternoon, after I heard the apprising shouts of the rest of my party returning on the trail. But when I dropped to the earth again, the earth that fawned and groveled around me, I was forever cleansed from all preferred emotions. Never again was I to be afraid to fear, or proud of courage or ashamed of resentment; cured of hating hate, of being ashamed of wrath or embarrassed by tears, or puffed up by capacity for laughter. All those conventions of pridefulness or despisings among the alterations of feeling-knowledge by which man has come to know himself as a separate soul, are ranged for me henceforth with the snobbery of despising the lowly forms in which the spirit has rested from age to age of man's ascending pilgrimage. There is a sea slug, called *holothuria*, which spits out its vitals when frightened and grows them again in security, which is probably a nearer cousin of mine than I had imagined. But the new set of vital reactions which had grown in me was out of older stuff than I had vomited forth in the sickness of terror, as old as the world before there were man-made preferences in emotions.

Made familiar with fear in this fashion, I was not to be entirely rid of it for some years, but was never again completely overcome by it for more than the split second of its onset. When fear finally left me, it was with no less surprising suddenness than when it first took me in its claws. That must have been seven or eight years after the incidents just described. I was camping at a place called

Seven Pines, on an island between two branches of a creek that came down from the snow fields of Kearsarge Mountain, where I would be often absolutely without human touch for several days at a time. I carried a gun, and learned to sleep with a warning sense wide awake, as is the habit of those who live much in the open; not a state of fear, but with fear ready to rise at need to its ancient function. There the Friend visited me, but remotely, as one who might be called, not intruding. It was my habit to fish one day up the creek and the next day down, or rather to make fishing my excuse for quiet expeditions in search of beauty, with caution awake, and pleasantly aware of the hot smell of bindweed and sulphur flowers and the glint of tall penstemons called red rain. It was past noon when at last I drew out from the creek and rested on the crisped grass, hearing the moan of the doves in the live oaks and the chuckle of the waters. One by one the outer rings of consciousness dropped flaccid as leaves in the windless air, while sleep drew around me like a soft cocoon.

And the first thing I noticed when I awoke was that I had lost something; something more than a piece of the bright day gone past recovery. Sleeping and waking out of doors gives one that sensation often, a slice of time, objectively, irrevocably missed . . . but it wasn't the day, which by the shadow clock had sipped two hours away . . . nor my rod, leaning against the pine, nor my gun which had fallen harmlessly from the holster among the grasses. I got up then and looked for my string of trout moored in a soddy runnel, and scrutinized the dust of the trail a hundred rods below. But nothing had passed there in the interval when I had lapsed out of the day as naturally as an animal, as naturally as the bob-cat that came out of the buckthorn thicket and eyed me indifferently, as though I had been another of the same kind, scarcely turning out of the trail for me. By that very failure of avoidance I knew that I had lost the smell of fear. It was a little time longer before I realized that fear itself had gone, the unconscious tension of awareness, leaving me sib to the earth again, equally unterrified and uncourageous. The Friend came out from under the silver firs and walked back to my camp with me, and all night sat outside my tent where I slept with the flap open, unalarmed.

Looking back, I realize that those years in which fear hung on the fringes of my consciousness and occasionally became a factor in all outdoor experience, coincided with the years in which I had lived most actively in my life as a woman. It was not until I had penetrated deep into the garden behind the Garden that was lost, that I understood the significance of that. For the time it was enough to know that fear would not surprise me again in desert or mountain, nor in any of the places where I was afterward to experience the Friend.

Never in cities . . . only once in Hyde Park when the rhododendrons were in bloom it came skirting under the trees to me, and in old English gardens, and along the Cotswold roads . . . around Cirencester there were fauns playing under the hazel copses, little lost fauns that had come over with the Romans and could not find their way home again. I felt their eyes bright and wistful on me from among the fern. If there had been no one else about, and if I could have remembered my Latin. . . . Among the rushing rivulets at Tivoli, or at Paestum on a summer twilight, wherever there were any wilds not wholly man infested, there would be presences of the wild, the same that I had known at home, and yet each subtly distinct, native to its land. In England the Friend was a small wild creature tamed a little by sufferance, but never to be trained to the ways of man. In Italy I understood how the Presence could have entered into the passions of mankind, as faun, as satyr, as Dionysius and as Pan. It is twenty years since I was in Italy, but I recall that I understood very well then that this distinction was somehow related to the several kinds of beauty felt there; felt, before it was apprehended, by creature *as* creature, —simple instinctive creature to whom everything was creature kind . . . the swift ebullience of spring as procreant female shape, the fine warm rain as silver footed nymph. That was how I came to realize that the third great river which circled Eden was the aware-

194

ness of beauty as significance, undefined; *felt* as the significance of things not yet perceived by the intelligence. It seemed to me that when I was in Italy I understood much more than this of the relation of beauty to the Friend-in-the-Wood. But it was about that time that I crossed the fourth river by which the moon had established itself a dead world, and the tricksy, stroking, sharp-toothed rain had been divided from beauty to become aqueous vapor falling inconveniently from the skies. Also it seemed to me that the point at which any people ceased to improve upon the creature concepts in which the experience known to me as the Friend, had been expressed,—to make God out of gods—was the point at which, for them, intellectual perceptions began to be valued more than feeling-knowledge. That's why in England the Friend-in-the-Wood is more ancient seeming, shyer and of less insistence. The English have always prided themselves too much on sense and not enough on sensibility. But along the Mediterranean, feeling-knowledge ran a longer course before it was overtaken by the habit of correcting one intellectual error by another, which is called science.

It was in Italy that I began that search for all the words and ways by which feeling-knowledge can be communicated. I think if I should ever find anybody whose stock of words and ways in the equivalent of mine, so that we can piece them together in a pattern of communication, that for me the Friend will cease, as for my contemporaries it disappeared with the finding of the mate. That is why I am making this roadside heap of my little stock of words and ways, from which I shall presently steal quietly away. I own that if the Friend-in-the-Wood turned into however subtle a certainty, I should miss him very much.

It was after I came back from Italy that I ceased hoping that the vouchsafed nearness of the Friend-in-the-Wood might somehow provide those informing conversations which would mean so much to youth if only they could be carried on in the vocabulary of the Garden. For by this time I had realized that the illuminations which came from those silent sessions in the wild were of the sort which set in motion the search for words, for nice distinctions of definition, for intricate unfoldings of smooth-pointed buds of suggestion. When the Friend comes out of the wood, even if the wood is no thicker than these sparsely spaced, low junipers which are nearest to my home, every living thing within a little space around takes on intention, pricks itself on the mind, looks me in the eye. Even stick and stone, as well as bush and weed, are discovered to be charged with an intense secret life of their own; the sap courses, the stones vibrate with ion-shaking rhythms of energy, as I too shake inwardly to the reverberating tread of life and time; they are each in its sphere as important to themselves as I to me. Now and again I have that sharp impress of virtue in a plant or beauty in a flower, of which the Indians say, "It speaks to me." I have such passages of intimacy with small furry creatures as we had when I was furry and fourfooted myself.

Other times when I sit quietly with the Friend, I begin to be aware of the soundless orchestration of activities beyond the ordinary reach of sense, the delicate unclasping of leaves of grass, the lapsing of dry petals into dust, the dust itself impregnate by the farthest star. At such times I am most aware of me behind myself, this eye of mine, the instrument dividing red from blue and green, reporting the shape of the universe; this ear reaching imperfectly but happily along its little range of sound; this hand which knows its way with an intelligence not mine but far more sure.

At times like this the flesh grows translucent and I am aware of the glistening white bones of me moving, intaught, to turn this lamp of my mind every way to catch the smallest ray from the concave universe. Presently all there is of me—blood, tissue, and the infinitely divided net of nerves—is no more than a film between me and that universe, through which the Friend is perceived as it was in the beginning, as it is ever beginning, *Wakonda*, Uncarnate Spirit pressing toward life adventure. Then I recall a man I knew whose work was complicated with test tubes and instruments of precision who told me how, when he would no more than have his hand on his laboratory door—sometimes on the passage to it—he was aware of a presence warm within, that called and warmed him all the hours he was away from it. That was the Friend for him, as for another it might have been uncarnate spirit in the urgent planless crowd, or in stone and steel or metal of the mine; the voiceless passion of spirit toward form that has no hope but to be broken into multiples of form, more subtly implicated, as who shall say it is not in the wild brier to be a rose, the granite mountain to be grass, the grass to be a man.

Hours like this with the Friend, without thought, resting in the feeling-knowledge out of which later thought is to proceed, Life affirms itself to me as an entity, a thing, more explicit and entirely aside from the by-product of living processes. Enmeshed in these, tangled in the complex of materiality which gives it form, nevertheless it has Being, and that mysterious quality which, stepped down through the particular instrument of glands and ganglia, is called personality. Such hours, the life that is me,—that I behind myself—makes, by virtue of its separateness, an indent on the uncarnate life which haunts the Wood. The word comes to me out of some forgotten book of the East to express the mutual interpenetration of Life and lives; the mark of Uncarnate Spirit on its media, ions, all that subtle scale of vibration known to us as color, sound, power; the imprint of the incarnate spirit of man on his material, by which he comes into workable relations with it—the sculptor with his clay, the inventor with his metal, stone, crystal, the horse trainer with his stock. This is the Friend-in-the-Wood; the ever living and as yet uncreated Life, pressing to be shaped as tree and shrub, as beast and man; never so urgently felt by me, who am nearest by nature to these things, as in the Wild; felt by others each according to his endowment, as my friend feels it along the white tiled corridor to his laboratory, the Spirit of Life Uncarnate calling, "Come and use me!" Do we not take too much credit to ourselves supposing that the work of our hands is ours? How shall we be certain that it takes no portion from the pressure of spirit to become substance and form, the insistence of the voice-less, wistful Friend to pierce the thin film of primary substance toward wider levels of perception, the unidentified factor of all evolution? Well might it withdraw itself from all who turn from its calling to find their fulfillment in creature satisfaction or, equally might it produce terror, showing its teeth and claws frighteningly to the willing subject of an evolution, by whatever sanctions of the times and the mores, evaded.

Once let the intelligence work at it, I am sure that a good case could be made for the Friend-in-the-Wood—whether as Friend or Fear—as the notice registered on the creature by its creator, the trope of the light-turning flower to the sun, the return of the sun on its orbit. But for me, who distrusts all intelligence which is not illumined by feeling-knowledge, to know the Friend is more esteemed than to know about it. That is why I have asked to be buried not in any formal plot, but anywhere in the wild, and not too deeply, so that I may the more swiftly resolve my substance to new incarnations of tree and grass, live again in my flesh even as the lowliest; so that I myself shall most readily seize on familiar and friendly stuff of the spirit.

ꞏ≈ꞏ

Notes

Introduction

1. Letters from Peggy Pond Church to John Espey, August 26, 1972, in the Peggy Pond Church Papers, Albuquerque, N.M.

2. Ibid.

3. Ibid.

4. Letter from Peggy Pond Church to Mary Austin, October 8, 1929, in the Mary Austin Collection, Henry E. Huntington Library, San Marino, Calif.

5. Ibid.

6. Letter from Peggy Pond Church to John Espey, August 26, 1972.

7. Unpublished journals of Peggy Pond Church in the Peggy Pond Church Papers.

8. Unpublished notes of Peggy Pond Church in the Peggy Pond Church Papers.

9. Ibid.

10. Ibid.

11. Ibid.

12. Unpublished journal of Peggy Pond Church, in PPC Papers. Fink's biography, published in 1983, is titled *I—Mary*.

13. Unpublished notes of Peggy Pond Church.

14. Quoted in unpublished journal of Peggy Pond Church, September 13, 1971.

15. Letter from Peggy Pond Church to Harriet Stoddard, July 3, 1972.

16. Letter from Peggy Pond Church to Harriet Stoddard, July 17, 1972.

17. Letter from Peggy Pond Church to Harriet Stoddard, n.d.

18. Mary Austin, *The Lovely Lady* (New York: Doubleday, Page, 1913), p. 124.

19. Letter from Peggy Pond Church to Harriet Stoddard, June 17, 1972.

20. See Carolyn Heilbrun, *Writing a Woman's Life* (New York: W.W. Norton and Co., 1988).

Writing Nature

1. *Mary Austin, a Memorial,* ed. Willard Hougland (Santa Fe, N.M.: Laboratory of Anthropology, 1947), p. 22.

2. Mary Austin, "Greatness in Women," *North American Review* (February 1923): 200.

3. T. M. Pearce, *The Beloved House* (Caldwell, Idaho: Caxton Printers, 1940), p. 17. Pearce retells the observation that Austin made in *Earth Horizon.*

4. Eudora Welty, *One Writer's Beginnings* (New York: Warner Books, 1983), p. 75.

5. "These Modern Women, Woman Alone," *Nation* 124 (March 1927): 228.

6. Mary Austin, *Earth Horizon* (Boston and New York: Houghton Mifflin, 1932), p. 187.

7. Ibid., p. 187.

8. Mary Austin, *The Friend in the Wood*, Mary Austin Collection, Henry E. Huntington Library, San Marino, Calif., p. 20.

9. "Woman Alone," p. 229.

10. Ibid.

11. Ibid.

12. Ibid., p. 230.

13. Austin, *Earth Horizon*, p. 330.

14. Letter from Mary Austin to Alfred Kidder, Mary Austin Collection, Huntington Library.

15. *Mary Austin, a Memorial*, p. 126.

16. Letter to Arthur Ficke, March 27, 1930, quoted in James Ruppert, "Mary Austin's Landscape Line in Native American Literature," *Southwest Review* (Autumn 1983): 389.

17. Carl Van Doren, "Mary Austin," *Scholastic Magazine* 21 (September 29, 1934): 23.

18. Austin, quoted in Pearce, *The Beloved House*, p. 86.

19. Mary Austin, quoted in T. M. Pearce, *Mary Hunter Austin* (New York: Twayne Publishers, 1965), p. 63.

20. *The Friend in the Wood*, p. 21.

21. Ibid., p. 20.

22. Mary Austin, *The Land of Little Rain* (Boston and New York: Houghton Mifflin, 1903), p. 186.

23. Letter from Charles Minton to Peggy Pond Church, April 15, 1968, Peggy Pond Church Papers, Albuquerque, N.M., n.p.

24. Mary Austin, *The Flock* (Boston and New York: Houghton Mifflin, 1906), p. 106.

25. Letter of Ambrose Bierce to George Sterling, February 3, 1906, quoted in Dudley Wynn, *A Critical Study of the Writings of Mary Hunter Austin*, New York University, 1941, p. 22.

26. Mary Austin, *The Lands of the Sun* (Boston and New York: Houghton Mifflin, 1927), p. viii. This was a reissue, with slight changes, of *California, the Land of the Sun*.

27. Ibid., p. viii.

28. Ibid., p. 34.

29. Mary Austin, "Walking Woman," Mary Austin Collection, Huntington Library, p. 13.

30. Mary Austin, "Fire, a Drama in Three Acts," *The Play-book* (Wisconsin Dramatic Society) 2, no. 6 (November 1914): 19–20.

31. Mary Austin, *The Land of Journeys' Ending* (New York and London: Century, 1924), p. 40.

32. "The American Forum of the Novel," *New Republic* 30 (April 12, 1922): 6.

33. Austin, *The Land of Journeys' Ending*, p. 264.

34. Quoted in *Time Magazine*, October 14, 1988, p. 32.

35. Carolyn Heilbrun, "The Masculine Wilderness of the American Novel," *Saturday Review of Literature* (November 22, 1974): 46.

36. Harriet Monroe, introduction to *The New Poetry*, eds. Harriet Monroe and Alice Corbin Henderson (New York: Macmillan, 1917), p. iv.

37. Austin, "Walking Woman," p. 4.

38. "Going West," in *The American Rhythm, Studies and Re-expressions of American Songs* (New York: Harcourt, Brace, 1923), p. 35.

39. "When I Am Dead," *New Mexico Quarterly* 4 (August 1934): 234–35.

40. Austin, "Woman Alone," p. 230.

41. *Notes on the Validity of Modern Mysticism*, Mary Austin Collection, Huntington Library, p. 4.

42. Denise Levertov, *The Poet in the World* (New York: New Directions, 1973), p. 69.

SELECTED BIBLIOGRAPHY
MARY AUSTIN

American Rhythm, The. Studies and Re-expressions of American Songs. New York: Harcourt, Brace, 1923; Boston and New York: Houghton Mifflin, 1930.

Arrow-Maker, The. A Play. Produced at the New Theatre, New York City, 1911. New York: Duffield, 1911; revised ed., Boston: Houghton Mifflin, 1915.

Basket Woman, The. A Book of Fanciful Tales for Children. Boston and New York: Houghton Mifflin, 1904.

California, the Land of the Sun. London: A. and C. Black, 1914; New York: Macmillan, 1914; revised ed., *The Lands of the Sun,* Boston and New York: Houghton Mifflin, 1927.

Can Prayer Be Answered? New York: Farrar and Rinehart, 1934.

Children Sing in the Far West, The. Boston and New York: Houghton Mifflin, 1928.

Christ in Italy, Being the Adventure of a Maverick Among Masterpieces. New York: Duffield, 1912.

Earth Horizon: An Autobiography. Boston and New York: Houghton Mifflin, 1932.

Everyman's Genius. Indianapolis: Bobbs-Merrill, 1925.

Experiences Facing Death. Indianapolis: Bobbs-Merrill, 1931.

Fire. A Play. Produced at the Forest Theatre, Carmel, Calif., 1912.

Flock, The. Boston and New York: Houghton Mifflin, 1906.

Ford, The. Boston and New York: Houghton Mifflin, 1917.

Green Bough, The. A Tale of the Resurrection. Garden City, N.Y.: Doubleday, Page, 1913.

Indian Pottery of the Rio Grande. Pasadena, Calif.: Esto Publishing, 1934.

Isidro. Boston and New York: Houghton Mifflin, 1905.

Land of Journeys' Ending, The. New York and London: Century, 1924.

Land of Little Rain, The. Boston and New York: Houghton Mifflin, 1903; Garden City, N.Y.: Doubleday, Anchor Book, Natural History Library, 1962.

Lost Borders. New York and London: Harper and Brothers, 1909.

Love and the Soul Maker. New York: D. Appleton, 1914.

Lovely Lady, The. Garden City, N.Y.: Doubleday, Page, 1913.

Man Jesus, The. New York and London: Harper and Brothers, 1915; reprinted as *A Small Town Man,* 1925.

Man Who Didn't Believe in Christmas, The. A Play. Produced at Cohan and Harris Theatre, New York City, 1916. Published in *St. Nicholas Magazine* 45 (December 1917): 156–62.

Mother of Felipe and Other Early Stories. Collected and ed. Franklin Walker. Los Angeles: Book Club of California, 1950.

No. 26 Jayne Street. Boston and New York: Houghton Mifflin, 1920.

One Smoke Stories. Boston and New York: Houghton Mifflin, 1934.

Outland (under the pseudonym of Gordon Stairs). London: John Murray, 1910; New York: Boni and Liveright, 1919, 1920.

Santa Lucia, a Common Story. New York and London: Harper and Brothers, 1908.

Starry Adventure. Boston and New York: Houghton Mifflin, 1931.

SELECTED BIBLIOGRAPHY

Taos Pueblo. Photographed by Ansel Adams and described by Mary Austin. San Francisco: Grabhorn Press, 1930.

Trail Book, The. Boston and New York: Houghton Mifflin, 1918.

Woman of Genius, A. Garden City, N.Y.: Doubleday, Page, 1912; Boston and New York: Houghton Mifflin, 1917.

Young Woman Citizen, The. New York: Woman's Press, 1918.

A comprehensive list of Mary Austin's publications in magazines may be found in *Mary Austin, Bibliography and Biographical Data*, California Library Research Digest, Monograph 2 (Berkeley, 1934). However, since this is not a complete list, the footnotes in this bibliography provide additional references to her publications in other periodicals. The primary collection of correspondence, research materials, and unpublished manuscripts may be found at the Huntington Library, San Marino, California. A smaller collection, containing originals and copies of letters to some of her friends, is housed in the Coronado Room, Special Collections, at the University of New Mexico Zimmerman Library, Albuquerque, including the Peggy Pond Church research and notes for *Wind's Trail.*

INDEX

Alber, L.J., World Celebrities
  Lecture Bureau, 15
Alice's Adventures in Wonderland
  (Carroll), 90, 91
Alton (Ill.), 42
"Alumni Banquet, The"
  (*Blackburnian*), 166
"American Elements in Literature"
  (Austin), 167
"American Fiction and the Pattern
  of American Life" (Austin
  speech), 15
"American Indian Art" (Austin
  lecture), 15
American rhythm, 16, 24
*American Rhythm, The: Studies and
  Re-expressions of American Songs*
  (Austin), 13, 24
American self, 26
Anasazi, x
Andrews, W.E., 137
Andrews, William 153-4
Animus, xv, xviii
Applegate, Frank, 14
Arrow-Maker, The (Austin), 12,
  22, 29
Art, 123, 141, 156
Art and Archaeology, 16
Art Department (Blackburn
  College), 135
Atlantic Monthly, 9
Audubon, John James, 54
Austin, Mary Hunter (1868-1934):
  abroad, 12; on American
  writing, 24; appearance, 5, 10,

35, 36, 39-40, 47, 143-4, 145,
146, 169, 170; astrological sign,
36; autobiographical novel (*see
Woman of Genius, A*);
autobiography (*see Earth
Horizon, An Autobiography*);
biographer (*see* Church, Peggy
Pond); birth, 5, 35-6, 37;
birthplace, 6, 37, 38; brothers
(*see* Hunter, George Jr.;
Hunter, James M.); in
California (1884-1912), xvi, 8,
9, 11, 19, 21, 114, 142, 145,
148, 173-80; childhood, xviii,
5, 6, 51, 58-80, 89, 95-120;
college (*see* Blackburn College;
State Normal School); community theater promoter, 15;
cousins (*see* Burns, Anna;
Dugger, George; Farrell, John;
Farrell, Minnie; Lane, George);
creative life, xvii-xviii, 4, 5,
8-9, 10, 11, 16, 94-5, 116, 120,
134, 138, 140-41, 151, 154,
162-3, 164; daughter (Ruth),
xvi, 9, 10, 11, 130; death, 49;
depression, 105; and desert, 8,
11, 19, 101, 153, 175, 179;
diaries, 141, 166; divorce, 11;
doll, 111-12; domesticity, 3, 4,
49; education, 7, 8, 10, 84-8,
112-13 (*see also* Blackburn
College; State Normal School);
environmentalist, 15; essays,
xx, 3, 4, 7, 18, 27, 159, 167,

168; on experience, xii-xiii, 4,
31, 97-8, 111, 154; family
relationships, xv, xviii, xxi, 5,
44, 52-3, 58-60, 68, 109-10,
125-6, 170-71, 172; fantasy life,
xv, xviii, 45, 47, 73-4, 79, 80,
84, 99, 100, 102, 157 (see also
"I-Mary"); father (see Hunter,
George); feminist, 11-12, 13,
17, 28-9, 30, 125-6; fiction,
xix, 3, 9, 11, 12, 13, 16, 18,
29, 51, 100; fiction, childhood,
97; fiction, first, 9; fiction, last
(see Starry Adventure); grandpar-
ents (see Graham, Hannah
Dugger; Graham, Milo);
great-grandparents (see Dugger,
Jarrot; Dugger, Polly (Mary)
McAdams; Graham, Janot;
Graham, Theda Case); health,
135, 137-8, 140, 141, 143; and
Hispanic culture, 9, 13, 14, 15,
180; homesteading, 9; husband
(see Austin, Stafford Wallace);
imagination 61-2, 68, 80;
intuition, 17, 18, 27, 63, 114;
and Johnson Street house,
121-2, 125; library card, 91;
library promoter, 15; literary
gift, source of, 52-3; loneliness,
17, 123; male characters, 29,
146-7, 150, 166; marriage, xiv,
9, 10, 13, 148; meditation, xii;
Mexican government consultant, 15; in Mexico, 15; in
Missouri, 141; mother (see
Hunter, Susanna Savilla
Graham); mystical experiences,
5, 6-7, 17, 71-2, 74-9; and
mysticism, 13, 16, 23-4; mythic
themes, xv, xviii, xxi, 12, 22-3,

24, 26-8, 31, 157-9, 178;
namesakes, 40-41; and Native
American culture, 9, 11, 12,
13, 14-5, 21, 23, 24, 25, 142,
160, 179, 180; and nature, xii,
xviii, 7, 8, 10, 11, 14, 18-22,
24, 25, 59, 69-72, 111, 115,
159, 163, 179, 180; New
Mexico visits, 13; in New York
City (1912-1924), 12, 13, 123;
nieces, xi, 55; nonfiction, 9,
11, 12, 13, 16, 18, 21, 25;
painting, 141; personality, xii,
xv, xx, 3-4, 36, 66, 120, 168;
plays, 12, 22-3; as poet, xi, 9,
10, 12, 15-16, 20, 24, 28, 134,
141, 155, 157, 159, 161, 163,
165, 167, 168-9, 178; psychic
powers, interest in, xii, 4, 8, 18;
publicist, 133; reading, xii, 7,
8, 18, 86, 88, 90, 91, 96-7,
113, 116-17, 119, 156, 159,
162, 172, 174; in Santa Fe
(1924-1934), ix, x, xii, xiii, 3,
12, 14-16; self-image, xix, 6, 7,
10, 30, 36, 52-3, 95, 139, 140,
161-2, 163, 165-6; sister (see
Hunter, Jennie); on the
Southwest, xii, 15, 16, 19; as
speaker/lecturer, 12, 13, 15, 23;
on true love, 12-13; war effort,
13; and WCTU, 128-32; and
womanliness, xviii, xix, xxi, 4,
5, 127, 131, 138; women
characters, 29; in writers'
colonies, 11, 12; writing,
criticism of, xv, 16, 17, 21;
writing, universal quality of, 16,
17, 30
Austin, Stafford Wallace, 9, 11,
19, 130, 138

Harte, Bret, 172, 174
Hawthorne, Nathaniel, 174
Heaven, 68-9, 78, 110
Heilbrun, Carolyn, xx, 26
Henderson, Alice Corbin, xi, 26
Hiawatha (Longfellow), 113
Hodge, Frederick Webb, 9
Homesteaders, 8, 174
Hoover, Herbert, 12
Hough, Emerson, 9
Houghton Mifflin (publisher), 133, 155
House at Otowi Bridge, The (Church), x
Hunter, George, xix, 5, 38, 39, 40, 41-4, 45, 52, 58, 59, 60, 61, 65, 69, 74, 77, 89, 90, 91, 95, 96, 97, 99, 101, 102, 110, 126, 127, 129, 148; death, 103-4, 105
Hunter, George (Jr.), 96, 101-2, 108, 110, 112, 170, 173, 177
Hunter, James M. (Jim), 6, 10, 40, 59, 60, 61, 64, 65, 66, 67, 79, 91, 104, 108, 110, 116, 118-19, 126, 135, 136-7, 140, 141, 146, 147, 159, 170, 171, 172, 173, 174, 176-7, 179
Hunter, Jennie, 5, 59, 60, 61, 64, 66, 67, 68, 101, 102, 103, 106, 107; death, 106
Hunter, Susanna Savilla Graham, 6, 44-5, 46, 49, 50, 52, 53, 59, 64, 99, 101, 122, 123, 137, 144, 147, 149, 151-2, 170, 171, 173, 174, 177, 179; Chautauqua lectures, 59, 113; conflict with Mary, xix, 7, 10, 40, 42, 52-3, 59, 60, 61-2, 63, 66, 67, 68, 70, 89, 90, 91, 94, 106-7, 110, 117, 118, 119, 120, 126-7, 134,

143, 163, 172; marriage, 38-39; Methodist, 5, 58-9, 69, 77, 132, 134; public speaker, 136; and WCTU, 5, 59, 128, 129, 130, 131, 132, 134, 135; widowhood, 103, 108-9, 121
Hunter, William, 41
Huntington Library (Calif.), xiv, xvii

Illinois, 37, 38, 175, 177
Illinois River, 73
Imagists, 26
"I-Mary," 6, 64-7, 104, 107, 135, 140, 141, 157
Improvement of the Understanding (Spinoza), xii
Indians, 37-8; *see also* Austin, Mary Hunter, and Native American culture
In the American Grain (Williams), 24
Inyo County (Calif.), 19
Isidro (Austin), 11, 28, 155
Ivanhoe (Scott), 98

Jackson, Helen Hunt, 172, 174
Jersey Lily, *see* Langtry, Lily
Johnson Street (Carlinville), 121, 123, 176
Jonson, Ben, 96
Jordan, David Starr, 9-10; Effie Vancil, 145, 146, 147, 169, 171
Jung, Carl, xv, xviii, 22, 26

Keats, John, 162

Ladies Home Journal, 16
"Lady of Shalott, The" (Tennyson), 91, 92-3

Laela (*Fire*), 23
Land of Journey's Ending, The
(Austin), 25, 92
Land of Little Rain, The (Austin),
9, 11, 19-20, 37, 116, 155
Landseer, Edwin Henry, 123
Lane, Charles, 174; George, 175;
Mary Hunter, 174, 175
Langtry, Lily, 124, 130, 143;
placque, 123, 124, 125
Lawrence, D.H., 14
Letters (Mansfield), xii
Levertov, Denise, 31
Literary and Scientific Circle, 113
Literary Digest, 16
Little theater movement, 125
Logan, John A., 159-60
London, Jack, 11
"Lone Tree" (*One Smoke Stories*),
164-5
Long, Haniel, xi
Longfellow, Henry Wadsworth,
113, 136, 174
Los Alamos (N.M.), ix
Los Alamos Ranch School, x, xi
Los Angeles (Calif.), 11, 173-4,
176
Lost Borders (Austin), 11
Love and the Soul Maker (Austin),
12
Lovely Lady, The (Austin), xix,
13, 28, 99
Luhan, Mabel Dodge, 3, 13, 14,
145
Lummis, Charles Fletcher,
9, 10

McClure, J.E., xviii, xix, 161,
165, 166, 167, 168
McGee, Ellen (*A Woman of
Genius*), 77-8, 80, 82

McGuffey, William Holmes, 89,
91, 104, 128
McNath, Valda, 12
Macoupin County (Ill.), 142
Macoupin Creek, 73
Malarmé, Stéphane, 31
"Man and the Place, The"
(Austin), 159
Man Jesus, The (Austin), 13
Mansions of Philosophy, The
(Durant), xii
Markham, Edwin, 9
Marlborough School (Los
Angeles), x-xi
Meem, John Gaw, 14
Methodists, 5, 29, 40, 50, 78,
123, 128, 131; Free, 109
Mexico, 15
"Middle Place of the Mind," *see*
Sacred Middle
Millais, John Everett, 124
Miller, Hugh, 7, 8, 18, 113,
114-16, 153, 156, 178
Milton, John, 113
Minton, Charles, 20
Mississippi River, 73
"Mother of Felipe, The" (Austin),
9
"Mother-wit," 46, 48
Muir, John, 19
Munsey's Magazine, 9
Museum of Natural History (N.Y.),
122, 123

Nation, 16
National Endowment for the Arts
and Humanities, 15
National University (Mexico), 15
Nature of the Physical World
(Eddington), xii
Neith (*No. 26 Jayne Street*), xix

New England, 174, 175
New Mexico, xii, xiii, 13
New Republic, 16
New York Legislative League, 13
NMS (secret society), 144
No. 26 Jayne Street (Austin), xix, 13
Nuclear scientists, x

"Oak Leaves" (Austin), 163-4, 165
Observation, habit of, 152
OIO, *see* Oioparthenian
Oioparthenian (OIO) (Blackburn girls' society), 135, 136, 160
Old Red Sandstone, The (Miller), 7, 18, 113, 114, 116, 117, 178
Oliver (*The Trail Book*), 122
Olivia (*A Woman of Genius*), 29, 77, 80, 81-4, 102, 103, 104, 117, 121, 125, 126, 128, 135, 143, 150, 157, 162, 166
One Smoke Stories (Austin), 16, 164
Oppenheimer, Robert, x
Oratorical Contest, 136, 137
Orthopatetic (Blackburn men's literary society), 137
Otowi (N.M.), ix, x
Outland (Austin and Sterling), 12, 89, 148
Out West (magazine), 9
Overland Monthly, 9
Owens River water issue, 11

Paiute, 8, 11, 19
Paradise Lost (Milton), 110, 113
Pasadena (Calif.), 170
Patchen, Mary, 41, 43, 44-5
Pattern, *see* Austin, Mary Hunter, creative life

Pearce, T.M., 16; Collection (Univ. of N.M.), xiv
Penitente hymns, 14
Pepper-pot soup, xiii
Petrie, Flinders, 159
Pierce, Edward T., 9
Pilgrim's Progress (Bunyan), 91, 110
"Play to be Sung" (Austin), 97, 99-100, 101
Plum Street farm (Carlinville), 61, 67, 105, 108
Poetry, 16
Polk, Mrs. James A., 46
Pound, Ezra, 27
"Primitive Drama" (Austin speech), 15
Primitivism, 14
Pueblo Indians, x, 14, 25

Railroads, 142, 170, 172
Ramona (Jackson), 174, 175
Rhodes, Eugene Manlove, 9
Rinaker's Hill, 74
Robertson, Charles, 18, 153
Robertson Hall (Blackburn College), 156
Romantic poets, 8
Roosevelt, Theodore, 119
Ruskin, John, 119, 149

Sacred Middle, 13, 18, 139, 158, 159
Sacrifice of self, 29
St. Nicholas (magazine), 9, 96, 98, 117
Saloons, 128-9
San Francisco (Calif.), 173, 175
San Joaquin Valley (Calif.), 145, 171, 173, 176, 180

Walnut tree, 71-2, 74, 177
Warner, Edith, ix, x
WCTU. *See* Women's Christian
  Temperance Union
Webster, Daniel, 159
Wells, H.G., 12
Welty, Eudora, 4
Wetherall, Peter (*The Lovely
  Lady*), xix, 99
Whatnot, 122, 123, 156
"When I am Dead" (Austin), 28
Wick-i-up, 11
Wilde, Oscar, 124
Willard, Frances, xix, 10, 130-34,
  135
Williams, William Carlos, 24
Wilson, Harry Leon, 11
Winning of the West (Roosevelt), 119
"Woman Alone" (Austin), 7, 29
Woman of Genius, A (Austin), 13,
  28, 29, 77, 80-84, 102-3, 105,
  117-18, 121, 124-5, 126, 128,
  135, 143, 150, 162, 166

"Woman-soul," xiv
Women's Christian Temperance
  Union (WCTU), 5, 59, 128,
  129, 130, 131, 134, 149;
  newsletter (*see Union Signal*)
Women's University Club (Los
  Angeles), 15
Woods, *see* Carlinville,
  woods
Words, 88-9, 93, 135
Writing a Woman's Life (Heilbrun),
  xxi
Wynn, Dudley, xv, 19

Yale University, 15
Young Women's Christian
  Association (YWCA), 160

Zuni, 160
Zuni Folk Tales (Cushing),
  160